Family Violence

A CANADIAN INTRODUCTION

Family Violence

A CANADIAN INTRODUCTION

JULIANNE MOMIROV WITH ANN DUFFY

James Lorimer & Company Ltd., Publishers
Toronto

James Lorimer & Company Ltd., Publishers acknowledges the support of the Ontario Arts Council (OAC), an agency of the Government of Ontario, which in 2015-16 funded 1,676 individual artists and 1,125 organizations in 209 communities across Ontario for a total of $50.5 million. We acknowledge the support of the Canada Council for the Arts, which last year invested $153 million to bring the arts to Canadians throughout the country. This project has been made possible in part by the Government of Canada and with the support of the Ontario Media Development Corporation.

Cover image: iStockphoto

Cover design: Meghan Collins

Library and Archives Canada Cataloguing in Publication

Momirov, Julianne
    Family violence: a Canadian introduction / Julianne Momirov and Ann Duffy. — 2nd ed.

Order of authors' names reversed on 1st ed.
Includes bibliographical references and index.
Issued also in an electronic format.
ISBN 978-1-55277-902-6

    1. Family violence--Canada. I. Duffy, Ann II. Title: Duffy, Ann. Family violence. III. Title.

HV6626.23.C3M64 2011   362.82'920971   C2011-903863-3

James Lorimer & Company Ltd., Publishers
117 Peter Street, Suite 304
Toronto, ON, Canada
M5V 0M3
www.lorimer.ca

Printed and bound in Canada.

CONTENTS

1

UNDERSTANDING FAMILY VIOLENCE FROM A SOCIETAL PERSPECTIVE

FAMILY: SAFE HAVEN OR DANGEROUS SPACE?

Thirty-year-old Mark[1] sits, staring at the floor in a small room, waiting for someone to unlock the door and take him to the van that will drive him to his first court date. He has been charged with domestic assault after punching and shoving his pregnant wife, Jen, so hard that she fell down the basement stairs. Her fall caused her to lose their child. She had several broken bones and was bleeding internally. His five-year-old son had been taken away by child welfare workers. He feels like his life is over. He *wishes* it were over because he knows how messed up it is.

Mark was an abused and neglected child who grew up witnessing his father's violence against his mother. When he could not see what was happening, he could hear it, even through the pillow he would hold tightly over his head. He was tormented by guilt because he could not defend his mother. He had tried on many occasions when he was younger, but his father had beaten him then hurt his mother even more, telling Mark that it was his fault because he had not "minded his own business." He had dreamed of killing his father but never had the courage to do it.

By the time he was fifteen he was living on the street, once again surrounded by violence and predators who preyed on street kids like him. Mark eventually found refuge in a youth centre with people who genuinely cared about him and introduced him to kindness. For the first time, he felt like a worthwhile, valuable human being and was encouraged to dream of a future. With his self-esteem tenuously raised through counselling, he managed to obtain his high school diploma. Then fortune truly smiled on him when he got a good job with a local construction company and impressed his supervisor enough to be enrolled in the carpentry apprenticeship program. While attending community college for his first round of classes, he met Jen, the kind of girl he had always considered too "high class" for someone like him. They began to date and Mark experienced romantic love for the first time.

Jen introduced him to her world and, in spite of feeling like an imposter for the first few years, Mark found that he enjoyed it. It was comfortable. He liked being part of a social sphere where people lived in nice houses, husbands did not beat their wives, parents were kind and loving to their children, and kids grew up feeling valued and good about themselves. It was the world he had imagined when he was a child in the schoolyard, watching the other children from his hiding place. He and Jen got married and, within a couple of years, put a down payment on a small house in a suburban neighbourhood. That house became his pride and joy and he tirelessly worked to improve it, fixing things, landscaping, endlessly tinkering.

After a few years, Mark dared to believe that he had closed the door on his past and that it would no longer haunt him. His brutal childhood seemed so far away. He thought of himself as an entirely different man from the one he had been when he was young. One day he was brave enough to tell himself that he was actually *happy*.

Then, as suddenly as his luck had changed for the better, everything went sour. When the economic downturn hit his town, the company where Mark worked announced that it was bankrupt. At first, Mark and Jen were able to get by on his unemployment insurance and her pay. He stayed home and played "house husband," caring for their little boy to save on daycare costs. He did not mind because he thought of it as a break before going back to full-time work. But his unemployment benefits ran out and he was still unable to find a job. Financial worries began to plague them. Their hard-earned savings and retirement funds were evaporating. So was his self-esteem.

Mark decided to start his own renovation business but he soon discovered that he was not a very good businessman. He took on more work than he could handle, and because he could only afford to hire the cheapest helpers, many of whom were incompetent, unreliable, and stole his tools, he ended up losing everything and being sued to boot.

Feeling like an utter failure as a man, as a husband, and as a father, Mark began to drink heavily. His relationship with Jen suffered as he began to resent her. He resented it when she was promoted and got a raise because it made him feel like more of a failure. He resented that she controlled the money and expected him to account for what he spent, even though he knew it was because he was spending it on alcohol rather than groceries. For the first time in their relationship, there was an element of latent violence to their fights. Mark even slapped her during one of their fights over money. Jen took their son and went to stay with her parents. She would not return until he begged her to forgive him, promising it would never happen again.

He had meant it. He was frightened by what he had done, remembering how he had raised his hand and struck his wife across the face, awakening the memories of his father doing the same thing to his mother. Mark had sworn to himself that he would never be like his father. But things just kept getting worse. They could not meet their mortgage payments and pay the utilities during the same month. His pride and joy had become a huge financial burden. Jen's parents bailed them out for a couple of months but then they could not help anymore. His parents were not in a position to help themselves, let alone Mark and his family. As the house slipped through their fingers, Mark's anger and drinking escalated, feeding on each other.

Sometimes Mark hated Jen and, more frightening than that, there were fleeting moments when he wanted to hurt her. He began to distance himself from her and their son because he was afraid of himself and what he might do to them. He drank from the moment he opened his eyes in the morning to dull the pain of his inner torment and anger. On the same night that he told Jen he wanted to separate, she told him that she was pregnant. He wanted to kill her as the enormity of the thought of bringing another child into their nightmare struck him. Maternity leave? Another mouth to feed? His anger exploded. Blind to the presence of his son, he started yelling threats and insults and punched Jen in the stomach. He shoved her backward as hard as he could. She fell against the door to the basement, which flew open under her weight. Mark watched her tumble down the steep stairs, ending up in a crumpled tangle of limbs, like a rag doll. His son was screaming.

Although Mark, Jen, and their son are fictional characters, their story is based on research that reveals patterns of outcomes for individuals who witnessed violence against their mothers, as well as being abused and neglected as children. There are certainly Canadians whose families continue to suffer from the same, or similar, outcomes. Family life is still being devastated by violence. Individuals' lives are still being damaged and destroyed by violence committed by those closest to them. For this reason, despite decades of research into the problem of family violence and years of intervention, it is still imperative to educate ourselves about this serious social issue.

Family violence is a subject that a lot of people find nauseating and unfathomable at the same time. Both reactions generally stem from the belief that the family is a "haven in a heartless world" (Lasch 1977) where the members love one another unconditionally and support one another at all times, a safe place where people retreat to escape strangers and the harshness and alienation of the world. If we believe such things about the family, we are then more horrified to discover that in many families individuals are beaten, threatened, humiliated, and sexually assaulted. The usual response is to convince ourselves that the people perpetrating such acts of violence must be "sick" and ought to be "locked up." If the victim[2] is an adult, the inevitable question is then "Why doesn't she or he leave?" These responses assume that if social authorities imprison perpetrators or victims leave, the violence will disappear, or at least decrease significantly. They ignore the fact that family violence has a rather long and persistent social history.

How can the family be a place of violence? Gelles and Straus (1988), the two "fathers" of the sociology of family violence, list eleven traits of the family that contribute to its violent character. These traits include the amount of time family members spend with one another, the intensity of their interactions due to their emotional ties, the range of activities in which family members engage, and the intermingling of different genera-tions and sexes. Ironically, other analysts (Straus and Hotaling 1979) sug-gest that these same traits can also make the family a loving milieu.

The irony of such traits is that intimacy and intensity may lead to love *and* violence. This twofold reality demonstrates how violence can take place within a close, loving environment. While family members may draw comfort from one another and give support, they may also prey on one another. Sharing joy and venting frustration may go hand in hand within the family fold.

In addition, not all types of families are "created equal." Common-law (or cohabitation) unions appear to be at least twice as violent as mar-riages. Brownridge and Halli (2000) examine research indicating there are differences between families founded on a marital union as opposed to a common-law one and, even with variations in methodologies, they conclude that in terms of overall physical violence, common-law couples suffer twice as much as married couples. When severe violence is examined, common-law couples experience over four times more violence than mar-ried couples. Cohabiting women are more likely to be killed by their male partners. The Winnipeg Family Violence Court from 1990 to 1992 heard many more cases where the accused was part of a common-law couple rather than married. The authors suggest that the differences are possibly due to of the type of people who choose to cohabit with their partners rather than marry them. They found that cohabiting individuals were more likely to be lower in maturity, more nonconventional, and more willing to take risks. The relationship differences ascertained were that they were less happy, there was less commitment, and they frequently had poor-quality relationships with parents and friends. Brownridge and Halli conclude that combining both types of families when conducting research could make it more difficult to understand the true nature of violence against women.

An article by the same authors a year later provides a further analysis of married couples, comparing women who previously cohabited with another man prior to their present marriage with women who had not.

11

Their examination reveals that PC (previously cohabited) marriages involve even higher rates of violence than common-law couples. Brownridge and Halli (2001) speculate that the social problem of violence may increase in Canada due to the rising rate of cohabitation. As a sidebar to this observation, it should be noted that the 2006 Canadian census reveals that common-law couples have grown most since 2001, now accounting for 15.5 per cent of all census families (up from 13.8 per cent in 2001 and 7.2 per cent twenty years ago). (See Statistics Canada website at www.statcan.gc.ca for the 2006 Analysis series.)

Based on the research discussed previously, it should be interesting to see whether the legalization of same-sex marriage in Canada in 2005 has had an effect on Brownridge and Halli's rates of family violence.

TAKING A SOCIETAL PERSPECTIVE

Blaming the pathology of violence on general traits of family life or types of family unions still does not explain why there is violence present in some families and not in others. Therefore, we should explore other possible reasons for the occurrence of violence. To do so, we need to broaden our focus. By keeping our focus narrow, we inadvertently preserve the popular myth of the family: the family-as-haven and the street-as-threat. This way of thinking allows us to continue to believe that family violence is a private matter rather than a social one. Our focus should shift to the social context in which the family is embedded. We can accomplish the task of viewing the social context and its relation to violence within families by using what the sociologist C. Wright Mills (1959) termed "the sociological imagination." In essence, what this means is that we should understand that personal biographies are linked to history. To put it another way, we as individuals live out our lives in a particular time and place, otherwise known as a historical period. What happens and has happened in the world around us influences our personal histories by constraining us or allowing us to accomplish things that at other times and in other places would have been impossible. For example, anyone born around the year 1980 would have grown up in a computerized world in which the Internet is pervasive. Thanks to social interactive websites such as MySpace, Facebook, and Twitter, people who have never met face to face—and probably never will—form friendships and keep one another up-to-date (sometimes minute by minute) on what is happening in their lives. It is commonplace to find romantic partners on websites and go on "virtual" dates, something that would have seemed outlandish—the stuff of sci-fi movies—a scant twenty years earlier.

We should take an intellectual step back to view our individual histories within their social context, and to understand how one influences the other. In this way, we are able to recognize that what is happening to us in our personal lives is tied to what is happening in the world around us. Our private troubles are often linked to public issues. When we move between our personal biographies and the socio-historical context of our lives, we are exercising our sociological imaginations. This unique perspective helps us understand that family violence is a social phenomenon, not a private matter. Violence is not inherent in individuals and their psyches, nor in particular families, but in the nature of relationships.

In addition, we have to address the nature of family violence. Some prominent social researchers consistently show that men and women are equal actors when it comes to family violence. Their studies show that, not only are both sexes capable of being perpetrators as well as victims, but *women may be more likely to abuse men* (Straus 2004 and 1993). However, there is some concession to the fact that women are more likely to be victims of severe violence and to suffer serious injuries as a result (Straus 2004). Other researchers insist that family violence is *gendered*—and that gender is masculine. According to them, there is such a gender imbalance when it comes to family violence that they argue that "family violence" should rightfully be renamed "male violence." Not only are males largely responsible for committing violent and abusive acts within the domestic sphere, but females are predominantly their adult victims. Although a number of researchers have conducted studies showing that husbands are abused as much as—if not more than—wives, their studies are problematic. (These studies are explored in more detail in Chapter 2.)

Johnson (1995) proposes that both these groups of researchers are somewhat correct. That is, there are at least two different types of family violence based on sample groups. More recently, Johnson and his colleagues have refined their research to indicate that there are, indeed, at least four types of family violence (to be discussed in detail in Chapter 2). Now that there is more research on other violent relationships within families and intimate groups—notably same-sex couples—indicating that significant numbers of men are, indeed, the victims of violence and significant numbers of women are, indeed, perpetrators (against other women), it is imperative to re-examine and refine our convictions about the gendered nature of family violence.

In this book, we take a sociological and feminist approach to family violence.[3] We show that family is rooted in society, that individuals are socialized into particular patterns of behaviour, that these patterns are difficult to change, and that power systems external to the family itself have an enormous impact on the processes taking place within the family. Intersectionality, an approach developed in the nineties, is our guiding principle. It refers to a type of feminist theory that recognizes that women are not simply products of a patriarchal power system, but are also disadvantaged by race, class, homophobia, and age. Viewed in this way, each and every woman represents an intersection of oppressions or disadvantages which mediate her experiences of family violence. These intersections should be recognized by anyone who seeks to understand her experiences and make sense of them. Developed by Patricia Hill Collins in the nineties, using a term first introduced by Kimberlé Crenshaw in the eighties, it was initially employed to discuss African-American feminism. (For more explanation and discussion of the development of this theory, see Bograd 1999; Association for Women's Rights in Development 2004.)[4]

We will also endeavour to answer three important questions: What is family violence? What forms does it take? Where does it originate?

Family violence is a social problem that affects all of us and that has serious material and social ramifications. The material costs put a strain on the shrinking public purse as a result of the many services required to deal with the aftermath of family violence, such as police officers, social workers, courts, and prison officials. The social costs are evident in the breakdown of relationships within our societies. Relationships among family members are severely damaged by violence; and family members themselves are harmed in many ways. To put it bluntly, violence harms society, not simply individuals. One way individuals are harmed is through humiliation, which results from being violated by someone else. Such violation could be physical, sexual, or psychological. It is perhaps particularly humiliating when the person committing the violation is a trusted loved one. The shame will probably be shared by both the perpetrator and the victim, although not necessarily at the same time. Humiliation will be experienced by the victim when she or he realizes that she or he has been victimized. The perpetrator, however, will likely not experience humiliation until she or he internalizes what she or he has done or is publicly labelled by the criminal justice system. (For interesting social-psychological discussions of shame and the resulting damage to the self, see Scheff 1990; Goffman 1963.)

The Government of Canada and various provincial and territorial governments have initiated numerous programs to help combat the problem of family violence, including the introduction of domestic assault courts, changes to laws concerning restraining orders, and myriad other services.

Clearly, family violence cannot be contained within the boundaries of an individual family. It damages perpetrators, victims, and witnesses, both physically and psychologically. These damaged people then go out into our society and have relationships with others. Logic suggests that these relationships, too, will become damaged by the legacy of violence. As the damage spreads throughout our society, it involves more and more people whose relationships are tainted as a result. Societal institutions, such as social service agencies, the police, the courts, and the penal system, become involved in the attempt to stem the flow of this toxicity. Yet family violence does not simply originate with families; its origins can be found in aspects of Canadian society as well.

THE VIOLENCE OF SOCIETY

Society is violent. We all know this. Turn on the television, go to—or rent—a movie, play a video game, read a book, pick up a newspaper or a magazine...go to a bar or dance club on a Saturday night where it is almost certain that a fight will break out, go to a hockey game, witness the road rage displayed by drivers in heavy traffic. Violence is pervasive.

Sociologists have long recognized and accepted the presence of conflict, as well as consensus, in social relations.[5] Lewis Coser, a pre-eminent American sociologist (1956), argues that conflict can be functional or beneficial for society in that it can bring about social change. Another sociologist, Thomas Scheff (1990, 7) distinguishes between "good" and "bad" conflict, asserting that if the social bond among members of a society is intact, then conflict may serve a constructive purpose; on the other hand, if the social bond is broken or profoundly threatened, then conflict is likely to be destructive.

Conflict can take many forms, from disagreement to actual aggression, from controlled to chaotic. As a society, we do not like chaotic conflict—riots, angry mobs, and high levels of street crime give us cause for fear. We are more willing to tolerate conflict from particular kinds of individuals or groups because we perceive conflict as part of their accepted societal role. For instance, in our society, aggression is often considered acceptable in males as part of their socially defined masculinity. In addition, when violence is used as a means to an end—to achieve specific goals—it is often considered acceptable. One example is the high tolerance for, and even encouragement of, corporal punishment of children as a means of discipline by some parents and educators. Until quite recently, physical aggression of husbands against their wives was tolerated. It may be argued that there is still a great deal of tolerance of violence against women, children, and other marginalized groups in our society—such as the elderly—despite the public commitment of the government to end such behaviour.

The pervasiveness of conflict and violence tends to legitimize it. Since it inhabits most of our waking moments, we tend to see it as a natural component of our social life.

Canadian society is especially violent for certain social groups—the poor, women, and First Nations peoples, for example. The lives of First Nations peoples in this country are often characterized by violence, both on and off the reserve. From domestic violence to racism, First Nations peoples suffer victimization as individuals and as a group (see Griffiths and Yerbury 1995). This situation is also true for many women. Not only are they in danger when they venture outside their homes, particularly at night, but they are also in danger in their own homes, where the men they love, and who supposedly love them, may threaten and harm them (DeKeseredy, Burshtyn, and Gordon 1995). Sexist attitudes victimize them further when blame is attributed to them by themselves and others if they are attacked by a male in a public setting (Walklate 1989, as cited in DeKeseredy et al. 1995, 71). When the attack takes place inside their own home, women are even more likely to be subjected to intense scrutiny by others who want to discover whether there is any possibility that she somehow instigated the violence perpetrated against her. Despite what we know about men and violence, we are still programmed to assume that a man would not mistreat his wife or girlfriend without good reason.

Some scholars have argued that the family reflects the violence of society, that it acts as a "mirror" for the social context (Lynn and O'Neill 1995, 272–73). The family "reflects" the inequalities and power relations of the society in which it is grounded. This reflexivity would then account for violent behaviours manifested among family members. Although this characterization is true to some extent, it fails to capture the whole ethos of family violence. Such an assertion makes the family seem excessively passive. Instead, we should be willing to examine power relations and social processes involved in family life and within the violent family specifically. Otherwise, the "mirror" metaphor presents the question: Why, then, aren't all families in Canada violent?

Much more insidious than these overt signs of societal violence, however, are the deeply entrenched covert aspects. These less obvious features are to be found in our culture and social structure, specifically in our mode of production—capitalism—with its attendant economic inequality among groups of people, rendering some to abject poverty. Also, fundamental beliefs embedded in our culture about human beings and conditions pertaining to them (liberal democratic philosophy) are not obvious. Few people are able to identify these elements as having any bearing on family violence. This lack of vision stems from people's inability to connect what happens to individuals in their private context to the social context in which they operate. The belief in "individuality" and "uniqueness" obscures their ability to see how similar they are to so many. Thus, they fail to see that the conditions of the social context ground their thoughts and behaviours. Patriarchy, which functions as both culture *and* social structure (and genders all of society), also contributes substantially, both overtly and covertly, to the violence of men's and women's lives.

Thus, we see that conflict and violence are endemic to the Canadian social context. They are not peripheral or alien elements; they are, in fact, part of our everyday lives in some form. Most of us cannot successfully escape them. The implication is that all individuals have internalized conflict and violence in some way. Many people believe that life without conflict, including family life, is not possible—or even desirable. For them, a certain level of conflict is considered to be "healthy."

Despite the knowledge of the existence of family conflict and violence, the discipline of sociology has been rather slow to incorporate these issues into its general study of the family.

DEFINITIONS AND MEASUREMENT

Definitions and measurements of family violence pose a unique problem because of the nature of family relationships. Violent interactions usually take place in private, so public officials are not in a position to scrutinize such incidents. There are few, if any, witnesses. Any witnesses who are present may be extremely reluctant to admit to what they have seen, even to themselves. So researchers frequently have to rely on self-reports or official statistics.

Official statistics (such as police reports, data from public agencies) often contain what is called a "dark figure"—these are the cases that do not come to the attention of officials but are still occurring. For instance, a woman reporting on the violence she has suffered from her husband may tell a researcher that her husband has struck her ten times in the past six months, excluding the numerous incidents in which he threatened to strike her or verbally abused her. The researcher, on the other hand, may consider that the threats and verbal abuse are part of the definition of violence and should be included. In this scenario, according to the researcher's definition, there would be many more incidents of violence, but because of the woman's definition, some of the incidents have been obscured or left "in the dark." We cannot know what that dark figure is. A dark figure will always be present in self-reporting because people have varying definitions of violence that are, to a great extent, inaccessible to researchers. Also, research often focuses on one or the other partner, not both.

Avoiding these problems requires that terminology be as precise as possible when applied to empirical phenomena. A precise definition of a social problem means that we can determine exactly when "normal" or permissible behaviour crosses over into abusive behaviour. Such precision also requires that the language be completely lacking in ambiguity and that it be interpreted in a particular fashion. However, both language and behaviour are highly ambiguous and dependent upon their context for meaning.

Jones uses "a veil of words" to introduce her argument that the terminology used to discuss the problem of violence within the family often obscures more than it reveals. She argues that using the terms "domestic violence" and "family violence" create the illusion of gender-neutrality when describing violence within the family. "Male violence disappears in euphemism," she charges. Furthermore, a term like "battered woman" highlights only one facet of a woman's experience, reducing the rest of her identity to a single variable. It also implies that she is a passive victim of abuse, rather than an active resister or survivor (Jones 1996, 17–18), and ignores the possibility that she may resist being identified in that way.

Another point that Jones raises is that we generally tend to talk about violence in the passive voice: "women are beaten," "wives are abused," "children are abandoned," and so on. This type of terminology focuses only on the victim, disguising the identity and motivations of the perpetrator. When we are informed about the perpetrator, he or she is usually obscured by an abstract noun: "women are threatened by aggressive behaviour" or "they are battered by the relationship" (Jones 1996, 21). Rarely are we given the explicit details of exactly what was done by whom to whom. The point is that the use of such euphemistic terms makes the language of family violence imprecise—which, in turn, makes family violence difficult to define and understand. (For an excellent critique of how even feminists contribute to the problem of the focus of sexual violence being on female victims instead of male perpetrators, see Mardorossian 2002.)[6]

Definitions of violence against women vary widely in the research literature. Psychological and emotional abuse may be included under the rubric of "family violence," along with financial abuse, verbal abuse, and sexual coercion (see Johnson 1996). The same ambiguity exists for violence against other family members, such as children, siblings, and elders. Neglect, abandonment, denial of human needs, "rough-housing," "sibling rivalry," spanking, incest, murder—all these terms arise when researchers begin to discuss violence among family members. Some research instruments include terms like "severe violence" and "very severe violence" with lists of what types of actions belong under each heading.

This wide variation raises substantial questions about how broadly or narrowly family violence should be defined. Is it more precise to count blows or bruises? Or should we spend our time trying to ascertain the meanings behind people's actions? Or their feelings about them? Or both?

Measurement is also a problem, especially when it comes to the instruments used in empirical research. According to Johnson (1996), a number of statistical sources for family violence are problematic. For example, the Uniform Crime Reporting Survey gives an account of criminal acts that have come to the attention of the police in Canada. The most significant problem associated with reliance upon such a survey is the dark figure, which is inherent to all official statistics. Also problematic is that once mandatory arrest policies were put into place, police discretionary powers were largely eliminated. There is some suggestion that, to show their displeasure, police officers tend to arrest both parties when they are called to a scene of family violence, even if the victim was defending herself or retaliating against her abuser.

Family violence is especially prone to under-reporting because the family is considered to be a private institution. The ethos of the family makes victims too ashamed to report any violence they experience, while dependency on the abuser or sheer terror may keep victims from making their abuse a matter for the public record. Similarly, a sense of obligation to keep the family intact or a desire not to get too involved in "private" disputes may keep police officers from reporting violent acts between family members as domestic violence.

Another reason it is so difficult to clarify the dimensions of violence within families is what sociologists refer to as "social desirability." This term refers to instances when individuals will say and do things—or refrain from saying or doing things—in front of others to make themselves more socially acceptable. In the case of family violence, many perpetrators under-report or downplay the seriousness of their violence because they know that being abusive to their family members is not socially acceptable.

Another source of statistics is clinical samples (Johnson 1996). These samples are studies that look at the behaviour of victims who have sought assistance from agencies such as rape crisis centres or shelters for battered women, or of perpetrators who have been incarcerated. These studies are highly problematic. For example, generalization is difficult due to improper sampling methods, which result in samples of subjects that do not represent the population as a whole. Thus the findings may be pertinent only to the subjects of the study, not to all victims of family violence. Self-selection (subjects volunteering for the study) results in a sample of victims that may consist only of a particular type or subsample, rather than a wide variety. Perpetrators who have been convicted of offences may be characterized as having had bad luck or insufficient resources to effectively escape prosecution, rather than as guilty of a serious crime. On the other hand, they may be the most vicious of perpetrators. For these and other reasons, clinical samples are highly unreliable.

Population surveys—usually conducted by telephone—are used as another statistical measurement. One of their strengths is that they complement police statistics, since the surveys often uncover incidents that were never reported in addition to those that were. They are also often rich in detail. The problem, however, is that the accuracy of those details is almost impossible to determine. Given the freedom of anonymity, interviewees might be tempted to say anything; or the spontaneity of the telephone call may result in the interviewee's inability to recall specific details. In addition, the language of the questions may lead some respondents to omit certain data. There may also be some degree of embarrassment due to the sensitive nature of the topic or a certain amount of paranoia about the confidentiality of the call, the identity of the caller, and so on (Johnson 1996). (A lengthy discussion about the implications of different types of methodologies and samples on defining and understanding of the dimensions of family violence, relying on the work of Michael Johnson, will be pursued in Chapter 2.)

It is evident that family violence is a complex and somewhat elusive phenomenon. Definitions change as power balances in society shift. The measurement of social relations so complex and sensitive is a task that requires a refined instrument. However, the instruments that have been used so far have drawn criticism for the frequency of inaccuracies. We should therefore be cautious when we read reports of family violence, since the findings may have more to do with the methods used for measurement than with empirical reality.

REASONS FOR OPTIMISM

In spite of all the above, we feel it only right to include some studies that suggest there are reasons to be optimistic about the futures of families who have suffered violence and rates of family violence in general.

Felson, Ackerman, and Yeon (2003) point out that when comparing rates of family violence with those of violence outside of families, the rate of the former is only 11.7 per cent of assaults reported in the National Crime Victimization Survey in the United States. They concede, however, that family assault is probably under-reported. From their research, they hypothesized that verbal altercations (and, by extension, violence) between family members were more likely than between strangers. Their findings reveal that this is not the case. Despite high levels of contact and conflict, violence is not more likely to flow from verbal altercations between family members than strangers; in fact, violence is *less* likely between family members.

Another bright note with respect to family violence may be found in Johnson (2003), who argues that, contrary to popular belief, it is not inevitable that if a male partner assaults his female partner, the violence will become more frequent and intensify over time. Her secondary analysis of the data gathered in the 1993 Canadian Violence Against Women Survey indicates that 60 per cent of women whose marriages were intact, but within which they had experienced violence, had experienced only one occurrence. The frequency and severity of violence were also factors related to the continuation of violence. Men who had engaged in minor violence against their wives were more likely to have stopped being violent. The man's age, the type of union (cohabitation vs. marriage), and length of relationship were also predictors of the continuation of wife assault. Therefore, the author suggests that early intervention in a marital relationship within which violence occurs, along with greater social disapproval of wife assault, may stop male violence in its tracks.

Thus, without undermining the seriousness of the problem of family violence in Canada, these studies allow us to believe there is the possibility that the problem can be solved.

CONCLUSIONS

When we look at the social context of family violence, we see that Canadian society has various structures and components that tolerate, contribute to, and maintain violent behaviours. Through socialization into this society—accomplished to a great extent by our family—we learn to adapt to this environment. As a result, some may adopt violence as a way of life and internalize it into their identity. Family violence is thus the result of learned ways of interacting, which we perpetuate due to socialization (unless we consciously decide to change our behaviour) and, perhaps even more importantly, due to power relations. If we do not feel powerful in our lives, we may very well seek to exert power over others who are already socially defined as less powerful. Consequently, family violence seldom has to do with the pathology of individuals or families. The sociological approach to family violence is to understand it as a social problem. As such, it affects all of us and is everyone's responsibility.

2

INTIMATE PARTNER VIOLENCE OR WOMAN ABUSE?

Lisa turns the key in the lock of the door with peeling paint and walks into the shabby little apartment with the stale smell of smoke in the air. She looks around, remembering the beautiful home she had lived in with her husband. Although she has given up a lot, Lisa feels that it was worth it. Her husband was a highly successful lawyer, but he was also an abusive alcoholic who tormented her with malicious insults and forced her to have sex with him whenever he commanded. In spite of sacrificing an affluent lifestyle and fearing what the future will bring for her and her little boy, Lisa feels safe for the first time since she became pregnant. She has not worked in years and has no idea what kind of job prospects await her—certainly nothing like the six-figure income earned by her husband. She fears that her husband will fight her for custody of their son just to ensure that he does not have to pay her any child support. Lisa thought she would never find herself in this position, having grown up in a home where her father was violent toward her mother. She had sworn that she would not end up like her poor mother—she thought she knew better than to marry a man who hit her—but had been attracted to her husband's confidence and strength. Their relationship had been a good one as long as her life revolved around him. When she had become pregnant, he had become jealous of their child. His jealousy and resentment had grown after their son's birth, when the baby's care occupied most of her time and attention. She had tried to leave before but had always returned, each time more browbeaten than before. Then she discovered that children who were exposed to family violence were considered to be abused and suffered lasting psychological damage. At that point, Lisa understood why she was in her current situation and that she had to save her son regardless of the cost to herself.

Those of us who grew up in the sixties in Canada knew that women were being abused by their husbands and boyfriends, but we did not know the dimensions of the problem or how pervasive it was. Such things were considered "private." We just hoped it did not happen to us. It was not until the sixties when the feminist movement brought the problem to centre stage in the public forum that most women began to think about what was really happening to so many of us and what to call it. We began to realize just how many women were being treated this way and how serious the problem was. We also started to understand that it was not a random occurrence. Thanks to political activism and scholarly interest, the portrait of violence grew clearer until the government could no longer sweep it under the carpet. By the turn of the twenty-first century, there was an explosion of information available from research that fuelled controversies over who was being victimized, whose victimization was not being revealed, and the best way to reveal the truth about abuse in intimate relationships. These are the themes that will be discussed below.

NAMING THE VIOLENCE

Naming the issue of violence against women in the sixties was such a fundamental turning point in women's history that it is now difficult to understand the era that preceded it. Prior to the mid-nineteenth century, the list of constraints on women's rights and opportunities was almost endless. Denied political, legal, employment, marital, and social freedoms, women's adult existence was typically conditioned by marriage, childbirth, and child rearing. This pattern reflects the deep patriarchal roots of our society, in which women (and children) figured primarily as men's property (Lerner 1986, 212).

Husbands expected wives to directly provide services and produce children (preferably male) who would also become productive members of the family. While women were important, even key, to the day-to-day functioning of the household, their well-being depended upon the good-will of the patriarch. If she failed to fulfill her responsibilities (for example, to produce male children) or if she dared to challenge the patriarchal order, there were few social constraints on his means of discipline.

As property owner, the male had the right to exercise physical force to control and dominate his wife and children. Records of criminal court and divorce proceedings indicate that men made ample use of their right to use violence. Public complaints emerged only when the violence was so excessive that it led to serious injury or death, or created a public commotion. As with whipping and beating children, as long as the husband or father remained within the bounds of socially acceptable violence his actions were condoned and even encouraged (Pleck 1987).

The social legitimation of such abuse was first questioned in the nineteenth century. The emergence of the temperance movement in North America and Britain led some advocates to link male drunkenness to domestic violence. The temperance reformers presented excessive wife assaults as further evidence of the ills of alcohol (Strange 1995; Pleck 1987). In Britain, these initial steps taken by temperance advocates led to a variety of efforts to reform the status of women. In 1857, for example, early women's rights activists founded the Society for the Protection of Women and Children. This society sought to provide woman and child victims with legal advice and observers in courtrooms. It also set up the first shelter for victims of assault. Indeed, it was in Britain in 1857 that the term "wife beating" was first used (Pleck 1987, 63, 64).

While these efforts failed to end the social legitimation of wife abuse, they did initiate a few legal reforms. By the early twentieth century, special courts had been established in Canada and the United States that attempted to remove family issues from the criminal justice system and provide a "curative rather than punitive approach" (Pleck 1987, 126). The Toronto Women's Court, for example, provided private counselling to couples in conflict and attempted to dispense informal, equitable justice (Strange 1995, 301). These reforms had little effect, however. Police still continued to routinely minimize "domestics" and sought simply to "patch things up." Courts, preoccupied with preserving the family unit, offered women and children little in the way of protection or support. For myriad reasons, women tended to withdraw their charges. Indeed, their best strategy was often to lay charges to control their husband's violence and then later to withdraw the charge. Typically, they and their children were reliant on the abuser's income. Since divorces were extremely difficult to obtain and it was impractical and impossible for most single mothers to acquire sufficient employment income, single motherhood was not a viable alternative. Even if—as rarely happened—the husband was imprisoned, it was typically for six months or less.

This general pattern, which tended to legitimate male violence while trapping women in abusive relationships, persisted well into the fifties. Violence against women was common in Canadian communities, but hidden; and societal responses were inadequate and piecemeal. Family violence was still assumed to be typical of the "lower classes" and, as such, held up to ridicule. Frequently, the woman—in particular her housekeeping skills, or lack thereof—were assumed to be the root cause of the couple's conflict. With the popularization of psychology, more sophisticated analysts blamed her for her own victimization by suggesting she must be "masochistic" to stay (Pleck 1987, 139, 193). A husband's drunkenness was also frequently used to explain away his aberrant behaviour.

It was only with the emergence of modern feminism in the sixties that these practices and the age-old beliefs that supported them were finally challenged in the public arena. English feminist Erin Pizzey, who wrote *Scream Quietly or the Neighbours Will Hear* in 1974, is usually credited with "naming" the violence and establishing the foundation for feminist analyses of woman abuse. Her work was widely read and tremendously influential amongst the many women meeting at women's centres, working in consciousness-raising groups, or simply reading the new women's literature. In 1980 Linda MacLeod's *Wife Battering in Canada* was published. This Canadian publication became the cornerstone of the battered women's movement in this country. By this point, the shelter movement in Canada had already set down its roots and the lives of all women—including abused women—were being fundamentally altered.

27

THE NAME GAME TODAY

Today, now that it is recognized that this violence exists and is unaccept-able, wife abuse may seem to be a fairly straightforward issue.[7] Husbands and wives have arguments; sometimes the arguments escalate into physi-cal conflicts, and the husbands make use of their greater physical strength to dominate their wives. However, this basic scenario is far from accurate. The incidence of violence against women in intimate relationships is much more complex, contradictory, and multi-dimensional than simple misun-derstandings, marital fights, or conflicts. It is also much more serious, and sometimes deadlier, than arguments that have just gotten out of control.

First, the term "wife abuse," since it suggests that the abuse is restricted to women in formal marital relationships, is unacceptable to most activ-ists in the field. Today, with growing numbers of families being headed by common-law couples—the number of common-law unions in Canada has quadrupled between 1981 and 2006[8]—such a narrow definition would ignore a large segment of the population (La Novara 1993, 10). As a result of these considerations, activists in the battered women's shelter move-ment tend to opt for more inclusive terms like "woman abuse" or "woman battering."

Secondly, some social researchers argue that the focus on male perpetra-tors and female victims is inaccurate. One of the newer terms employed is "intimate partner violence" (see Ahmad et al. 2007; Moore and Stuart 2005; DeKeseredy 2007). We would like to emphasize that our preferred term is "woman abuse." As we will show, while women are clearly capable of violence in intimate relationships, the prevailing pattern in our society is still one of male violence against female partners. Females engage in physical violence against their partners but it is often—though not always—reactive violence; that is, they are reacting to physical violence rather than initiating it.

Finally, the term "abuse" is not clear. The assumption that abuse typi-cally takes the form of physical violence (hitting, shoving, and so on) and that physical violence is the most serious form of woman abuse is ques-tionable. Not surprisingly, much of the research literature has focused on physical violence, since the resultant injuries are less subjective and more easily identifiable. However, it is important to keep in mind that woman abuse has many manifestations that may or may not be accompanied by acts of physical violence, including sexual abuse, economic deprivation, emotional or psychological violence, and social battering (Todd and Lundy 2006).

National Institute of Justice statistics in the United States indicate that about two-thirds of women who were physically assaulted by their intimate partners also experienced sexual assault. Almost 80 per cent of these women reported that they had been sexually assaulted within the relationship more than once. The vast majority of these women did not report the sexual assault after the first occurrence. Only 6 per cent of the women reported to the police after the first incident, and only 8 per cent of them applied for a protective order. Significantly, the women who did report to the police were 59 per cent less likely to be assaulted by their intimate partner again, even if he had not been arrested. The figure was even higher (70 per cent) for the women who had applied for a protective order, whether or not they had actually obtained one. Caucasian women waited the longest before applying for a protective order (an average of eight years). Hispanic women waited about five years, and African-American women waited the least amount of time—three years. Even the shortest waiting period is still a long time, particularly in light of the finding that women who had endured sexual assault suffered from worse mental and physical health than those who had only been physically assaulted. Their children suffered as well— almost 90 per cent of them had been exposed to their mothers' assaults, the majority from the age of three (Taylor and Gaskin-Laniyan 2007).

Economic abuse is also an important dimension of abuse. Women who seek refuge in shelters often report that their husbands provide them with inadequate funds to run the household or feed the family. These same husbands often actively oppose their wives' efforts to obtain paid employment. Economic dependency and insecurity can be a key aspect of the abuse pattern since it effectively locks the woman into the relationship.

Abuse may also take the form of psychological or emotional battering, which frequently accompanies other forms of abuse but can also be a separate and distinct form. Recent research suggests that the underlying motivation for psychological abuse is the desire to control and to destroy victims' self-esteem. It is often misunderstood as trivial when contrasted to the obvious injuries of physical violence. However, psychological abuse may be much more devastating to the victim because damage to mental health may be more far-reaching and profound than physical damage. The 2004 General Social Survey (GSS) indicates that it is 2.5 times more common than physical abuse between intimate partners (Doherty and Berglund 2008).

Even though reported rates of emotional and/or financial abuse are similar for men and women (17 per cent of men and 18 per cent of women), the effects appear to be more negative for women (Doherty and Berglund 2008). In a relationship marred by violent episodes, tone of voice or slamming doors may create acute fear and anxiety in the abused partner, who knows the next violent episode may be imminent. Lastly, abuse may take the shape of social isolation. Abused women often report that their partners restrict or stop contact with family and friends and lock them into the destructive intimacy of their relationship. Significantly, victims of physical and psychological abuse often indicate that it is the non-physical forms of battering that are harder to bear than the physical pain (Straus and Sweet 1992). Wounds and injuries heal, but the pain of lost dreams and shattered trust lasts a lifetime.

A study of rural women in southwestern Ontario experiencing psychological abuse explores the frustrations of these women. They have access to few resources and are often not treated as legitimate victims of abuse because, as stated in the following quote, "there's no marks." In addition, rural communities may be more conservative, and their small size and greater intimacy among inhabitants makes it more difficult for abused women to find appropriate assistance (McCallum and Lauzon 2005). As one victim states:

> ...There was really no where [sic] to go. And if he wasn't beating me I wasn't really eligible to go into the woman's shelters. I had to have something from the police, I had to prove that I had been abused and you can't really prove verbal abuse...[if] there's no marks, no crime's been committed. (McCallum and Lauzon 2005, 133)

Based on the foregoing considerations, we define woman abuse as a pattern of violence—physical, psychological/emotional, sexual, economic, or social—that is intentionally inflicted on a female partner in the course of an ongoing dating, common-law, or marital relationship, or after one or both partners has ended this relationship. The intent of the abuse is to dominate and control the woman and, in this pursuit, violence is conditioned by a social context in which men as a group tend to have more power and authority than women as a group.

EARLY EXPERIENCES WITH ABUSE

Romantic love is held in high esteem in our society. From an early age, girls are socialized to believe that the pinnacle of personal achievement in their lives will be finding "Mr. Right" and sharing a passionate loving relationship with him, usually in a marital (or quasi-marital) situation with the children of their union. This is still true, despite the fact that many girls are now also raised to believe that they should pursue a career as well. Nothing supersedes the romantic relationship, however, as demonstrated by the innumerable movies, books, and TV programs that relish in depicting lonely, unfulfilled career women who foolishly choose career over love and live to regret it. The musty scent of the "old maid" still lingers in twenty-first-century culture. Even girls who are lesbians and grow up to have relationships with other women are steeped in images of romantic love and personal fulfillment through a passionate attachment.

Such brainwashing makes women vulnerable to exploitation in romantic relationships, even if the exploiter is not necessarily the man with whom she is involved. Women are exploited by a society that demands that they sacrifice themselves and their own best interests to raise children, care for husbands and elderly parents, act as housekeepers, chauffeurs, and counsellors. And they embrace this role willingly and enthusiastically, generation after generation. Dating is an apprenticeship for adult romantic relationships, so what girls learn about love and interaction with intimate partners while they are young trains them to have certain expectations for deeper future commitments. With their perception clouded by the dreamy notions of true love promoted by popular culture, girls may be even more vulnerable than their youth dictates. If they are led to believe that it is normal to

31

be abused by the person they are dating, it is likely they will expect that marital unions will also involve "the bad with the good" and develop a tolerance for maltreatment.

Pursuing the romantic dream, girls who have been maltreated as children tend to begin dating at an early age. Unfortunately, their early training in romantic love sometimes also provides them with training in being the victims of violence. Research on youth involved with child protection agencies indicates that youth who have experienced family maltreatment as children may repeat their experiences in dating, as victims or perpetrators of violence against their dating partners. Dating, having sex, and using alcohol are ways to practise "being grown up" and enacting roles that were modelled in their own homes (Wekerle, Leung, Wall, MacMillan, Boyle, Trocmé and Waechter 2009).

According to the Canadian Department of Justice Dating Violence Fact Sheet (CDJDV Fact Sheet), dating violence may consist of a single act of violence—physical, psychological/emotional, or sexual—against an individual with whom the abuser is in any stage of an intimate relationship, or it may be a series of acts. Escalation of abuse is common in such relationships, as with other types of intimate violence. The Fact Sheet also allows for the possibility that the abuser may not be acting alone, but with a group. It concedes that definitions of dating violence differ among studies, which makes it more difficult to understand the dimensions of the problem.

The Fact Sheet goes on to state that there are few studies focusing on teens as young as twelve or thirteen, the ages at which dating and dating violence may begin. Nevertheless, existing information indicates that dating violence is a common occurrence, particularly when measuring the full spectrum of violent behaviours from psychological to sexual abuse—the latter experienced by far more females than males. Significantly, Price, Byers, Sears, Whelan, and Saint-Pierre (2000, 7) found that on all six scales used as measurement in their study, "boys were more accepting of psychological, physical, and sexual dating violence than girls." In this study, boys tended to believe that intention was more significant with respect to abusive behaviours, while among the girls, it was the impact of behaviours that was more salient. Mann (2007, 68) indicates that men have differing motivations for the use of violence, including the need to control, punish, and get respect and sex from their female partners. Women tend to slap, punch, scratch, and sometimes use weapons to wound the men with whom they are involved. Men tend to "just walk away" from the violence inflicted upon them and do not usually feel terrorized by the women.

The Fact Sheet also describes a 1993 Canadian National Survey of university and college students that questioned them about their elementary school dating relationships. The study focused on men as perpetrators and women as victims. Two per cent of the males who responded admitted that they had threatened physical force to get their girlfriends to have sex with them, while 2 per cent admitted *using* physical force. Four per cent had been physically abusive and 19 per cent admitted to being emotionally abusive. Of the female students who responded, 3 per cent had been threatened with physical force by their boyfriends to force them to have sex with them, 4 per cent of the women admitted their boyfriends had *used* physical force to make them have sexual relations with them, 24 per cent stated their boyfriends had been emotionally abusive, and 7.2 per cent reported that they had experienced physical violence. Recall that these university and college students were not describing current or even high school dating relationships, but those from their *elementary school* years (CDJDV Fact Sheet 2010).

The same 1993 Survey also delved into violence in high school dating relationships among the same sample. Men were asked about their abusive behaviour while women were asked about their victimization. One per cent of male respondents admitted they had threatened to use physical force against their partners to force them to have sex with them, 2 per cent stated that they had actually used physical force, and 33 per cent reported that they had emotionally abused their girlfriends. One per cent also admitted that they had used physical force to hurt their partners. Of the female respondents, 8 per cent stated that their boyfriends had threatened to use physical violence to force them to engage in sexual relations, 14 per cent stated that their boyfriends had used force, 50 per cent reported that they had been emotionally abused by their boyfriends, and 9 per cent admitted that they had been physically hurt by their dating partners (CDJDV Fact Sheet 2010).

Some studies appear to indicate that male and female dating partners are equally likely to be abusive. However, the same methodological problems plague this area of study as that of spousal violence: using scales that count acts as opposed to behaviour embedded in context or consequences. As we will discuss, there is also a gender gap in terms of self-reporting, in that females tend to over-report their own use of violent methods while males tend to under-report. One thing is certain, however: women report being victims of sexual abuse far more than males (CDJDV Fact Sheet 2010).

There is a possible connection between playground bullying and dating violence, despite the relatively few studies that have focused on dating rela-tionships among twelve- and thirteen-year-olds (CDJDV Fact Sheet 2010). One study recently done by Laporte, Jiang, Pepler, and Chamberland (2009), comparing 471 adolescents aged twelve to nineteen in child protec-tion with those from the community, indicates that childhood experience of family violence affected their intimate relationships. Teenage girls who had been victimized in their families were more likely to be victimized by their boyfriends. Teenage boys who had experienced family violence were at higher risk of using aggression against their girlfriends, especially if "harshly disciplined" by their fathers. Boys who had been harshly disci-plined by their mothers were not at greater risk for aggression toward their girlfriends, suggesting that masculine gender socialization in youth plays an important role in adult abusive behaviour. This study also examined the amount of violence perpetrated by the adolescents against their parents. As it turned out, "the more frequently the adolescents reported hitting their parents, the more frequently they reported being aggressive with their dat-ing partners" (Laporte et al. 2009, 17).

From these figures, it is evident that abuse in dating relationships begins early in women's lives and frequently escalates as they mature. Consequently, it is imperative to examine these early relationships, as they appear to be a training ground for adult behaviour. An international study conducted by Murray Straus, involving students from thirty-one universities in sixteen countries and using the Conflict Tactics Scale (CTS), concludes that studying students is important because they are "at a formative period in their lives, especially in relation to the development of appropriate pat-terns of behavior with a partner. The patterns manifested at this age are often enduring features of their relationships" (Straus 2004, 792).[9] Straus also notes that studies of violence among dating partners in the United

States and Canada have demonstrated that the rate of physical violence is very high, with 20 per cent to 40 per cent reporting one or more assaults in the preceding twelve months (2004, 791). As is common among studies using this scale to measure violence, the rate of violence by females against their male partners was slightly higher than that of males against their female partners. The rate of physical violence among the dating students at the median university was about 29 per cent during the previous twelve months and 7 per cent of the students had physically injured their dating partner. Straus concedes that, when considering the degree of injury inflicted, men are more likely to inflict more serious injuries on women than the reverse. In contrast, Price et al. (2003), using a revised version of the CTS, found that the scale was more helpful in understanding the scope of adolescent dating violence and its variations when used along with other measurements, including focus groups. Their research did not support the "violence parity" results of Straus and other researchers who had restricted their measurement to the CTS, once again indicating the significant shortcomings of strictly quantitative measurement of violence in intimate relationships.

Anderson, Simpson-Taylor, and Herrmann (2004) examined "rules" of appropriate behaviour that may lead to the acceptance of rape myths among young men and women at the middle school, high school, and university levels. They argue that it is important to study middle school youths because there is little existing research on this particular group, even though 12 to 13 per cent of younger adolescents and 14 to 25 per cent of young women report that they have been raped or sexually assaulted. Also, adolescence is when dating behaviour and sexual activity typically commence (Anderson, Simpson-Taylor, and Herrmann 2004, 78). Results indicate that boys and men are more likely to hold rules that support rape than are girls and women. In the same gender group, middle school boys held the most rape-supportive rules while university men held the fewest. There was less overlap between the sexes among younger students, suggesting that as boys and girls get older and more educated, their understanding of gender relations in intimate relationships becomes somewhat more sophisticated and egalitarian. Middle and high school girls and boys agreed that if a woman exhibits behaviour such as kissing or petting a man, or teases a man about his sexual performance, then she has broken a "rule," making it acceptable for a man to force her into sexual relations. However, both university men and women felt that if a woman does not physically or verbally resist a man's sexual advances, it was all right for a man to assume that she wanted to have sex with him, based on the age-old notion that men are sexual aggressors and women are gatekeepers. The authors found that the more rules that were endorsed by a male, the more likely he was to have sexually coerced a female, but there was no significant correlation between a girl or woman's endorsement of rules and her experience of sexual coercion (Anderson, Simpson-Taylor, and Herrmann 2004, 87).

It is not only the women who report their earliest dating relationships as abusive who are victims of intimate violence, however. Woman abuse cuts across race and class, and it may start at any time during a relationship. Some women indicate that the violence did not start until they were married. Yet others reveal that physical violence appeared in their relationship only when they became pregnant with their first child, or after separation from their male partners. As noted above, the earliest moments of an abusive relationship may not be characterized by physical or even psychological violence so much as by overwhelming romantic intensity. In dating relationships, a young woman may find herself flattered by the extreme attention her boyfriend focuses on her. He wants to be involved in every aspect of her life, including what she wears, who her friends are, and where she goes. He calls or texts her on her cell phone dozens of times a day or requests/demands that she check in with him everywhere she goes so that he knows that she is "safe." With the popularity of Facebook, Twitter, and other social networking sites and apps for cell phones, such constant monitoring is easily facilitated and may appear more innocent than in less technological times. The real intent of such a degree of interest is easily obscured, at least in the beginning.

A LOVE SO GREAT...

Q: When does a persistent lover become a stalker?
A: When his behaviour feels threatening and makes you fearful for your safety.

36

This characterization is somewhat simplified but it goes to the heart of the matter of criminal harassment, colloquially known as "stalking." Criminal harassment is a very particular type of violence that undermines the victim's sense of safety and personal integrity. It has psychological and sometimes physical dimensions. Section 264, the criminal harassment provisions, first appeared in the *Criminal Code of Canada* in 1993 (compared to 1990 in California, the first U.S. state to enact such a law). According to a brochure published by the Royal Canadian Mounted Police (2007), the definition of this crime states:

> *Generally it consists of repeated conduct that is carried out over a period of time and which causes you to reasonably fear for your safety or the safety of someone known to you. Stalking does not have to result in physical injury in order to make it a crime. The law protects you even if the conduct of the stalker is not done with the intent to scare you. It is enough if the conduct does scare you. This may be an advance warning of the possibility of future violent acts.*

This definition clearly indicates that what constitutes criminal harassment is what the victim considers to be harassing behaviour. Unlike other crimes wherein intent by the perpetrator is an important element of culpability, stalking is considered to be a crime even in the absence of perpetrator intent; in other words, if the victim *feels* threatened or fearful, regardless of whether the perpetrator has clearly indicated that he wishes to cause harm of some kind, criminal harassment has occurred. Stalkers are considered to be obsessed with their victims. The majority have been in some kind of relationship with the victim, though not necessarily a serious one. Frequently, however, they are former lovers or spouses who refuse to recognize that the relationship is over and are trying to force the former loved one back into the relationship. Some are suffering from a mental illness and others are in love with the higher-status victim and believe that he or she would return their love if not for something keeping them apart. Obscene phone calls are the most frequently reported stalking behaviour reported by women (RCMP 2007; AuCoin 2005; see Tjaden and Thoennes 1998).[10]

According to a report published by the Canadian Centre for Justice Studies (CCJS) in November 2000, the number of incidents of criminal harassment reported to the police between 1996 and 1999 increased by 32 per cent.[11] Among ten Canadian cities, Edmonton had the lowest rate in 1999 with 11 incidents per 100,000 population, while Montreal and Saskatoon had the highest with 73 and 75 respectively (Hackett 2000, 3–4).

Between 1999 and 2004, among women fifteen years of age and over, more than one in ten (about 11 per cent) were victims of stalking by men, while about 7 per cent of men were the victims of stalkers (AuCoin 2005, 34). Most victims are stalked by one particular individual but about 28 per cent (men more frequently than women) had been stalked by more than one. The majority of stalkers are male, regardless of the sex of the victim. This means that even men are predominantly stalked by men. About 5 per cent of stalkers are female and in fewer than one in ten situations both the victim and stalker are women. However, when the stalkers are female, their target is primarily another female. Thus, the majority of victims of male or female stalkers are women (see also Hackett 2000 for earlier figures). Kropp et al. (2002) speculate that the small number of male victims may be due to the fact that males do not feel as threatened by females and, therefore, are less likely to report being stalked (as cited in AuCoin 2005, 36).

Research indicates that the closer the relationship between the victim and stalker, the more likely it is that the victim will experience diverse types of stalking behaviours. For example, a female victim might receive obscene phone calls from her former intimate partner as well as being spied upon. Two-thirds (67 per cent) of female victims and 54 per cent of male victims reported experiencing multiple forms of stalking by a former intimate partner. These figures suggest that the more intimate the former relationship between victim and stalker, the more the stalker knows about the victim and is able to use that knowledge to harass her or him (AuCoin 2005, 36).

About 21 per cent of respondents who had been stalked by a former spouse reported that the stalking had lasted more than a year. Twenty-nine per cent of female respondents as opposed to 21 per cent of males had been stalked from one to six months, while 31 per cent of males reported having been stalked for a week or less (AuCoin 2005, 38). The CCJS report for the period of 1995 to 1996 indicates that stalking may even start while the victim and her stalker are still living together. Stalking usually occurs at or near the victim's home regardless of the relationship between victim and stalker; however, the closer the relationship between them, the more likely the stalking will occur within the home. Only a small percentage (less than 2 per cent) of stalking victims report physical injury, although threats of possible harm were present in 52 per cent of the incidents reported to the police (Hackett 2000, 6–9).

The issue of cyberstalking was also raised in the CCJS report. Also known as "online harassment," cyberstalking occurs in chat rooms, message boards, and e-mails where stalkers send threatening or harassing messages to their victims who are, once again, more likely to be women. Victims and cyberstalkers may be known to one another. The Internet provides new possibilities for harassing victims. For example, "Other incidents have involved the cyberstalker campaigning against the victim by posting information about the intended target on discussion groups or poster boards (possibly by pretending to be the victim). In these incidents, the cyberstalker may elicit a third party to harass and threaten the victim" (Hackett 2000, 11). Occasionally, cyberstalking becomes actual stalking. It may be difficult to prosecute cyberstalkers due to the anonymity afforded by the Internet and the fact that victims and stalkers may live in different countries (Hackett 2000, 11). Unfortunately, this type of violence may be the wave of the future with children and youth who are growing up steeped in increasingly sophisticated technology. Further research on cyber-relationships is important in order to understand if, and how, violence against women may be perpetrated.

DIMENSIONS OF VIOLENCE AGAINST WOMEN

Woman abuse came out of the closet in the late sixties and early seventies in Canada. At this time, women were responding to the contemporary women's movement, were being challenged by new feminist authors, and were coming together in consciousness-raising groups and at newly founded women's centres. They quickly identified violence as a key issue in their own and other women's lives. Although women have been abused throughout history, the social movement energized by modern feminism waged a successful campaign to document the pervasiveness of this violence and its devastating impact on women's lives, and to challenge the societal beliefs and values that trivialized and privatized women's suffering. Almost at once feminist analysis translated into social activism, of which one immediate focus was the creation of shelters (at first called transition houses) for "battered wives." In 1972, the first shelters were established in British Columbia and Alberta. By 1980, there were seventy-one transition houses or hostels across Canada accepting battered women (MacLeod 1980).

No doubt these early efforts would have fizzled if they had not been responding to an actual need. It rapidly became clear that violence against women in their homes was not uncommon or insignificant. In 1978, social researcher Linda MacLeod assembled statistics from forty-seven Canadian transition houses and, based on the results, estimated that about 15,000 women across Canada would stay in a transition house each year. In addition, an estimated 12,000 women requested help from (but did not stay at) transition houses "because they were physically battered by their husbands" (1980, 16–17). These results, along with the ongoing demand for shelter services, demonstrated that the abuse of women was not simply a private, personal trouble rooted in individual pathology. If only one or two Canadian women were victims of abuse, it made sense to focus on their personal background and idiosyncrasies. When thousands of women were asking for assistance, the problem was clearly societal and systemic. As early activists argued, this abuse was a public issue that warranted the attention of all Canadians and reflected on the fundamental beliefs, values, and structure of our society. MacLeod updated her research in 1985 by collecting statistics and interviewing battered women and transition-house workers at 110 shelters. At this juncture, she estimated that 42,000 women were accommodated at the 230 shelters across Canada every year, and almost every shelter had been forced to turn "a large number of women" away (1987, 6–7). The publicity surrounding these and earlier figures further motivated social activists, researchers, and policy analysts to determine the actual extent of the problem.

MacLeod's research, while a landmark effort, was exploratory. There was no way of knowing how many abused women were unable or unwilling to contact a shelter, or how many were able to use other forms of escape from a violent relationship. What was needed was a much more extensive—and costly—national picture of woman abuse. However, as previously discussed, woman abuse by its very nature is extremely difficult to research. In all survey research, there is the problem of respondents being unwilling to honestly report their behaviour or attitudes (Northrup 1997). This difficulty is greatly compounded because abusive behaviour and experiences are often seen as stigmatizing and shaming. Creating and funding research that would explore this complex and contentious issue on a national basis while protecting the rights and safety of respondents was an enormous challenge.

Throughout the eighties, considerable academic research addressed the dimensions of woman abuse by employing survey techniques and, in particular, the CTS, formulated by one of the pioneer researchers in family violence, American sociologist Murray Straus (1979), and referred to by some as "the gold standard" in measuring domestic violence (Hegarty, Bush, and Sheehan 2005). The scale consists of eighteen items intended to identify a continuum of non-violent and violent strategies that may occur in interpersonal conflict. For example, respondents (husbands or wives) are asked to indicate how often, if ever, in the past year they have insulted, slapped, pushed, shoved, threw an object at, or kicked their partner.

A number of Canadian researchers have used the CTS to measure woman abuse in Canada (DeKeseredy and Hinch 1991, 21–23). Few studies have attempted to measure woman abuse at a national level, which is not surprising given the expense of national surveys. However, even city-based surveys suggest that a significant number of Canadian men and women have experienced abuse—even severe abuse, which involves a high level of harm. Smith (1987), for example, reported that in his Toronto sample of 604 women who were currently or formerly married or in a cohabiting relationship, 14.4 per cent had been abused in the past year and 5.1 per cent had been severely abused.

However, as a number of researchers have been quick to point out, the popular CTS approach is not without its flaws. (For excellent discussions, see Todd and Lundy 2006; Dobash and Dobash 2004; and DeKeseredy and Schwartz 1998, 2005.) The introduction to the CTS item list identifies the "strategies" as ways that couples seek "to settle their differences." However, many abusive incidents are not precipitated by conflict or disagreement—some victims report violence erupting without warning.[12]

41

Given the introductory remarks to the CTS, it is not clear which incidents respondents would include. In addition, the CTS continuum format implicitly makes the questionable assumption that physical violence is worse than psychological abuse. It also assumes that some "minor" forms of violence (slapping) are less physically injurious than "severe violence," and leaves out other abusive actions such as scratching and burning.

Further methodological problems are raised by the fact that research indicates that men and women do not report—and perhaps do not perceive—the same reality when it comes to violence. For example, Brinkerhoff and Lupri (1988) found that women report their abusive acts against their husbands more readily than men report their abusive acts against their wives. Other studies reveal that men's and women's reports on the occurrence and frequency of violence in their relationship are widely discrepant. Clinical studies with violent men also indicate that these men tend to minimize their violent acts and the injuries they cause. In addition, it is not clear from CTS reports whether or not women's violence is a response to male violence or if women's violence is as potentially injurious. Finally, by simply counting the violent acts, the CTS approach ignores the larger context of violence. For example, in a society where men tend to be principal wage earners for the family and are still often assumed to be the "head" of the household, one violent act by the man may have a much more definitive impact on the household than several violent acts by a rebellious wife (DeKeseredy and Hinch 1991, 23–25; Johnson 1996, 56–60).

Another important shortcoming of the CTS is that it operates under the assumption that the terms "conflict," "abuse," and "hit" are interpreted in similar fashion by men and women—which is, according to feminist theory, unlikely given that the social construction of gender takes place within the structures and processes of a patriarchal society. Further, to assume that meanings are the same across gender when other social positions—such as race, ethnicity, social class, and age—also significantly exert their influences on an individual's perceptions and interpretations, may be to take dangerous liberties with variables that could contribute to reducing validity in social research (Fox and Murry 2000).

Significant advancements toward understanding the dimensions of woman abuse were achieved in the early nineties when the Canadian

Violence Against Women Survey (CVAWS), funded by the federal Department of Health, was conducted through the auspices of Statistics Canada. This national survey, which involved telephone interviews with a randomly selected representative sample of 12,300 women and used a modified CTS approach, provided Canadians with invaluable insight into the nature and extent of male violence. This pioneering effort not only provides an informed base for national policies, but also stands as a model that has been replicated by other countries wishing to address the costs and consequences of violence against women (Johnson 1995).

The CVAWS produced powerful evidence that intimate violence is a pervasive and significant issue in women's lives. The researchers found that one-quarter of the women surveyed (aged eighteen or older) had experienced violence at the hands of a past or present marital partner from the age of sixteen. This means that one in four Canadian women will in all likelihood be pushed, grabbed, shoved, threatened, slapped, kicked, bitten, hit, beaten up, or sexually assaulted at some point in their marital lives. While "severe" violence such as "choking" or "using a gun or knife" was relatively uncommon in the reports (7 per cent and 5 per cent of respondents, respectively, reporting these types of violence), more than one in ten of the women who reported violence in a current marriage indicated they had at some point felt their lives were in danger. This severity is perhaps not surprising since 39 per cent of these women reported more than one violent episode in their current marriage and 10 per cent reported more than ten episodes (Statistics Canada 1993).

Holly Johnson and Valerie Pottie Bunge (2001), in examining the prevalence and consequences of spousal assault in Canada, indicate that although rates of violence among men and women are more or less equal, "…women are almost four times more likely than men to fall into the most serious and potentially injurious category of assaults: being beaten up, choked, threatened/assaulted with a gun or knife, and sexually assaulted (3.8 per cent compared to 1.1 per cent of male victims), and more likely to be pushed, shoved or slapped (3 per cent compared to 1.7 per cent of men). Men, on the other hand, are three times as likely as women to be kicked, bit, hit, or hit with something (3 per cent compared to 1 per cent of female victims)" ("The Severity of Spousal Violence," para. 3). Women were also three times more likely than men to report physical injuries, twice as likely to report ongoing assaults (more than ten), and five times as likely to report that they feared for their lives. Female victims were also more likely to state that they suffered negative emotional consequences ("Consequences and Outcomes of Spousal Violence," para. 2).

After the mass murder of young female students at Université de Montréal's École Polytechnique and sociological survey data that indicated high rates of wife abuse in the late eighties and early nineties, public outrage convinced the Canadian government to commit $176 million between 1988 and 1996 to family violence initiatives, particularly those dealing with woman abuse. The CVAWS was one of the results of this commitment, as was the Canadian National Survey on Woman Abuse in University/ College Dating (CNS). Both of these surveys addressed the problems inherent in earlier survey methods popular among American researchers such as Steinmetz, Straus, and Gelles. Despite international praise for these surveys, a backlash movement led by fathers' rights groups and men's rights advocates developed, complaining that men were being discriminated against by "prostituted science and scholarship" and that intimate partner violence is gender symmetrical.[13] Conservative MPs, such as Roger Gallaway, who was Joint Chair of the 1998 Special Joint Committee on Child Custody and Access (SJC), have lent their support to such groups. The SJC concluded that, as there was evidence that men, too, were the victims of violence by women, it would not recommend the use of a gender-specific definition of family violence in any family or divorce legislation proposed. Murray Straus supported this position, stating that the CVAWS had excluded elements of his CTS dealing with violence by women in order to avoid political embarrassment. Statistics Canada then moved away from an explicitly feminist approach toward a gender-neutral one in its ensuing General Social Surveys (GSS), which gathered data on family violence commencing in 1999. The GSS now more closely resembles the original CTS, and because of this has come under critical attack by many researchers. Notably, there is no support for the notion of "battered husband syndrome" by the researchers who conducted the 1999 GSS (DeKeseredy and Schwartz 2005). It should be noted that in both the 1999 and 2004 waves of the survey, results for severity and constancy of violence, severity of injuries, threats to harm or kill, level of fear, and the nature and level of violence witnessed by children indicate that women are the primary victims. Also noteworthy is that about 30 per cent of male victims in the 2004 wave, as opposed to only about 6 per cent of females, stated that the violence had "little or no impact on their well-being" (Mann 2007, 59–60).

DeKeseredy and Schwartz (2005) note that, unlike most surveys based on the CTS which find that at least 10 per cent of both male and female respondents have experienced violence in the preceding twelve months, the 1999 GSS found that only 3 per cent of women and 2 per cent of men with current partners had experienced violence during that same period. Even if the time period is extended to the preceding five years, the rate of victimization is 8 per cent for women and 7 per cent for men. The authors state that these curiously low rates are explained by researchers as the effect of presenting the study as a "crime victimization" study. In other words, if victims of violence at the hands of their intimate partners do not consider their partners' acts criminal, they will not report them and thus they will not become part of the statistical evidence.

In 1998 Statistics Canada began to publish its annual profile entitled "Family Violence in Canada," which provides the most current information on the various types, incidence, and prevalence of family violence, indicating trends and focusing on a different aspect of the problem each year.[14] The annual report relies on police-reported data, therefore certain limitations are inherent; nevertheless, it provides an overview of the extent of the problem in general and within certain specific family relationships. The 2009 report indicates that reported violence between "spouses" (including married, common-law, separated, and divorced couples) has declined over the past decade by about 15 per cent. This type of violence accounts for about 12 per cent of all violent crimes reported to the police, with common assault being the most frequently reported behaviour, followed by major assault, uttering threats, and criminal harassment, also known as stalking. Over 80 per cent of the victims are female. Charges were laid in about three-quarters of all reported assaults and those in which the victim was female were more likely to result in charges (Statistics Canada 2009, 5).

Two themes emerge from the research literature of the nineties: the first is the importance of distinguishing between different types of violence, motives of perpetrators, and social and cultural contexts; the second is rec-ognizing the issue of control (Johnson and Ferraro 2000). The researchers assert that there are actually four distinctive patterns of partner violence that reflect definitional and methodological differences. Common couple violence (CCV) is not characterized by a generalized pattern of control; it arises within the context of an argument that escalates to the point of vio-lence, when both partners are likely to strike one another. Johnson states that CCV does not usually entail severe violence, nor does it escalate over time. He contends that this is the type of violence most frequently reported by general samples.[15] Intimate terrorism (IT), on the other end of the con-tinuum, is all about control by one partner over the other (Johnson and Ferraro 2000). The violence is not mutual in this pattern, and emotional abuse is frequently part of the strategy for control. It is also noted that the violence involved in IT is much more frequent than in CCV. Comparing fre-quency, escalation of violence, severity, and response by females, Michael P. Johnson (2006) concludes that IT and Situational Couple Violence (SCV), a later characterization, are very different phenomena. SCV involves violence by both partners but neither is controlling. Violent resistance (VR) is the pattern that often appears to be gender symmetrical in violence among intimate partners, since it includes women's attempts to resist abu-sive control by their male partners. The fourth and final pattern, mutual violent control (MVC), consists of couple violence wherein both husband and wife are violent and controlling. In other words, it consists of two intimate terrorists struggling for control. According to Johnson and Ferraro (2000) there is little known about this particular pattern. They emphasize that studies that find there is gender parity in violence between intimate spouses produce such results because they lump together male-perpetrated IT, CCV (perpetrated by slightly more men than women), and mostly female-perpetrated VR. Such an aggregation of essentially different patterns of violence obscures rather than clarifies the dimensions of family violence.

Johnson and Ferraro (2000) state that to call studies in which "gen-der symmetry" is based on the percentage of men and women who have committed at least one violent act is to ignore the differing frequencies of male- and female-perpetrated violence, as well as the disparity in physical consequences. The debate between the "family violence" and "feminist" schools of thought and their associated research methods precipitated, among other things, a revision of the CTS and renewed discussions about sampling. It is important to clarify what type of violence is being measured (such as in the 1995–96 National Violence Against Women Survey) to understand figures gauging the experience of violence among Asian (13 per cent), African-American (26 per cent), American Indian and Alaskan Native women (31 per cent), and mixed-race women (27 per cent), as opposed to white women (21 per cent) (Johnson and Ferraro 2000, "Demographics, Social Location, and Identity," para. 6). In other words, is the violence CCV or IT? Johnson and Ferraro assert, "We cannot develop good theories about race differences until we make such distinctions" (2000, "Demographics, Social Location, and Identity," para. 7). They also question how much of the variations depend on factors involving race and ethnicity as opposed to socio-economic status.[16]

The second major theme emerging from research in the nineties discussed by Johnson and Ferraro (2000) is that of control. They point out that perpetrators of violence are attempting to gain some measure of control in their own lives and over their partners, although their motives are likely to differ; and that gender is no longer sufficient to explain such differing motives, particularly in light of research on same-sex couples. There should also be an account of differing motives in terms of CCV and VR. Other continuing themes discussed by Johnson and Ferraro (2000) include coping with partner violence, psychological and behavioural consequences of partner violence, and social consequences of partner violence. They conclude that the nineties represent a time of tremendous growth in the breadth and scope of research on the subject.

Michael P. Johnson (2006) also points out that it is erroneous to believe that samples drawn from agencies that provide services to battered women are definitive. These workers most often characterize their clients' experience as IT, but most couples who experience violence are involved in CCV/SCV. In order to avoid sampling biases that skew the picture of intimate partner violence, he suggests that research instruments should include an assessment of control tactics and ask questions about both partners' use of violence in order to fully understand what is really happening.

Kelly and Johnson (2008) offer the most recent typology of intimate partner violence, describing five different types: coercive controlling violence, violent resistance, situational couple violence, separation-instigated violence, and mutual violent control—although they reiterate Johnson's point (2006) that little is known about this final type. It is important to differentiate among the various types of intimate violence so that, once the dimensions of each type and the best way to deal with them have been identified, screening and responses can be developed to address each individual type more effectively. Coercive controlling violence was first called "patriarchal terrorism," which evolved into "intimate terrorism," but was later altered again due to reluctance to use such terminology in courts. The more neutral term recognizes that not all controlling violence is perpetrated by men, and not all coercive and controlling behaviour stems from patriarchal structures and processes. Separation-instigated violence involves the particular type of violence that commences when a couple separates, as opposed to violence that *continues* throughout the separation period. Kelly and Johnson point out that coercive controlling violence is usually perpetrated by males in heterosexual relationships, but it is important to recognize that in lesbian couples, it is of course women who use such violence against their partners (Kelly and Johnson 2008).

While acknowledging these persistent debates about research methodology, it seems fair to say that a vastly improved research base has confirmed that violence against women in intimate relationships is a pervasive and persistent social problem. No longer is it necessary to rely on estimates or impressions. Newspaper items that call attention to the "epidemic of violence against women" or refer to the "pervasive abuse of women" now have added credibility. Research has also given us a much more solid understanding of the parameters of abuse—who the typical victims and abusers are, what the nature of the violence is, where it occurs, and so on.

Since MacLeod's landmark research in the late seventies, researchers have been interested in documenting not only the extent of the violence but also its distinguishing characteristics. Clearly, analysts hope that by understanding who is victimized and when victimization occurs, they will gain insight into why violence occurs and how to end it.

GENDER PATTERNS WITHIN VIOLENCE

Violence in families between intimate partners is not a random phenomenon. There are distinct patterns with respect to those most likely to be victimized. Using some of the categories of analysis involved with intersectionality (except for homosexuality, which will be covered in Chapter 4), we will examine some recent research below.

Michalski (2004) conducts an extensive comparative, cross-cultural examination of trends in intimate partner violence using a social structural approach. He begins by observing that violence against women occurs across all geographical regions and in all types of society (see Pinheiro 2006 as well). Michalski is critical of the cultural approach to analysis, which argues that violence against women stems from patriarchal beliefs and values or from a violent culture; instead, he argues that it is "the social structures within which violence tends to be embedded" (Michaelski 2004, 653) that have greater explanatory power. He believes that violence is one possible strategy for handling grievances—that it might be a "type of moralistic response or social control" against the object of the grievance. He isolates six sociological factors within which the social relationship is embedded, and which contribute to the choice to use violence against female intimate partners by males: social isolation, or the degree of social support—possibly political or economic—available to the woman; integrated networks, or cross-cutting ties and interdependent networks, which could apply pressure on the male perpetrator to not use violence; inequality, particularly between men and women; relational distance, meaning the level of intimacy between the parties (the more intimacy, the less likely the man will choose to be violent against his wife); centralization of authority (if all or most of the authority, decision-making power, or political resources rest in the hands of the man); and violent network exposure, which describes a man's social network that supports violence and its use against a wife or girlfriend. Michalski (2004) suggests that, were public policy to be directed to reducing or eliminating these factors from the social structure rather than focusing efforts on individuals, violence against women might be reduced.

Although research suggests men are more likely to be the instigators of serious, repetitive violence, women are also capable of serious violent acts.

In some cases, the woman was reported to be responding to years of endur-ing violence and abuse. For example, in 1994 a forty-eight-year-old Ontario woman was acquitted of all criminal charges after drugging her unfaithful husband and cutting off his penis. Her lawyer argued that she was suffer-ing from "battered wife syndrome and was acting in self defence...because she feared [her husband] might kill her that night" (Crook, *Toronto Star*, 2 October 1992).

It is now widely accepted that some instances of woman-initiated vio-lence are the result of *battered woman syndrome*. This term, popularized by Leonore Walker (1993), one of the pioneer activists in the movement against woman battering, refers to the theory that women victimized by intimate physical, sexual, or psychological violence may eventually feel so helpless and hopeless that they cannot extricate themselves from the abusive relationship. When they feel their own or their children's lives are in imminent danger, they may respond by attacking and killing their abuser. This psychological state—an aspect of post-traumatic stress disorder[17]—has been successfully used in Canada and the United States to defend women who have killed their abusive male partners (Walker 1993). As a result of a landmark Supreme Court of Canada ruling in 1990, which recognized battered woman syndrome as a legal defence, a 1997 report to the federal government recommended that seven women incarcerated for murder be freed from prison, pardoned, or have their sentences reviewed since they had been defending themselves against abusive partners.

Recent research into lesbian battering has also been presented as evidence that women are potentially as violent as men. Certainly, some aspects of violent lesbian relationships are highly reminiscent of heterosexual patterns of abuse; however, the fact that lesbians can be violent does not mean that women in heterosexual relationships are likely to act in a similar fashion. Lesbian violence is conditioned by the relationship between the couple and their social context. As women, the lesbian couple is likely to be treated by the larger society as equals; however, as lesbians, they are both socially defined as members of a generally stigmatized group. In addition, the les-bian community—in its established dissonance with mainstream society—is likely to provide a context that is more prominent in the relationship as well as more supportive of healing the couple than the typical suburban community (Card 1995).

Similarly, heterosexual women's violence is structured by its social context: a context in which women are more likely to be poor, less well paid, less educated, and so on. Heterosexual men and women do not typically confront one another as equals in this society. Regardless of their personal qualities and abilities, they live in a society with the inevitable knowledge that this society is frequently—although with some notable exceptions—led by men, financed by men, and designed by men. When a woman hits her husband or male lover, she does so with the knowledge of these gender inequalities. She knows, for example, that if the marriage ends, she will probably take custody of the children and will, in all likelihood, struggle financially. She knows that at forty-five or fifty years of age she, but not he, has a greater chance of being considered a marital long shot. She may not like these social conditions, but she will be aware of them and they will be part of the meaning of her actions.

Acts of violence are socially constructed, and it is the social meaning of the violent act that is most significant. For example, if someone unintentionally drops a rock on your foot, you may be injured and angered but your reaction is tempered by understanding the social meaning: the other person did not intend to hurt you. If, however, the act was intentional or part of a pattern or historical tradition in which other people like you have been injured or violated, it acquires dramatically different implications. While lesbian battering does confirm that women are capable of severe violence—even murder—it cannot stand as a parallel to the violence in heterosexual relationships.

Criminal justice statistics corroborate a gendered pattern of victimization. It is women who file the overwhelming majority of domestic violence complaints with police; it is women who are most likely to appear in hospital emergency rooms with injuries from domestic violence; and it is women who are more likely than men to be killed by their marital partner. Between 1977 and 1996, 75 per cent of all spousal homicides involved men killing their wives—three times the number of men killed by their wives (Statistics Canada 2000, 28). Crime statistics consistently document that extreme violence, such as homicide, is a primarily male phenomenon. Not only are men more likely to be victims of homicide (67 per cent of all homicide victims are male), men are much more likely to be accused of homicide (87 per cent) (Johnson 1996, 179). The most dramatic and violent acts of family violence, familicides—where the wife and children (sometimes along with other family members) are killed in one incident—are also a distinctly male phenomenon, with men committing 94 per cent of famili-cides (Wilson and Daly 1994, 4).

Koziol-McLain, Webster, McFarlane, and Block (2006) state that an examination of studies done in the U.S., Australia, Canada, and Sweden indicates that 25 per cent of intimate partner femicides are followed by the perpetrator's suicide, compared to 5 per cent of non-intimate homicides. They note that there are common factors associated with femicide: it often occurs after an estrangement; in relationships where the male partner has battered his female partner repeatedly; and in some countries, such as Canada, if a firearm was used. Koziol-McLain et al. (2006) analyzed data gathered from 1994 to 2000, from a multi-site study of risk factors for inti-mate partner femicide, to explore whether there are unique femicide-suicide risk factors among women in violent relationships. Not surprisingly, they discovered that the most significant risk factor for femicide-suicide was prior domestic violence against the victim (72 per cent). The use of a gun in the incident was also strongly predictive (61 per cent). This figure was reflected in a study done in Quebec by Bourget et al. (2000), where a gun was used in 61 per cent of homicide-suicides as compared to 27 per cent of homicides only (as cited in Koziol-McLain et al. 2006). Two additional risk factors unique to femicide-suicide were prior suicide threats made by the perpetrator, and marriage between the perpetrator and victim at any point (i.e., not necessarily a current marriage). One notable factor that the researchers did not consider to be significant was use of illicit drugs by the perpetrator—although 50 per cent of femicide-suicide perpetrators had apparently used drugs prior to the incident. In terms of racial factors, both victims and perpetrators were more likely to be white, Hispanic, and Asian rather than African-American. Psychologically, perpetrators of femicide-suicide may have a higher stake in conformity and may appear, prior to the incident, to be somewhat less lethal than other perpetrators. The implications for those working with victims of partner abuse are that women should receive specific interventions if they are considering separation from their husband; and that men who use violence against their wives should not be allowed to own a gun and should be scrutinized by health professionals for risk factors, especially if they are going through separation (Koziol-McLain et al. 2006).

Umberson, Anderson, Williams, and Chen (2003, para. 1) examine the literature regarding stress/coping and masculinities to understand how "culturally defined images of masculinity might shape men's response to stress with violence." Their review of these literatures led them to hypothesize that men who adopt a masculine identity consisting of repression of negative emotion and physical and emotional withdrawal as coping mechanisms for stress, and who exercise control over themselves and their intimates, are more likely to express that masculine identity through the use of violence. A small sample of men with a history of domestic violence and a comparison group of non-violent men were asked to keep a structured diary for at least seven days. The diary entry included daily answers to questions about their relationship, general sources of stress, personal control, and emotional state. Their results indicate that non-violent men are more likely to express their emotions in daily conflict situations with their partners, while, as hypothesized, men who repressed their emotions or had difficulty expressing negative emotions (or any emotions at all) were more likely to lose control and lash out. These men were also likely to view their partners as provoking these violent incidents, holding them responsible.

Based on this evidence, we reject notions that men's and women's participation in marital violence is equal. However, we do not want to imply that violent women should be invisible in studies. Rather, we believe the focus should be on male violence in intimate relations since this violence is currently exacting the heaviest personal and societal costs in terms of the number of women and children in shelters, police intervention in domestic disputes, and spousal homicides.

RACE AND ETHNICITY PATTERNS WITHIN VIOLENCE

A similar relationship between race and woman abuse has been documented in the United States. Research there indicates that "wife abuse" is significantly more common amongst the unemployed and poor and amongst African-Americans and Hispanics (Gelles 1993, 33–34). This relationship between racial/ethnic minorities and abuse does not, however, imply causality. Two recent events suggest that cultural values and practices (such as arranged marriages) are responsible for producing woman abuse. In two well-known incidents, a prominent Filipino-Canadian woman was killed in a domestic dispute, and nine members of a British Columbia Sikh family were killed by a jealous ex-husband. Analysts dismissed any causal link and pointed out that woman abuse, sexism, and misogyny know no racial or ethnic boundaries (Cordozo, *Toronto Star*, 16 April 1996). These violent incidents more likely reflect the stresses of economic and social marginalization, rather than subcultural values that permit or endorse wife abuse. Since economic marginalization and minority group status tend to intersect, it is to be expected that woman abuse would be more evident in minority communities. Poor and minority groups may also be more subject to police and judicial scrutiny and, as a result, the violence is more likely to become part of the public record (Todd and Lundy 2006).

The CVAWS did not ask respondents to identify their ethnic or cultural background and little other research of the time focused on this issue (see DeKeseredy and Hinch 1991, 28).[18] Recent research, however, has indicated that Aboriginal women may be particularly subject to woman abuse. Aboriginal people appear to be three times more likely to be victims of spousal violence, at 21 per cent overall. Twenty-four per cent of Aboriginal women reported suffering violence at the hands of a common-law or marital partner in the five years preceding 2004, compared to about 8 per cent of non-Aboriginal women (Elizabeth Fry Society 2010). Activists and academic researchers support the conclusion that intimate violence against women is particularly acute in Aboriginal communities (LaRocque 1994; Baxter et al. 1995).[19]

This appears to be a particularly thorny issue in light of Aboriginal activism in the judicial system. Aboriginal people have lobbied extensively for alternative justice approaches that are more culturally sensitive to their needs; however, progress is prevented by a conflict of interest within the Aboriginal community. This conflict is starkly demonstrated in the 2004 Watson Lake, BC, case in which former Kaska chief Daniel Morris beat and sexually assaulted his common-law wife, Elizabeth Dickson, injuring her severely enough to require a three-day stay in hospital and resulting in continuing problems with her vision. Morris was sentenced to two years probation on four charges, in spite of a letter from the Liard Aboriginal Women's Society, signed by forty-nine Kaska women, requesting a custodial sentence for him. Despite the fact that the judge's decision was based on consideration of the social devastation suffered by Aboriginal communities, including poverty, alcoholism, and systemic bias, it may have been (perhaps unwittingly) supporting a largely male Kaska leadership that is biased against women and wishes to silence them (Pope 2004).

Nwosu (2006) argues that the domestic violence endured by Nigerian-Canadian women in Toronto is part of their larger experience of being immigrants in this country. Nigerian men attempt to recreate their cultural gender role, which socializes them to believe that they should be the head of the household and have control over their wives. Nigerian women often find themselves being the main breadwinners, yet still having to shoulder traditional women's roles in the family without assistance from their husbands. Should these women become empowered by their new role in Canadian society and try to negotiate power within the family, they may find themselves victims of abuse. Unfortunately, a lack of culturally appropriate services and the conservative constraints of their ethnic community may make it impossible to seek assistance.

Abused immigrant women seem to have little faith in the criminal justice system in Canada as a means for solving the problem of domestic violence. They believe that police intervention may exacerbate the "isolation, inequality, control, and unequal power dynamics" that initially contribute to the violence (Wachholz and Miedema 2000, 315). Community support and culturally sensitive services may be of more assistance.

AGE-RELATED PATTERNS WITHIN VIOLENCE

The CVAWS results suggested that the typical abuser is most likely to be a young man under the age of twenty-five. More than one in ten men aged 18 to 24 were reported to be violent toward their partners, while only one in one hundred men aged 45 and over engaged in woman assault in an intimate relationship (Johnson 1996, 149; see also Gelles 1993; Kennedy and Dutton 1989; and MacLeod 1987). Since youth is understood to be a difficult period in modern life and the young often lack the resources or experience to make appropriate decisions, this pattern is understandable. It is also reflected, for example, in high rates of violent crime amongst young men (Coté and Allahar 1994, 62). A Canadian survey in 2000 confirms this age-related pattern, indicating that 33 per cent of women aged 15 to 17 were victimized by their male partners, compared to 14 per cent of women aged 18 to 24, and 8 per cent of women aged 25 to 44 in the preceding year (as cited in Wiebe and Janssen, 2001, 437).

However, as with every other "typical" characteristic of the batterer or victim, it should be emphasized that there are numerous exceptions. Abusers are generally, but not always, young. Woman abuse is not the exclusive domain of angry young men. Given the relative youth of many abusers, it is to be expected that many are in common-law relationships, have low levels of family income and education, and are often unemployed (Edelson et al. 1985; Smith 1990b). The CVAWS (1993) reported, for example, that "men living in families where the joint income is less than $15,000 and unemployed men had rates of violence twice as high as those in more affluent families and employed men." Not surprisingly, youth and low socio-economic status (and common-law marital status) were correlated; that is, very likely to occur together. It seems likely that these features interact with each other in complex ways—for example, youthful immaturity, economic insecurity, and low level of relationship commitment—to result in increased rates of intimate violence against women.

CLASS-RELATED PATTERNS WITHIN VIOLENCE

> *Poverty and violence play a kind of toxic dance in women's lives. Poverty marginalizes women, increasing their risk of victimization, while violence also isolates women, as the mental and physical effects grind away at women's sense of well-being, limiting what is possible.*
>
> - Gurr, Pajot, et al., *Breaking the Links Between Poverty and Violence Against Women*

The majority of what constitutes "the poor" in Canada is made up of women, particularly those who head lone-parent families. Poverty takes a heavy toll on these women in all aspects of their lives; violence has similar effects. Violence and poverty present a "formidable barrier to women's equality, well-being, and full participation in society" because "[b]oth reflect unequal relationships of power which result in the systemic discrimination of women" (Gurr, Pajot, et al. 2008, 4). Systemic discrimination results in a reduced likelihood of getting a good job with benefits, pension, and an income that would allow for a good quality of life for women and their children. When poverty and violence intersect with Aboriginality, living in a rural location, disability, and/or being an immigrant or refugee, the effects increase exponentially; the result can be women's virtual imprisonment in abusive family relationships. The human and social costs of such a situation are crippling for all Canadians, as human resources are lost when women and their children are unable to develop their full potential, and social resources are lost in the attempt to pick up the pieces of devastated lives.

While it is important to be aware of this pattern, it is also crucial to keep in mind that according to both survey and clinical research, men from all classes and occupations batter their wives.[20] For example, an examination of the lives of military wives in Canada found that abusive violence emerged as a significant concern in these women's lives regardless of their husband's rank (Harrison and Laliberte 1994). The well-to-do are not immune to woman abuse (although they may be better able to avoid public and police scrutiny) and violence against women is not endemic to the working class.

Kaukinen (2004) examined physical and emotional violence with status compatibility (relative contributions to family economic well-being between men and women in intimate relationships). She discovered that higher income in general reduces the risk of physical violence, but when a woman's status is higher than her partner's (i.e., her contribution is greater than his), she is at greater risk of being emotionally abused. Other research indicates that status parity (when men and women make equal contributions to the family income) contributes to more egalitarian marriages, which are less likely to be marred by violence and indicate generally higher levels of marital satisfaction.

According to latent structure analysis conducted by MacMillan and

Gartner (1999), there is little evidence to support the argument that women who are employed are less vulnerable to being victimized by their intimate partners. They also find no evidence to support the idea that a man's employment decreases the likelihood that he will abuse his female partner. What they found was that there is a relationship between the partners' employment statuses. That is, when a woman *and* her male partner are both employed, she is at less risk of being abused; however, when the man is not employed, her risk of abuse is substantially increased. Their position is that employment is a "symbolic resource" in a relationship because it measures relative status between them. Cultural expectations about gender still emphasize male authority and female dependence. MacMillan and Gartner state that their findings therefore "emphasize the importance of symbolic, rather than economic, considerations for understanding the etiology of spousal violence" (1999, "Discussion and Conclusion," para. 6). That is, it is not actual socio-economic resources, such as income, that influence whether a woman is at risk of being abused by her male partner, but income-earning, and possibly being the main income-earner, as a symbolic resource. A man who does not have such a symbolic resource may use violence in an attempt to dominate and control his female partner. They conclude that their "research demonstrates the need to incorporate dimensions of both interpersonal relationships and social structure into explanations of spousal violence against women and highlights the complex relationships between class, gender relations, and spousal violence" (1999, "Discussion and Conclusion," para. 8).

OTHER PATTERNS WITHIN VIOLENCE

Throughout the literature on woman abuse, alcohol figures prominently as an aspect of violence. Many abused women explain their husbands' actions in terms of drinking and, of course, many perpetrators use drunkenness in an attempt to excuse their violence. Predictably, the CVAWS reported that "perpetrators had been drinking in more than 40 per cent of violent incidents" against women and that drinking was most likely in cases of violence involving intimate partners (boyfriends, dates, and spouses) (Statistics Canada 1993, 5).

Most analysts agree that, despite the hopes and beliefs of both victims and victimizers, alcohol does not cause the violence and the violence will not necessarily stop if the drinking stops. Alcohol and drug use may provide the men with a "socially accepted time out," reducing inhibitions and potentially escalating the severity of the violence, but many men who are abstainers or moderate drinkers assault their wives, and many "heavy drinkers" are not "under the influence" when an incident occurs (Johnson 1996, 155–58).[21] The effects of alcohol abuse are reduced to non-significance when negative attitudes toward women are taken into consideration. Name-calling and emotional put-downs are a strong predictor of violence (Johnson 2000).

Studies on pregnancy and violence are as yet inconclusive, probably because of differences in sample types, assessments of victimization, and confounding variables. Nevertheless, it is worth exploring these figures as the idea of violence against a pregnant woman by her intimate partner—who is likely the father of her child—is profoundly disturbing.

One in five (21 per cent) of the women interviewed in the CVAWS report said that they had experienced violence by a previous or current partner during a pregnancy (Statistics Canada 1993, 4; see also MacLeod 1980). This has been explained both in terms of women's increased dependency and thus vulnerability during this time period, and in terms of the batterer's fear of increased family responsibility or increased competition for his wife's attention. A 1998 national Canadian survey reported that 40 per cent of women who had experienced abuse during their pregnancy stated that the abuse had commenced with the pregnancy (as cited in Wiebe and Janssen 2001, 437).

Jasinski (2004) found that data from the 1996 Pregnancy Risk Assessment Monitoring System (PRAMS) in the United States indicated that 2.9 per cent to 5.7 per cent of women from eleven states reported pregnancy-linked abuse. These figures are lower than those usually found in hospital- or clinic-based samples, likely because prevalence estimates from these sources indicate levels of violence among women who are pregnant—not among all women of child-bearing age, pregnant or not. Studies that have attempted to assess whether pregnancy affects the risk of a woman being abused by her male partner have not found that the condition increases their likelihood of experiencing violence; however, Jasinski notes that they have not found a decreased risk either (2004, 52). She also observes that the studies that have been done have not been specifically designed to examine the issue, which may account for the findings to date. Some studies have indicated that pregnancy is a time when abused women experience a respite, while others indicate the opposite. PRAMS data showed that a greater proportion of pregnant women reported less physical violence than prior to their pregnancy, and a study by Hedin (2000) showed that none of the women who reported abuse stated that it had begun at the time of pregnancy. Other studies have indicated that violence escalated throughout the pregnancy (almost one-third of abused women) (as cited in Jasinski 2004, 53). Goodwin et al. (2000) state that "…prevalence of abuse was greater when the male partner did not want the baby" (as cited in Jasinski 2004, 54). Women in this study were 2.5 times more likely to be abused. Stress may be a significant variable in these results. A variety of health problems for both mother and child may result from abuse during pregnancy, including increased risk of miscarriage. Jasinski (2004) suggests that future research should focus on more diverse variables and include a comparison group of women who are not pregnant in order to better isolate the impact of pregnancy itself on violence.

A study conducted in North Carolina (as cited in Wiebe and Janssen 2001, 437) found that among 486 women seeking abortions from a university abortion clinic, relationship issues as a reason stated for wanting to terminate the pregnancy was more common among those who had a history of abuse. Wiebe and Janssen's study encountered difficulties in administering the abuse questions to the 499 women who attended the abortion clinic, resulting in only about a 50 per cent response rate. However, among those women who responded to the abuse questions, 15 per cent admitted that they had been abused in the past twelve months. Of these, 8.3 per cent stated the abuse had been physical, for 7.1 per cent it had been sexual, and 8.3 per cent of the women admitted they were afraid of their partners (2001, 438–439). It is suggested that abused women are more likely to seek to terminate their pregnancies because it was not their choice to be pregnant at that point in their lives, or they did not want to bring a child into an abusive relationship.

Increased threats of violence and, in particular, life-threatening violence, often occur when the wife expresses a desire to leave or when she actually separates from or divorces her abusive partner. The CVAWS found, for example, that 19 per cent of women who experienced violence at the hands of a former partner reported that the violence occurred after or during separation, and one in three of these cases reported that the violence increased in severity when they separated (Statistics Canada 1993, 4; see also Johnson 1996, 169–70; Smith 1990b; Kennedy and Dutton 1989). In 2005, 34 per cent of women who had suffered violence during their relationship reported that it became more severe or frequent after separation (Statistics Canada 2005, "Spousal Violence: Risk Factors," para. 5).

As Smith points out, this pattern of abuse against women who have threatened to leave or who have actually left is important when thinking about explanations of women's actions (1990b, 55). Notions that abused women suffer from learned helplessness[22] or are masochistic or depressed are contradicted by the evidence that many abused women take dramatic steps to leave their abuser. The CVAWS found that 43 per cent of women who reported wife assault had indeed experienced increased violence when they left their partners either for a short time or permanently (Johnson 1996, 188).[23]

By the mid-eighties, the research literature revealed "exposure to parental violence to be the only consistent risk marker in women's victimization" (Hotaling and Sugarman 1986). Both perpetrators of violence and their victims are more likely to have been exposed to violence in their family of origin. MacLeod reported that 61 per cent of the husbands of women staying in shelters in 1985 had been abused as children, and 39 per cent of the women themselves had been physically abused as children (1987, 39). The CVAWS found that women with violent fathers-in-law were three times more likely than women with non-violent fathers-in-law to be abused by their marital partners (Statistics Canada 1993, 5).

One form of violence that is pertinent to disabled women, and that may not figure as prominently for other women, is neglect by a caregiver. This is defined as "failure to supervise or protect, leading to physical harm; sexual abuse; and failure to provide care or medical treatment" (as cited in National Clearinghouse 2004b, 2). Canadian statistics indicate that an estimated 83 per cent of women with disabilities are likely to experience sexual abuse in their lifetimes. Forty per cent to 70 per cent of girls with intellectual disabilities will be sexually abused before they reach eighteen years of age. Eighty per cent of psychiatric inpatients have been physically or sexually abused in their lifetimes (as cited in National Clearinghouse 2004b, 2). Their abusers are most likely to be men and/or caregivers (National Clearinghouse 2004b, 3).

In the five years preceding the study conducted by Brownridge (2006), it was discovered that the rate of violence among disabled women was 1.4 times greater than for non-disabled women. The violence also appeared to be more severe against disabled women. Young women with disabilities were most vulnerable. The male partners of disabled women were approximately 2.5 times more likely to behave in a "patriarchal dominating manner" and about 1.5 times more likely to display sexually proprietary behaviours than the male partners of non-disabled women. Unique to these women were forms of abuse such as the removal of an accessibility device (possibly a wheelchair or walker), withholding medication, and threatening institutionalization. With respect to the extended discussion on the shortcomings of the CTS, it should be noted that these types of abuse are not measured with that scale and, therefore, would not be captured in any study that uses it. It is noted by Brownridge (2006) that his study did not include disabled women who would have trouble understanding the questions or who would have required assistance to complete the telephone survey.

People with intellectual disabilities are those who have difficulties processing information; the term should not be confused with intellectual deficiency. These are people who may have problems with memory, learning, problem-solving, planning, and cognitive tasks. They frequently have other disabilities as well, such as epilepsy or cerebral palsy. Intimate relationships for these people include close caregiving relationships in group homes, nursing homes, and other communal settings. Violence can also occur between residents of the same facility. People with severe and multiple intellectual disabilities are less likely to date or marry and, therefore, dating and domestic violence may not be as common within this population. However, those with this type of disability have often experienced abuse from childhood, which makes them more vulnerable to abuse in intimate partner relationships since they have little expectation of any other kind of treatment. They may also have limitations that could make them easy targets for abusers (National Clearinghouse 2002).

HUSBAND ABUSE

Despite studies that indicate gender symmetry in family violence, and ardent advocates against "reverse discrimination" in legislation and popular culture, there is little evidence to support the idea that a significant proportion of men are as adversely affected by intimate partner violence as women (see, for example, Sarantakos 1999). Donald G. Dutton, a Canadian Psychology professor at the University of British Columbia, has studied the problem of relationship violence using the CTS (see DeKeseredy and Dragiewicz 2007 for a criticism of his recent book). In a 1999 study of gender differences in "rates, bidirectionality, initiation, and consequences of relationship violence in a representative sample," conducted in Alberta, Dutton, Kwong, and Bartholomew report that the rates of violence perpetrated by and against the men and women who volunteered information regarding the preceding twelve months were similar—husband-to-wife: 12.9 per cent men and 9.6 per cent women, versus wife-to-husband: 12.3 per cent men and 12.5 per cent women (1999, "Conclusions," para. 1). According to this study, on average, men stated that they and their female partners were equally likely to commit violent acts and initiate such actions, while women reported less victimization and more perpetration by themselves and less "male-only and male-initiated violence" (1999, "Abstract," para. 1). It should also be noted that the violence reported in the study was predominantly mild, minor, and infrequent, as is the case for the majority of findings in CTS-based research.

In the conclusions, Dutton et al. assert that "while more comprehensive study is needed, it appears that a substantial proportion of women's violence cannot be explained as acts of self-defense. Both genders reported that women do initiate violence and are sometimes the sole perpetrators of aggression in relationships" (1999, "Conclusions," para. 1). With respect to the small number of victims (of both sexes) of what they refer to as "asymmetric violence," meaning that one partner had inflicted at least five more acts of violence than the other in the previous year, they state that "these data indicate that only a minority of respondents reported clearly asymmetric patterns of violence in their relationships. Moreover, we found no evidence that male-to-female violence was more frequent than female-to-male violence in bidirectional cases" (Dutton et al. 1999, "Context and Consequences," para. 1). However, they acknowledge that abused women and violent men are probably unlikely to participate in surveys of the type undertaken (raising the question of why researchers continue to employ them). They echo Straus (1993) in moralizing about the importance of eliminating *women's violence* from society, citing the following reasons:

- spousal assault is morally wrong, regardless of gender;
- the acceptance of female violence may perpetuate traditional norms tolerating violence between intimate partners;
- here is evidence that women's violence may increase the probability of spousal conflict escalating into severe wife battery; and,
- all forms of spousal violence model violence to children and may be predictive of children subsequently being perpetrators or victims of relationship violence themselves (as cited in Dutton et al. 1999, "Conclusions," para. 2).

Loseke and Kurz discuss the issue of women's violence in detail, stating that:

> ...*without exception, all research using the CTS finds that women's and men's rates of violence are more or less equivalent. And, with few exceptions, only research using the CTS yields such images of gender similarity. There is something special about the CTS, or the way it is administered, that constructs a view of the world not found through the feminist research methodology of in-depth interviewing that invariably finds women to be the overwhelming victims of violence. [emphases in original] (Loseke and Kurz 2005, 82)*

They also observe that men *and* women tend to under-report men's violence as well as *over-report* women's violence, because men's violence is expected while women committing acts of violence *is not*. For these reasons and others, studies done using the CTS cannot provide reliable or accurate support for the case for husband abuse.

Minaker and Snider (2006) argue that the new "common sense" of male abuse as equivalent to female abuse is an example of feminist backlash. In this discourse, the husband-battering problem is not as evident as woman-battering because men do not report their abuse; because they are silent victims, their abuse does not appear in official statistics, nor do they seek assistance from shelters, apparently—a Vancouver shelter for abused men which was opened in the nineties had to shut its doors for lack of clients (a shelter for abused men in Britain suffered a similar fate). They argue that, rather than a lack of recognition of male victimization by women, there has been over-recognition, leading to a reduction of funding and resources to much-needed services for battered women.

One hundred and ninety interviews of ninety-five couples, analyzed both quantitatively and qualitatively by Dobash and Dobash (2004), revealed little evidence to suggest that women's violence against men is comparable in terms of nature, frequency, intention, intensity, physical injury, or emotional impact. Their findings reveal that, although women do commit acts of violence against men, the term "husband abuse" does not appear to be apt terminology. The women who participated in the study had all been abused by their male partners for years, but just over half had used violence against their abusers—none of which was sexual violence. Only a few had used serious violence or committed acts that had resulted in injury to the men. Thus, it was generally in self-defence that the abused women committed violence against their husbands/male partners. They did not perpetrate the kind of coercive or intimidating forms of violence that men frequently use against women and that are properly termed "abuse." Women's violence against male partners is usually within a context of male violence against them.

Michael P. Johnson (2006) also confronts the issue of "battered husband syndrome," pointing out that the study that started the gender symmetry debate, conducted by Steinmetz (1977, 1011), merely demonstrates the danger of taking data obtained by a general survey instrument as valid information about intimate terrorism—what he argues is "what we conventionally mean by 'domestic violence'" (1011). Steinmetz presented anecdotal evidence from men who had experienced IT at the hands of their female partners, followed by survey data that, Johnson argues, reveals situational couple violence instead—a markedly different type of violence. He concludes: "Serious as husband battering may be in each particular case, as a general phenomenon it is dramatically less frequent than wife battering" (M. Johnson 2006, 1011).

From this overview, then, it is clear that available research that goes beyond a decontextualized, mere counting of acts classified as "violent" (such as those in the CTS) does not support the notion that husband abuse is a serious social problem at this time, or one deserving of societal resources.

CONCLUSIONS

Several general conclusions can be drawn from the discussion in this chapter. First, since the inception of the modern women's movement, violence against women has been targeted as an important social issue. Secondly, researchers have responded to this concern by developing an increasingly detailed picture of both the parameters and features of violence against women in intimate relationships. This research remains at the centre of an intense political debate about feminism and gender equality. Despite the persistent criticisms of the research record, a growing body of findings provides unequivocal evidence that intimate violence against women is a prominent feature in the lives of a significant number of Canadian women. Thirdly, we have an increasingly clear picture of the dynamics of this violence. With this growing knowledge base, analysts are able to evolve a more fine-tuned understanding of the personal and societal roots of violence against women.

3

CHILD ABUSE: THE DENIAL OF CHILDHOOD

THE EXPERIENCE

Jade (now thirteen years old)

Jade, a quiet and keen observer, is credited by her mother and sisters as able to anticipate [stepfather] Hugh's violence. She mentally recorded and catalogued each incident of violence. One stands out for her. She was seven. The family was eating dinner when Hugh suddenly angered: *"He started hitting Mom for no reason. He was yelling and pushed her into the wall. She was crying. He broke her nose. I ran upstairs."*…She attributes his violence to an abusive upbringing and alcohol/drug usage. She is described as being withdrawn, acknowledges feeling very sad at times, experiences panic attacks if home alone, and frequently writes about dying. (Cunningham and Baker 2004, 36)

Malika (now fifteen years old)

Malika is the third oldest of seven children and she lived with almost daily violence until age 12. As one of the older children, she felt responsible for younger siblings but at the same time relied enormously on an older sister for protection and support. The violence in this family came to light when a neighbour called child protective services after the eldest girl was beaten for speaking with a neighbour boy, an innocent occurrence by Canadian standards but one which contravened the code of behaviour for girls in the family's culture…This depressed and traumatized child felt an overwhelming sense of guilt for not helping her sister…*"I felt like it was my fault 'cause I didn't call the police and we [oldest children and mother] didn't keep the little ones safe."* (Cunningham and Baker 2004, 54)

Perhaps even more than in the case of woman abuse, it is impossible to capture the complexity, diversity, and devastation of family violence experienced by children. The violence takes such a variety of forms and the perpetrators occupy such an array of relationships with the victims that any simple description overlooks as much as it encompasses. In addition, the lines between abuse and "normal" behaviour, between discipline and violence, are so murky in our society that victims themselves may have difficulty naming and assessing the violence used against them. The following overview attempts to identify some of the dimensions of the abuse while acknowledging the larger complexities and variations.[24]

One of the biggest questions that arises in the field of child abuse is whose rights should be paramount—those of the parents or those of the children? Certainly, parents are expected to control and properly socialize their children, often with little assistance and few resources offered by society. However, they are also expected to respect the integrity and rights of their children—again, with little clear assistance from society. However, children are much more vulnerable by nature than adults and deserve to be protected from all types of harm. It is also not beneficial for our society as a whole or for the future of families for children to be taught that violence is the best resource at their disposal and can be used to solve all problems. Achieving the appropriate balance between these two sides of the equation is a challenge for any society, and perhaps a greater one for societies like Canada, where individuality, self-reliance, and privacy are prized so highly.

Child abuse must be understood for its capacity to permeate our social systems and to inject poison into every facet of social existence. Not only do abuse victims frequently become adults who abuse their wives, husbands, and children, they become political leaders and generals who fight genocidal wars, authors who promote internecine hatred, religious leaders who sanction intolerance, managers who take pleasure in exploiting their workforce.

It is likely that all abused children struggle with some legacy of pain, shame, and anger. The impact of the experience is conditioned by the fact that they are children and by the position of children in society. However, there are enormous variations in the violence inflicted on children. The frequency and duration of the abuse, as well as the intensity of the violence, clearly affect the victim's experience. Many children are victims of "neglect": the parent(s) does not actively violate the children's rights but rather fails to provide the food, shelter, clothing, and care children need to thrive. There is a complex overlap between parental neglect and the neglect perpetrated by a society that has provided inadequate social support services. In many countries around the world, children are not only neglected but also prostituted or crippled in response to an economic order that offers little or no support to impoverished parents.

The complexities of domestic violence against children are also apparent in emotional or psychological patterns of abuse. Traditionally, abuse has been narrowly defined in terms of physical violence and obvious injuries. Only in recent years has attention increasingly turned to the psychological well-being of children. Emotional abuse should not be dismissed as a minor form of child abuse. For some children, it may take on nightmarish proportions. In punishment for any perceived infraction of parental will, they (or other loved ones) may be threatened with death, their possessions taken away or destroyed, or they are forced to witness the killing of a beloved pet. They might be forced, directly or indirectly, to witness physical violence between their parents. Despite the absence of physical scars, this kind of violence exacts an enormous price from its victims and has become a significant focus of research throughout the first decade of the twenty-first century.

Parental Alienation Syndrome (PAS), a phenomenon typically associated with divorce and custody battles, has also been called a form of emotional child abuse in which children are unjustifiably turned against one parent by the other, developing hostility and animosity toward the targeted parent (Cartwright 2002; Gardner 2002). Originally coined as a term by Dr. Richard Gardner, a child psychiatrist, in 1985, PAS consists of an alienating parent who manipulates and convinces a child to reject and despise the other parent—not because of anything that the targeted parent has done to the child, but to pursue her or his own personal agenda. The child participates in this rejection and believes that it is her or his own idea and not due to any influence from the alienating parent (Warshak 2000, 2001; Gardner 2002; McInnes 2003; Baker 2005). A controversial and landmark decision in May of 2008 by Justice James Turnbull of the Ontario Superior Court of Justice ordered that a thirteen-year-old boy who had been turned against his mother by his father was to be flown immediately to participate in a deprogramming workshop in the U.S. (Makin 2008). PAS remains a hotly contested topic.[25]

A qualitative study of thirty-eight adults who had been alienated from a parent as children indicated that they suffered from a number of negative outcomes that are similar to those suffered by victims of child abuse.[26] Low self-esteem (and sometimes self-hatred) due to internalization of the hatred of the targeted parent is one effect. Seventy per cent of the subjects suffered from depression. Drug and alcohol problems were reported by about one-third of the subjects. A significant minority of the subjects admitted that they could not trust others or even themselves. Female victims alienated from their fathers had difficulties with adult romantic relationships. Unfortunately, almost half the subjects admitted that they were alienated from their own children. Divorce was a common occurrence, at a rate higher than the national average. The divorce rate among them appeared to be the result of related issues, such as lack of trust, problems with alcohol and drugs, and depression. At the time of the interviews, all the participants were aware that they had been victims of PAS and some had reconciled with their alienated parents (Baker 2005). Clearly, the long-term effects of PAS are potentially as toxic as other types of child abuse and should not be discounted as just the unfortunate fallout from a bitter divorce.

Emotional and psychological violence also happens when children are sexually abused. The victimization includes not only the physical pain and suffering but also the violation of children's trust, destruction of their sense of safety in the world, and negative impact on their sense of self-worth. Some family members who sexually abuse children are also overtly violent and abusive. They may threaten their young victims with retaliatory violence if the child were to tell anyone.

The controversy over spanking still rages in this country and internationally. Some countries, like Sweden, have taken the position that physical discipline by parents is a criminal offence, while others, including Canada, take a more cautious position, reluctant to criminalize spanking but recognizing that physical discipline can escalate into deadly violence.

The experience of child abuse is a multi-faceted and complex phenomenon. Most children experience some level of family dysfunction, with parents who are immature, distant, or demanding. In addition, many children are directly or indirectly the victims of their parents' economic struggles. Economically pressed or insecure parents may take their frustrations and anger out on their children by physically hurting them, or may neglect their children—leaving them, for example, "home alone." Most children are subject, at least occasionally, to some degree of abuse, particularly psychological and emotional abuse. Indeed, most truthful parents would admit that they have on occasion failed their children by being neglectful, manipulative, or coercive. Although mercifully most instances of child abuse, as revealed by official statistics, are minor in nature, within the greater society there is a sizable subset of children who are subject to severe victimization and damage. These are the children who experience persistent or significantly injurious physical, sexual, and emotional violence, and these are the children often identified by social agencies and the courts. It is increasingly obvious that the experience of child abuse cannot be isolated from the ways our society constructs the experience of being a child.

NAMING THE ISSUE: FROM SPANKING AND SLAPS TO TORTURE AND MURDER

Although we all assume that we have some basic understanding of the term "child abuse," arriving at a workable, satisfactory definition is, in fact, not an easy task. Indeed, an important facet of much of the literature on child abuse is the question of definition. On a common-sense level, the term immediately evokes images of children who are beaten and bruised, neglected and abandoned. We may wonder how parents could perpetrate such violence on defenceless children, why they do not respond to the pain and suffering of "their own flesh and blood," but we rarely puzzle over what we mean by the term "child abuse." As with every facet of family

71

violence, closer examination, particularly from a feminist and sociological perspective, reveals a much more complex and contradictory reality—one that often has less to do with monstrous, unnatural parents and more to do with a hierarchical, power-oriented social system.

Good definitions are fundamental because they form the basis for theoretical explanations, empirical research, and policy initiatives. For example, if child abuse is conceptualized in broad and inclusive terms, research is more likely to uncover high rates of abuse, and such research is likely to generate a heightened public demand for public or private solutions. Similarly, if legal definitions are narrowly framed—for example, relying on physical injury as the defining characteristic of abuse—legal interventions will be restricted to a narrow range of behaviours.

With the introduction of the 1998 Canadian Incidence Study of Reported Child Abuse and Neglect—the first study to provide national estimates of child abuse and neglect reported to, and investigated by, child welfare agencies—researchers may in future have a more standardized definition for four categories of child maltreatment: physical abuse, sexual abuse, neglect, and emotional maltreatment. The authors of the report, however, point out how difficult it is to arrive at a consensus on definitions because there are so many different approaches, and contingencies within those approaches, including legal judgments and judgments made by professionals in the field. It should also be noted that under-reporting is a big problem with official agencies, which may affect definitions, since authors constructing studies may not be including all possible variations of each type of abuse. The importance of the CIS should not be underestimated. Having national statistics allows for international comparisons, and the opportunity to broaden our understanding of child abuse and the way that child protection agencies function in dealing with the problem (CIS 2001). For example, in 1998 it was noted that investigated and substantiated child maltreatment rates in Canada were lower than those in the U.S., but higher than Australia's rates (Trocmé, Tourigny, et al. 2003). Nevertheless, it is important to bear in mind that statistics on child abuse gathered by Children's Aid Societies are far from comprehensive. As with other types of family violence statistics drawn from official and/or agency sources, the dark figure looms in the background.

The most recent cycle of the CIS, conducted in 2008, divided child abuse into the categories of physical abuse, sexual abuse, neglect, emotional maltreatment, and exposure to intimate partner violence, broken down into thirty-two forms.[27] Based on approximately 85,440 substantiated child maltreatment investigations in 2008, 34 per cent belonged to the primary category of exposure to intimate partner violence, and another 34 per cent were primarily cases of neglect. Physical abuse made up 20 per cent, emotional maltreatment made up 9 per cent, and sexual abuse accounted for 3 per cent of all substantiated investigations. Eighty-two per cent of substantiated investigations were identified by a single category of abuse. Multiple categories were identified in the remaining 18 per cent, most frequently neglect and exposure to intimate partner violence, emotional maltreatment and exposure to intimate partner violence, neglect and emotional maltreatment, physical abuse and emotional maltreatment, and physical abuse and emotional maltreatment (in that order). The authors found very few cases in which sexual abuse was accompanied by other forms of abuse (Public Health Agency 2010, 30–31).

In 26 per cent of the cases of physical abuse, 21 per cent involved physical injury that was not considered to be severe enough to warrant medical attention, while 5 per cent of cases of physical injury did require medical treatment. No physical harm was found in 74 per cent of cases of physical abuse as the category also includes behaviours by caregivers that seriously endanger children but do not necessarily involve harmful actions. Eleven per cent of sexual abuse cases involved physical harm, with 8 per cent requiring medical treatment. When sexual abuse was the chief substantiated maltreatment, physical harm was present in 11 per cent of cases, and 8 per cent of them necessitated medical treatment. Although neglect may appear to be the most benign of the various types of child abuse, physical harm was identified in 6 per cent of the investigations in which neglect was the main substantiated maltreatment. Two-thirds of these required medical treatment. In the cases in which emotional maltreatment was the primary substantiated form of abuse, 3 per cent involved physical harm but very few required medical treatment. One per cent of investigations in which exposure to intimate partner violence was the chief substantiated maltreatment revealed physical harm, and in 1 per cent of those cases medical treatment was required by the victims (Public Health Agency 2010, 32–33).

Rates of emotional harm resulting from child abuse may have been underestimated in the study due to the way that information was gathered; that is, the study documented emotional harm as identified during the initial assessment period. The degree of emotional harm was measured by whether the child required treatment to deal with the symptoms of mental or emotional harm. From this, 29 per cent of substantiated child abuse investigations involved emotional harm; in 17 per cent of these the degree of emotional harm was enough to warrant treatment. Emotional harm was identified in 26 per cent of cases in which physical abuse was the main type of abuse, with 50 per cent of those cases requiring treatment. When sexual abuse was the primary type of abuse, it is perhaps not surprising that 47 per cent of cases also involved emotional harm and 44 per cent were identified by social workers as requiring treatment. Neglect also incurred a high level of emotional harm, as it was identified in 30 per cent of cases; 18 per cent of those were considered serious enough to need treatment. Emotional harm accompanied emotional maltreatment in 36 per cent of cases, and of those 23 per cent were severe enough to warrant treatment (Public Health Agency 2010, 33–34). The authors state, "While it may appear surprising to some readers that no emotional harm had been documented for such a large proportion of emotionally maltreated children, it is important to understand that the determination of emotional maltreatment includes parental behaviours that would be considered emotionally abusive or neglectful even though the child shows no symptoms of harm" (Public Health Agency 2010, 34). While emotional harm was found in 26 per cent of cases in which exposure to intimate partner violence was the primary type of abuse, only 15 per cent of these cases required treatment. Forty-two per cent of investigations involved a single incident of maltreatment, while the remaining 58 per cent involved multiple incidents. Physical abuse was most likely to be a single incident, while neglect was most likely to be a multiple-incident form of maltreatment (Public Health Agency 2010, 34–35).

In comparing the results of the three cycles, the authors of the 2008 cycle caution that changes in investigational methods make the newest cycle somewhat different from the previous two. Child protection practices changed relating to the investigation of risk of future maltreatment; the cases in which it was deemed that there was a risk of future maltreatment were not clarified in the 1998 and 2003 cycles. The number of investigations nearly doubled from the 1998 to 2003 cycles of the study, but there was very little increase in the number between 2003 and 2008. The age groups of those most likely to be investigated for child abuse did not change between the three cycles, as children under the age of one year were still most likely to suffer abuse, and rates of maltreatment consistently decreased with age (Public Health Agency 2010, 22–23).

Today, as noted above, a child's exposure to family violence is acknowledged as child abuse. Since the early eighties, a considerable amount of literature has documented the impact on children of exposure to their parents' violence, especially where the mother is beaten. Whether or not the children themselves are victims of other forms of child abuse (and, of course, many are), growing up in a violent family has long-term negative consequences for children and, in this sense, is abusive (see Rossman 1994; Jaffe, Wolfe, and Wilson 1990 for more information on the effects of exposure to family violence on children).

Some advocates urge the inclusion of prenatal abuse in the definitions of child abuse.[28] Many women continue to be subjected to abuse by their intimate partners during their pregnancies. Estimates for Canadian women are from 1.2 per cent to 6.6 per cent (as cited in Cunningham and Baker 2004, 55). Direct abuse of a developing fetus can include physical trauma to the abdomen, possibly triggering premature labour; creating an abusive environment in which the pregnant woman endures yelling, the arousal of fear, and maternal stress; and economic deprivation, possibly leading to the compromise of the pregnant woman's self-care and, by extension, care of the fetus. Indirect mechanisms involve risk factors correlated with abuse, such as smoking, self-medication with drugs and/or alcohol, and low weight gain, perhaps due to pressure from the male partner (Cunningham and Baker 2004, 56–57). Some of the outcomes of abuse during pregnancy are low birth weight, preterm birth, and neonatal or perinatal death (as cited in Cunningham and Baker 2004, 56). If children are vulnerable to abuse because of their dependence on adults, the fetus is considerably more vulnerable and at the greatest risk. Once again, however, the question of whose rights take priority arises in this scenario: does a woman—even a pregnant one—have the right to indulge in behaviours that may be potentially harmful to her unborn child, or is this child abuse? If an intimate partner causes harm to a pregnant woman that brings about a miscarriage, has he committed woman abuse or infanticide? Is this another slippery slope for women's rights?

What is missing from the discussion of the definition of child abuse is a consideration of the role that institutions and society play as children's caregivers and protectors. If we simply target individual families and attempt to hold them up to an unclear standard of adequate parenting, we ignore innumerable other areas where children are subject to abuse, including daycare centres, schools, courts, child care agencies, welfare departments, and correction centres. On a societal level, we would also fail to capture the many ways in which social policies result in vast numbers of children being inadequately fed, clothed, housed, and educated (Gil 1980). Accepting a definition that eliminates societal responsibilities, for example, means ignoring numerous abused and neglected children. While as a society we may agree that parents who intentionally injure or kill their children are abusive, researchers, policy advocates, and ordinary citizens do not yet agree on many other facets of child abuse (Gelles and Straus 1988, 52–59).

Nowhere does this struggle over "naming the issue" become more apparent than in the controversy over whether or not corporal punishment, including spanking, is a form of child abuse. One of the primary positions argues that corporal punishment and most physical abuse of children are to be found on the same continuum of force, and that the distinction between the two is a matter of subjective and cultural definition. In other words, there are no objective factors—such as injury—that distinguish physical punishment from physical abuse. Studies have shown that the most significant predictor of physical abuse is support for, and use of, physical punishment. Evidence also indicates that a good deal of physical abuse takes place within a context of corporal punishment. The other prominent position is that two situations can exist when it comes to violence against children: one in which parents are rational and intend to be correctional; and another when parents are out of control and reacting to factors that may not even relate to the child's behaviour. In other words, there are different patterns underlying punishment than those underlying abuse. Section 43 of the *Criminal Code of Canada* is an example of a law relating to corporal punishment that relies on this type of reasoning: that punishment of children is substantively different (with different underlying patterns of factors) than physical child abuse—the former being acceptable to some degree, the latter wholly unacceptable. The tricky part is distinguishing one from the other so that the latter can be stopped and prevented. A review of CIS data on parental punishment abuse concluded that violence that produced injuries and violence that did not produce injuries were not qualitatively different, nor did they appear to be generated by qualitatively different factors (Gonzalez et al. 2008). At this point, we are left with the sense that as long as parents are allowed by law to physically punish their children, the risk of physical child abuse is substantial and likely unpreventable. It seems apparent, then, that the role of culture and social systems are important in terms of the continued potential for child abuse.

In 1999 the Canadian Foundation for Children, Youth, and the Law commenced a constitutional challenge of section 43, arguing that it violates the *Charter of Rights and Freedoms* and the *United Nations Convention on the Rights of the Child*, which eventually led to the 2004 split 6–3 decision of the Supreme Court of Canada. The majority of justices found that section 43 did not constitute a violation of either the Charter or the Convention. The wording of the decision provided a kind of guideline for the forms of punishment that would be protected by section 43: it must be mild and not cause or risk harm to the child; it must not be used on children under two years of age or over twelve years of age; it must not be used on children with disabilities that would keep them from understanding the lesson or correction intended by the punishment; and parents must not use punishment out of their own frustration, anger, or "abusive personality" (McGillivray and Durrant 2006, 191–92). The minority justices all found that the law violated the Charter. The wording is ambiguous enough that it leaves a great deal of discretion in the hands of parents and caregivers. Ultimately, however, it also leaves the same high level of discretion in the hands of child protection investigators. The problem for society as a whole is that such ambiguity in the law virtually sets up parents to be labelled as child abusers.

While worldwide many parents find spanking, slapping, and other forms of hitting suitable and effective, many child care and family violence experts vigorously oppose the use of any form of violence against children. Murray Straus is a passionate anti-corporal punishment advocate who believes that children should *never* be spanked, under any circumstances. Despite decreases in the social acceptability of parental spanking, 94 per cent of parents in the United States spanked their toddlers. Despite opposition by professionals, including pediatricians, to spanking, these same professionals do not tell parents never to spank their children but rather to "avoid" spanking their children. Despite evidence disputing the notion that spanking is an effective means of discipline or more effective than alternatives, parents continue to spank their toddlers. Straus states that these paradoxes are rooted in cultural myths that spanking *is* effective and that it is harmless to children's well-being, particularly when incorporated into a loving relationship with parents. Recent prospective research has shown, however, that child recidivism is high regardless of what type of punishment is used, including spanking. Therefore, according to Straus, spanking does not work as an educative tool with toddlers and should be abandoned. Research has also shown that a child's cognitive function can be damaged by being spanked due to the fear and stress that it generates. Without an explanation, children do not understand the connection between the punishment and what they were doing; what they may learn is that their parent is the source of potential danger. They may not develop the kind of conscience that parents attempt to foster by using corporal punishment, because children learn to simply avoid detection by parents rather than choose not to engage in certain behaviours because they are wrong. Corporal punishment has also been shown to weaken the parent-child bond because of the resentment and anger children feel toward parents who spank them, even if they accept the legitimacy of the spanking. Parents continue to use corporal punishment, despite its ineffectiveness, because they *expect* it to be more effective than alternatives they might employ first. In other words, they focus on the ineffectuality of other types of punishment and ignore the ineffectuality of spanking. According to Straus, parents should learn to use alternative forms of punishment to correct their toddlers' behaviour with consistency, expecting that they will have to repeat the lesson over and over until the child finally learns (Straus 2006; see also Paintal 2007).

In addition to Straus's argument, numerous studies have revealed that corporal punishment—even if defined as mild forms that "do not risk or result in physical injury (spanking, slapping, pinching, smacking, hitting with hand or object)" (McGillivray and Durrant 2006, 184)—is associated with negative outcomes. Physical abuse in the 2003 CIS includes the subcategory "inappropriate punishment," recognizing that child abuse and "discipline" are closely related. A large Quebec study cited by McGillivray and Durrant (2006, 185) revealed that children were seven times more likely to experience severe violence if they had experienced minor physical violence, such as spanking. The fine line between "discipline" and "abuse" (considered by McGillivray and Durrant to be a false dichotomy) is sufficiently blurry that children who have been physically punished tend to have poorer mental health and more self-esteem issues, even if a generally supportive relationship exists between the parent and child (2006, 186). The parent-child relationship may ultimately suffer because the child identifies the parent as a source of pain and someone who has hurt her or him. Even though, in the short term, compliance is the reward parents derive from physical punishment of children, in the longer term compliance may turn into resistance, which increases the risk that the parent will cross the blurry line into physical abuse (McGillivray and Durrant 2006, 186–90).

After a shocking case in which a four-year-old girl was beaten to death by her stepfather, who was then acquitted, outraging the Swedish population, in 1979 Sweden became the first country to prohibit any kind of physical force being used to discipline children. Other countries have since followed suit, and numerous others are making progress toward banning corporal punishment (see also Paintal 2007). Sweden's Children and Parents Code was not meant to penalize or criminalize parents; it was meant to educate parents to find alternative ways to discipline their children that would honour the child's integrity and dignity as a human being. Significantly, the Ministry of Justice took major steps to familiarize Swedish citizens with the new law, creating a television and milk-carton campaign along with a brochure translated into a number of different languages and distributed to all households in which there were children. As a result, surveys taken in 1996 and 2000 indicated that there was very little support for corporal punishment among adults or children. In 1965, 53 per cent of Swedes supported it, while in 2000 only 11 per cent stated that they supported the mildest forms of corporal punishment. The greatest decline was among Swedes under thirty-five years of age, as only 6 per cent of them stated that they supported it. Reporting of assaults against children have increased, a sign that people have become more aware of the problem of child abuse; and prosecutions of people under thirty-five (the generation raised with the "no smacking" culture), and even of people *not* born in Nordic countries with corporal punishment bans, have decreased since 1984. In addition, most reported incidents do not result in serious injuries—another sign that the Swedish population has become highly sensitized to violence against children. Studies have shown that fewer children have suffered corporal punishment and the majority of them suffered only mild violence on isolated occasions. Those who had suffered severe corporal punishment were older participants. A questionnaire of schoolchildren revealed that 86 per cent had never been corporally punished by either parent (Durrant 2000; Hindberg 2001).

Happily, prosecution of parents in Sweden has declined and there has been no increase of parents in the criminal justice system, likely as a consequence of the law being part of the Parents Code, rather than the Penal Code. There has also been no increase in children being taken away from their parents and placed into care (Durrant 2000; Hindberg 2001). Sweden appears to have made a concerted effort to deal with the problem of corporal punishment in as humane a way as possible, focusing on assisting families rather than punishing them.

Perhaps the most positive result of the ban on corporal punishment and the public education campaign by the Ministry of Justice is that children and youth did not become undisciplined and unruly. Rates of youth crime have remained steady since 1983. The rate of theft among youth between fifteen and seventeen years of age declined by 21 per cent between 1975 and 1996. There was also a 75 per cent decline in this age group of suspects in narcotics crimes between 1970 and 1996. In addition, "[y]oung people's drug intake, alcohol intake, and suicide rates have also declined" (Durrant 2000, 6; see also Hindberg 2001).

A study of the acceptance of physical punishment in Europe included fourteen countries that were part of the European Union. Results indicate that, at the individual level, older men were the least educated, the most likely to believe that violence against children was not prevalent in their society, and more likely to support the use of corporal punishment. At the national level, laws prohibiting physical punishment of children and lower rates of child deaths resulting from maltreatment were both associated with lower levels of acceptability of corporal punishment (Gracia and Herrero 2008). This study suggests that a "no smacking" law has positive effects on societies. Considering the progress made in Sweden, it also appears that if the government makes a significant effort to educate people and provides support for families, a culture of anti-corporal punishment may be nurtured and more readily adopted by its citizens. More importantly, the positive effect on society may be enhanced by generations of young people who do not run amok due to lack of discipline, but whose self-esteem and emotional well-being are bolstered by being lovingly raised with dignity and respect.

Not surprisingly, much of this struggle around the use of physical discipline has shifted into a definitional debate regarding the meaning of "spanking" or "gently slapping," and the use of them as a "last resort." Indeed, some advocates of spanking seek to define the acceptable form as one or two slaps on the bottom with an open hand for children between ages two and six, and only in conjunction with other positive parenting techniques (Larzelere 1994, 204). The shifting terrain of definitional arguments will in all likelihood fail to resolve the public divisions on this issue, but they do underscore how central the issue of definitions is—not only to understanding but also to resolving child abuse. Enlarged definitions of child abuse necessarily expand the net of potential abusers, and more and more parents are forced to confront the uncomfortable question of whether abuse is external and foreign or part of their personal reality. Here, child abuse is defined as acts of commission or omission, usually by those entrusted with the care and nurturing of the child, which function to deny the child the reasonable opportunity to develop her or his potential as a human being. Such a broad definition, of course, allows for consideration of whether or not socially accepted standards of parenting are abusive and whether social agencies, entrusted with both the child's well-being and parental education—such as the education and social welfare system—are acting in the child's interests.

THE CHANGING HISTORICAL CONSTRUCTION OF ABUSE

One of the most important reasons these definitional conflicts persist is a long historical tradition (in many cultures, including Canada's) that endorses the use of violence—including sexual violence—against children. Under traditional patriarchy, children, like their mothers, belonged to the patriarch. It was his responsibility to control and provide for these dependents, and in pursuit of these responsibilities it was his right to employ violence—even deadly violence. At the moment of birth, the father in ancient times had the right to either acknowledge the infant or dispose of it. In many cultures, infanticide through exposure or denial of food was often practised both to limit demands on family resources and to eliminate children deemed defective. Needless to say, female children were particularly at risk of infanticide since they often required a dowry in order to be married and, as a result, were a drain on family resources. Also, as is still the practice in a number of countries today, children could be sold into slavery or prostitution if the family was in need. For centuries, children were seen as simply another form of property, much like a dog or a goat, and treated with a similar lack of sentimentality (Radbill 1980).

These paternal prerogatives over children's well-being and survival were typically buttressed by religious beliefs and values.[29] In the Judeo-Christian tradition, for example, the necessity of children's obedience to their fathers is a persistent theme.[30]

Traditional paternal rights over children extended beyond physical dominance and included sexual prerogatives. In ancient times, as recorded in the Talmud and Old Testament, female children were considered to be the father's property, betrothed while still toddlers and married off before they reached their teens. The rise of Christianity did not eradicate the sexual abuse of children. Although Canon law forbade child marriage, customary practice meant that many young girls were married off before their teens and even very young children were betrothed. While many of these practices were eliminated by the nineteenth century, child sexual abuse in the form of child prostitution remained prevalent. In England, the Victorian era was marked by the "cult of the little girl," a period when immature, preferably virginal, females between eleven and fifteen were considered the most desirable prostitutes. In part, this practice was the result of the growing fear of syphilis and the popular belief that having sexual relations with a virgin provided a cure for venereal disease (Rush 1980). These activities suggest a social context in which the sexual abuse of children was to some degree accepted and rationalized.

The redefinition of physical and sexual violence as abusive and unacceptable has a long and tortuous history. With the rise of education and modern individualism, childhood was reframed, and a more sentimental conception of children slowly emerged. Through changes associated with industrialization and urbanization, such as improved health care and birth control, there were fewer children in the family and they were more likely to survive into adulthood (Synnott 1983). Buoyed by these developments, social critics and social reformers began to insist upon more humane treatment for children. In the nineteenth century, for example, child labour laws were introduced in many Western countries to ensure that very young children were not employed and that children over the age of fourteen were not subject to beatings or unsafe working conditions. Middle- and upper-class "child savers" sought to help the numerous poor, abandoned, and orphaned children on the streets of the new industrial centres (Knudsen 1992, 7). Steps were also taken to safeguard children in the family with the creation of Societies for the Prevention of Cruelty to Children (SPCC) throughout the Western world—first founded in New York City in 1875 and modelled ironically on similar societies for the prevention of cruelty to animals—to protect children from abuse and forced prostitution (Radbill 1980).

While the United States and Britain played a leading role in responding to child labour and in the establishment of SPCCs, Canada and other Western countries quickly followed suit. In 1891 the first Children's Aid Society (CAS) in Canada was founded in Toronto. By 1901 there were thirty Children's Aid Societies in Ontario alone. In 1893 the Ontario legislature passed the *Prevention of Cruelty and Better Protection of Children Act*. Under the Act, local Children's Aid Societies were authorized to ensure that neglected children were cared for and that cruelty to children was punished.

Other provinces soon followed with similar legislation. Quebec, which had adopted legislation protecting the rights of children and youth in 1869, relied on church-sponsored institutions and did not introduce child welfare legislation until well into the twentieth century (Swift 1995).

Interestingly enough, in 2000 in Guelph, Ontario, the Humane Society and Family and Children's Services agencies "reunited in recognition of the association between animal cruelty and human violence" (Zilney and Zilney 2005, "Animal Welfare," para. 2), although they continue to pursue separate mandates and function independently of one another. The connection between child abuse (as well as other forms of family violence[31]) and animal abuse is becoming more and more the subject of research as we realize that animal abuse has been a training ground for some adult serial killers before they graduate to human violence (Zilney and Zilney 2005). Also, the likelihood of children who have been exposed to domestic violence (Currie 2006) and corporal punishment (Flynn 1999) demonstrating cruelty to animals was significantly greater. Males are much more likely than females to abuse animals if they were corporally punished by their fathers—a significant finding among a non-clinical sample of college students (Flynn 1999).

Needless to say, despite the advances achieved earlier, many of the more dramatic changes in social attitudes toward child abuse occurred in the latter half of the twentieth century. The landmark work of Dr. C. H. Kempe in the United States is usually cited as a crucial turning point (Kempe et al. 1980). By examining the patterns of bruises and fractures that often came to the attention of physicians attending abused children, Kempe was able to identify in 1962 what he termed "the battered child syndrome," which doctors could diagnose based on x-rays, bruises, and so on. That same year he chaired a conference on child battery, and out of these efforts emerged a model of child abuse law that, within five years, was adopted by every American state (Radbill 1980, 16).

While the United States took the lead in several of these developments, other countries, including Canada, very quickly followed. So much work on child abuse has been accomplished in Canada since the sixties that it is only possible to point out some of the landmark events. Certainly one of the critical milestones was the publication in 1972 (revised in 1978) of Mary

Van Stolk's *The Battered Child in Canada*. This book both raised the public profile of child abuse and brought together a variety of Canadian research and policy analysis. It was followed in 1980 by the Senate Report *Child at Risk*, which provided the earliest estimates of national rates of child abuse in Canada. Scientific documentation of some of the dimensions of child abuse was achieved in 1984 with the publication of Robin Badgley's 1,314-page *Sexual Offences Against Children*. This internationally acclaimed report included a survey of a nationally representative sample of Canadian adults. Based on the recall of these adults, the report determined that an astonishing one in two girls (53.5 per cent) and one in three boys (30.6 per cent) under the age of twenty-one had been subject to a sexual offence (ranging from being "flashed" to unwanted touching to actual or attempted sexual assault) (Badgley 1984, 180–82). Almost half the female and male victims sixteen years of age or younger were subject to attempted or actual sexual assault, including attempted or actual forced intercourse, sodomy using either a penis or an object, or forced sexual stimulation (Badgley 1984, 179–83). Predictably, this comprehensive and academically rigorous examination of the sexual abuse of Canadian children shattered many illusions and triggered widespread public demand for a societal response; in particular, an improved criminal justice response to intrafamilial child sexual abuse.

Throughout the seventies and eighties most provinces initiated extensive reforms to their child welfare and criminal legislation, establishing, for example, child abuse registers and mandatory reporting. Under the latter legislation, professionals who come into contact with abused children—such as physicians, social workers, and in some cases, average citizens—are required to report any suspected cases of child abuse. In recent years, laws tend to be less preoccupied with "neglect" and more concerned with children "in need of protection" (Swift 1995).

Also during the eighties and nineties, many private and public organizations emerged to combat child abuse. In 1983, the Ontario Ministry of Community and Social Services, in co-operation with the Canadian Children's Foundation, established the Ontario Centre for the Prevention of Child Abuse. In 1987, the Centre evolved into a private, non-profit charitable organization with a national agenda—The Institute for the Prevention of Child Abuse (IPC). Many other efforts were mobilized on the community level: grassroots feminist organizations, such as local rape crisis and sexual assault centres, set up support groups for adult female survivors of sexual abuse; and shelters for battered women developed programs to meet the needs of children who were either directly abused in violent homes or subject to indirect violence by exposure to a battering situation. In addition, shelters and sexual assault centres undertook public education campaigns in schools and in the community to challenge the beliefs and values that support patterns of family and interpersonal violence. Other groups, such as the International Order of Foresters (IOF), supported the distribution of public education pamphlets and films on family violence and child abuse.

Some sense of the intensity of the public response to child abuse (and to family violence in general) is apparent in the financial support for research, program development, and public education authorized by the federal government. In 1982, Health Canada established the National Clearinghouse on Family Violence to provide a national information and consultation service for professionals as well as a base for developing important sources of public education (for example, the Family Violence Film Collection). The Family Violence Initiative (also discussed in Chapters 2 and 6) was launched in 1988. Since 1996, annual funding of $7 million has been earmarked to be shared among seven departments to—among other things— collect national data and operate the National Clearinghouse, which disseminates electronic bulletins and publications online on such subjects as child abuse, neglect, and child sexual abuse. Also in the mid-eighties, the Canadian Council on Social Development, with funding from Health Canada, created *Vis-à-vis*, a national newsletter on family violence that provided quarterly updates on the latest developments across the country in research and policy (no longer in publication).[32] In 1992, Health Canada, in collaboration with the Social Sciences and Humanities Research Council of Canada as well as local organizations, foundations, and universities, established five new research centres on family violence and violence against women across Canada.[33] Other centres for research were established prior to 1992, such as the LaMarsh Research Centre on Violence and Conflict Resolution at York University (1980).[34]

This explosion of governmental, academic, and public concern about child abuse has fundamentally altered our awareness and understanding of the issue. However, as evidenced by the ongoing debate about spanking, all this well-deserved attention has not resolved the definitional disputes. Child abuse (along with other dimensions of family violence) remains contested terrain. Social movements have emerged that urge a stern response to disobedient and rebellious adolescents. Many fundamentalist and conservative spokespersons still endorse the use of physical punishment. Moved, as we apparently are as a society, by the plight of the defenceless child, many of us are not yet prepared to accord children the inalienable right to be free of violence.

MAPPING THE DIMENSIONS OF THE PROBLEM

The absence of any consensus about the parameters of child abuse makes undertaking research and setting policy extremely difficult. Only in 1997 was a decision finally made to collect Canadian national statistics on child abuse that resulted in the 1998 Canadian Incidence Survey on Child Abuse and Neglect.

Other sources of data provide some useful insights as well. Crime statistics, for example, tend to confirm that the family is one of the most dangerous institutions for children in our society. Forty-one per cent of violent crimes against children reported to police departments are perpetrated by family members, and almost half (48 per cent) of criminal sexual assaults are committed by a family member (La Novara 1993, 54). However, considerable numbers of violent crimes against children never come to the attention of police departments, and these statistics are more suggestive than definitive.

Official statistics are of limited use in understanding the societal dimensions of child abuse since they capture only those instances that have come to the attention of a reporting agency. As with many other aspects of family violence, it is reasonable to assume that many cases would be hidden due to fear, shame, and self-blame. Failure to report would be particularly true of cases of child sexual abuse, where even adult survivors have difficulty publicly confronting their abusers. In other instances, child abuse—physical abuse, neglect, emotional abuse—might be invisible to victims and the perpetrators who may define the behaviour as normal and socially acceptable. In other words, creating an accurate research picture entails numerous

87

difficulties. One solution, following Badgley's example in *Sexual Offences Against Children,* would be retrospective research with a nationally representative sample of adult Canadians. However, retrospective research is always problematic since it relies on the accurate recall of events that occurred years previously, and that—because they are painful—may be more likely to be forgotten or minimized. Research on adults that instead explores parental relationships with their children in the past year avoids these memory issues, but may still result in under-reporting as parents underestimate their physical or—especially—sexual violence. Certainly the best and most accurate information is likely to come from research that tracks a nationally representative sample of children across Canada (interviewing them at two-year intervals) from birth to early adulthood. Although such research involves considerable ethical concerns, it is the most promising avenue and is known as the National Longitudinal Survey of Children and Youth (Watchel 1994, 11). The survey was commenced in 1994 and covers subjects such as child development and behaviour, education, health, and well-being (see www.statcan.gc.ca).

Amongst the most influential and important American studies examining rates of unreported child abuse are Murray Straus and Richard Gelles's 1975 and 1985 national surveys. The Canadian counterpart to these American giants is arguably Dr. Nico Trocmé of McGill University, one of the developers of the CIS. Using the Conflict Tactics Scale (see Chapter 2 for a discussion of the shortcomings of this method) and a national probability sample, Straus and Gelles surveyed 6,002 households in 1985. Almost two-thirds (63 per cent) of parents in the sample reported hitting their child. In all, 19 out of 1,000 children were, according to their parents' reports, subject to severe acts of violence—that is, they were kicked, bitten, hit with a fist, beaten up, threatened with a gun or knife, or had a gun or knife used against them (1986, 469). Although these rates indicated a 47 per cent decline since 1975, they continued to indicate "extremely high" rates of abuse (1986, 474).

Gauging the number of cases of abuse is especially difficult when the focus is on specific types of violence. Sexual abuse (particularly male child sexual abuse) and emotional abuse are, for example, notoriously underreported in official complaints. Victims often do not come forward, even as adults. As a result, official case statistics will often grossly underestimate the size of the problem. Various research studies (such as Badgley's) have provided insight into the actual dimensions of these forms of maltreatment (Tower 1996, 137). Reviewing a variety of studies undertaken in the United States, Canada, and Britain from 1979 to 1988, researchers concluded that serious sexual abuse (unwanted or coerced sexual contact prior to age sixteen or seventeen) occurs against *at least* 15 per cent of females and 5 per cent of males (Bagley and King 1990, 56–77). A similar review by Tower on American research from 1978 to 1989 concerning male child sexual abuse reported prevalence rates ranging from 2.5 per cent to 17.3 per cent (Tower 1996, 141; see also Wallace 1996, 56; Manion and Wilson 1995, 8). The 1997 survey by researchers from McMaster University and the Clarke Institute of Psychiatry reported that one in eight girls and one in twenty-three boys is the victim of sexual abuse. Sexual abuse was defined quite narrowly for this study as "adults exposing themselves to a child more than once; threatening to have sex with a child; touching a child on the sexual parts of his or her body; and trying to have sex with a child or having sex with a child" (Gadd, *Globe and Mail*, 9 July 1997).

As evident from all of this research, one of the consistent features of the data has been the greater prevalence of female sexual abuse. However, some analysts are now suggesting that male child sexual abuse remains vastly under-reported, even in research based on self-report among an adult population (such as the McMaster/Clarke Institute study). The causes cited for this distortion are prevailing conceptions of masculinity and sexuality. Some researchers believe that in the future, as attitudes about victimization shift, research will reveal equivalent rates of sexual victimization of boys and girls (Tower 1996, 140).

What is clear from the statistical profile is that child abuse is an enormous social issue. In North America, literally millions of children are growing up without a childhood. The media images of children in popular television shows are just cruel reminders for many who do not live in a loving, supportive, and kind family. Violence, abuse, manipulation, and exploitation are the norm for them, and the emotional fallout from living through childhood years filled with fear, anxiety, self-loathing, and anger may plague them for much—if not all—of their adult lives.

GENERAL PATTERNS OF CHILD ABUSE

As with abuse against women, child abuse is not randomly scattered throughout the population. There are discernible (if disputed) patterns, and these patterns are the key to understanding the roots of violence against children and, perhaps as importantly, the key to understanding the politics of child abuse. Not surprisingly, child abuse tends to occur more frequently in families that rate high in conflict and in which there is "marital violence." Straus and Gelles report from their national U.S. survey that families where the husband had hit the wife in the course of the preceding year were 150 per cent more likely to disclose instances of child abuse than other families (1992, 254). Not surprisingly, parents who came from a violent home, particularly one in which they were physically punished, are more likely to engage in severe violence against their own children. Similarly, parents who simply witnessed violence in their family of origin are more likely to abuse their own children (1992, 255–56). Given the popular endorsement of both violence as an inter-personal tactic and discipline as a parental responsibility, it is not sur-prising that official child abuse statistics are as high as they are. Families affected by substance abuse are also viewed as more likely to abuse their children, particularly in the form of neglect and abandonment (Tower 1996, 114). Finally, families that are socially isolated (for example, lack-ing neighbourhood ties or involvement in organizations such as clubs, lodges, unions, church groups, and so on) are also more likely to be abusive (1992, 256–57). Given the breakdown of community in most modern industrial countries, this relationship between abuse and isola-tion is particularly important.

Research also suggests that certain types of children are more vulnerable to abuse. Children who are conceived or born outside of marriage and chil-dren who are born prematurely, as well as sickly babies and those born with physical or mental disabilities, are more likely to be abused. For example, in the provocatively titled book *When Children Invite Child Abuse*, the author details connections between child abuse and learning disabilities, child-hood depression, and nutritional problems (Gold 1986). In other words, any circumstances that add to the already considerable stress of becoming a parent appear to increase the likelihood that they will engage in some form of maltreatment (Tower 1996, 75).

The age profile of victims of abuse is far from clear. Statistics drawn from reported cases of child abuse suggest that children who are placed "in care" as a result of abuse concerns are spread evenly throughout the age range. Newfoundland reports the majority of its children in care are aged twelve to fifteen (30 per cent), while Manitoba indicates that reports of alleged abuse are most numerous for children aged four to ten (47.8 per cent of reports) (Federal-Provincial Working Group 1994, 24, 107). Needless to say, it is likely that abuse starts long before it comes to the attention of a reporting agency. Indeed, most analysts point out that in many cases child abuse starts before birth, as the child is often battered *in utero* in the course of violence against the mother, or subjected to the mother's abuse of drugs or alcohol. Not surprisingly, neglect and abandonment are most likely to occur in the period from birth to one year of age and are less likely to occur as the child matures. Deadly child abuse—that is, child abuse that results in the child's death—is most likely to occur before age four. Sexual abuse can occur at any age and has been reported against infants. However, research suggests that the average age for sexually abused boys is four to six, and eleven to fourteen for girls (Tower 1996, 101, 140; Bagley and King 1990, 70–72; Thomlison et al. 1991, 67).

The age patterns of abuse, in particular the young age at which so much abuse begins, are perhaps key to understanding why children—even when they are legally adult—remain with their abusive families, and why adult children have such difficulty addressing their victimization. As evident from some of the above statistics, abuse may be all the child has ever known. Indeed, despite images from the media and experiences in the families of friends, abuse may even seem "normal." More importantly, the child is profoundly connected with the abuser through their shared life history. However angry or enraged the child victim may feel, it may be enormously difficult to challenge her or his abusive parent or to place that parent in jeopardy by reporting the abuse to someone outside the family. Efforts to obtain outside help may simply confirm that children are rarely believed. Sometimes the abuse is muddied by "good times" with the abuser; sometimes the child victim has been taught to blame herself or himself for the violence or exploitation. Not surprisingly, a childhood of abuse may leave the child with few escape options: run away, lose oneself in drugs or alcohol, report the abuse, commit suicide, or commit homicide against the parents (Mones 1991).

Generally, of course, our social conceptions of age are crucial to any analysis of child abuse. We live in a society where children, simply because of their age, are denied a wide variety of social, legal, and economic rights. Unlike in other cultures and other historical periods, we assume that children should be treated as dependants, denied adult rights and prerogatives regardless of their abilities or family circumstances, and, in general, segregated from the mainstream of social life. While many would argue that these constraints are in the best interests of children, since they protect them from exploitation in child labour and ensure that they are given the opportunity to have an education, such social arrangements hinge on the presence of loving, supportive parents. The societal assumptions that children, by token of their age, should be powerless and dependent are precisely the assumptions that help set the stage for violence against children and prolonged abuse. Children are thereby made into a vulnerable group, and vulnerable groups are more likely to be abused. When children are made even more vulnerable due to marginalizing factors such as poor living conditions, inadequate housing, disabilities, race, and ethnicity, these intersecting inequalities compound their risk for abuse (Department of Justice Canada 2009a).

Children's exposure to family violence has become a highly significant topic of research in the early twenty-first century. As noted from the personal stories of children at the beginning of this chapter, being caught up in violence against their mothers is a traumatic experience and one that affects children to their very core. Children are conflicted in terms of their loyalties and feel guilt when they are completely blameless. Unfortunately, the recognition of exposure to family violence as a form of emotional abuse is a double-edged sword: mothers may now be held responsible by child protection agencies and the criminal justice system for exposing their children to the violence to which they are personally subjected. As a result, despite efforts they may have made to keep their children safe, mothers may end up being exponentially victimized. "Failure to protect" is considered by many child protection agencies to be sufficient grounds for a finding that a child is "in need of protection" (Strega 2006, 237). This characterization is highly unfair to women who are being battered, as demonstrated by Haight, Shim, Linn, and Swinford (2007) in their study. Women employ well-organized strategies for protecting their children, and they understand the complexity and importance of helping their children to understand and recover from the experience of family violence. They meet with child welfare and mental health professionals to develop ways to support their children through the trauma, provide them with hope for the future, to obtain information to help the children avoid getting involved with abusive partners in the future, and to find ways to communicate the separation of the spousal and parental relationships. How to best handle the home situation of abused women, as demonstrated in Chapter 2, is anything but clear-cut and simple.

Strega (2006) also points out that the biggest problem with child welfare is that men and their violence are invisible to the system. Odd as this may sound, as child protection workers focus their attention on protecting children, they tend to hold mothers responsible for children's exposure to violence, virtually ignoring the fact that it is *men* who are mostly responsible for perpetrating the violence in the first place. "Domestic violence" and "family violence" occur in these families, not male violence against women.

As Cunningham and Baker (2004, 3) point out, however, children are far from being passive victims of exposure to violence. They actively listen (or avoid doing so), hide, interpret, assess their role as the cause, worry about the consequences, try to protect themselves and others, and so on. They can also be drawn into the violence, injured as bystanders, or abused along with their mothers (Hayes, Trocmé, and Jenney 2006, 204).

GENDERED PATTERNS OF CHILD ABUSE

Given that the rights and roles of women was one of the central issues of the twentieth century, it is not surprising that gender issues emerge in the discussion of child abuse. Since family violence amongst adult members of the family is strongly structured by gender differences, it is reasonable to examine whether gender plays a significant role in child abuse (see, for example, Margolin 1992; Muller 1995). In particular, since men engage in considerable violence against women in our families and our society, are they more likely than women to use violence against children and are girls more likely to be victimized? Some researchers suggest using a feminist "power and control" analysis, which would lead to the position that child abusers are predominantly male, and victims are predominantly females or very young males. This analysis is based on the premise that child abuse primarily involves the exercise of power and maintenance of control over others. Rather than needing sexual gratification, for example, or lacking the ability to control his anger, the abuser is often seen as using and enjoying age-old prerogatives embedded in prevailing notions of masculinity. He believes he has the right to use his power to maintain control of the women and children in his life. This patriarchal male, socialized to exercise power and control and freely exercising his will to dominate his wife and child, presents a possible scenario for child abuse (Conway 1993). Similarly, given that men are socialized to be the sexual actors in our culture, male sexual abuse against girls may seem more likely than sexual assaults by females.

The existing statistical profile provides some useful information. Although the question of whether men are more violent and abusive to their children is far from fully answered, it does appear that gender is relevant to understanding violence against children—though not along the lines usually anticipated. The precise role played by gender depends on the type of abuse considered, and whether official or self-reported data are examined.

Vine, Trocmé, and Finlay (2006) report that in the 1998 cycle of the CIS, when two parents were present in the household, fathers were twice as likely as mothers to be physically abusive. Most of the perpetrators were family members (43 per cent) in substantiated cases of sexual abuse, but they were generally not the parents. Biological fathers were perpetrators in 7 per cent of the cases and stepfathers in 8 per cent. According to the authors, "[t]he relatively large number of stepfather perpetrators is surprising given that only 35 per cent of fathers living with their children in the CIS-1998 are stepfathers" (Vine, Trocmé, and Finlay 2006, 167–68). Interestingly, the 2003 cycle indicated that mothers and fathers were almost equally likely to physically abuse their children (53 per cent as opposed to 50 per cent, respectively), including stepmothers (3 per cent) and stepfathers (12 per cent). However, they note that these figures are somewhat skewed due to the fact that 30 per cent of child victims were living in female-headed single-parent households. In two-parent families, 67 per cent of substantiated physical abuse was committed by fathers, while mothers were 51 per cent of the perpetrators. Non-parental family members are most likely to commit sexual abuse, making up 35 per cent of the perpetrators; biological fathers were 9 per cent and stepfathers 13 per cent. Biological mothers made up only 5 per cent of perpetrators of sexual abuse (Trocmé, Fallon, et al. 2005, 51–52).

Forty-nine per cent of the victims of substantiated child abuse were girls in the 2008 cycle of the CIS (Public Health Agency 2010, 37). Other than this study and some data on the age and sex of victims,[35] the report of the third cycle, published in the fall of 2010, does not provide detail with respect to how gender and types of abuse intersect. The second cycle, conducted in 2003, demonstrated a gendered pattern of victimization. The 2003 CIS identifies that girls were 63 per cent of the victims of sexual abuse and 54 per cent of the victims of emotional maltreatment. Boys were more frequently the victims of physical abuse at 54 per cent, neglect at 52 per cent, and exposure to domestic violence at 52 per cent. Children over the age of fifteen were more likely to be victims of physical abuse at 70 per cent, and children between the ages of eight and fifteen were more likely to be sexually abused at 67 per cent (Trocmé, Fallon, et al. 2005, 6).

In contrast to the 2003 CIS, the 2009 Family Violence in Canada report indicates that, in 2007, male family members made up 96 per cent of the identified perpetrators of sexual abuse against children under eighteen, and 71 per cent of the perpetrators of physical assault. Fathers, including biological, step-, and adoptive, were involved in 44 per cent of those physical assaults, while brothers were responsible 13 per cent of the time, and other male relatives made up 10 per cent. In cases of sexual assault, 32 per cent of children under eighteen were victimized by fathers of any category. Brothers were responsible for victimizing siblings in 27 per cent of cases, while male extended family members were the perpetrators in 32 per cent of cases. Mothers were usually the ones responsible for physical assault of children when a female was identified as the perpetrator, at 20 per cent (Nemr 2009, 35). Much of the physical abuse may have started out as punishment for perceived misbehaviour.

The 2009 report further indicates that, among police-reported physical assault by family members, girls were more likely to be victimized than boys. Twelve- to seventeen-year-olds were also more likely to be victimized than younger children (CIS 2005, 33). For boys, the peak age for physical abuse was fourteen, while for girls the peak was age seventeen (34). Boys were more likely to be injured than girls (46 per cent as opposed to 36 per cent) but the majority of injuries suffered by either sex were considered to be minor—that is, not requiring treatment (35).

Leaving aside the issue of neglect, evidence does suggest that women may be physically violent and abusive to their children, but at a lesser rate than men, particularly if the amount of time spent taking care of children is taken into consideration. For example, Trocmé found that mothers were the perpetrators in 39 per cent of substantiated cases of physical abuse and in 1 per cent of sexual abuse cases (1994, 66–68). This appears to contradict U.S. national surveys that suggest that women are "at least as violent as men against their own children" (Straus and Sweet 1992, 247). Since these researchers also reported that women were as likely to assault their spouses as vice versa (see Chapter 2), these results must be scrutinized.

Considerable research indicates that women undertake the lion's share of parenting in this society. While there have been some shifts in the division of domestic labour, the bulk of child rearing remains the mother's responsibility. This is, of course, dramatically evident in custody arrangements, which almost always result in mothers assuming responsibility for the day-to-day child care. Consequently, given the relative amounts of time that women and men spend with their children, it would seem that women as a group are indeed less violent (Cole 1988). This is, of course, consistent with traditional gender socialization in which men are brought up to be both aggressive and dominant and the family disciplinarian.

Women were perpetrators of sexual assaults in only 4 per cent of cases and physical assaults in 29 per cent. Mothers were more often perpetrators than sisters or other female family members (15 per cent versus 4 per cent for each of the others). However, when the victims were children six years of age or under, mothers were ten times more likely to be the perpetrators than siblings and about six times more likely than other female family members (FVC 2009, 36). In recent years, however, as male sexual abuse has attracted more public attention and understanding, reported rates of male abuse have increased (Lew 1990; Genuis, Thomlison, and Bagley 1991). Some analysts predict that gender differences in child sexual abuse will eventually disappear; however, while both boys and girls may be equally likely to be victimized, age may continue to play a role in maintaining the discrepancy, since girls' victimization persists as they mature.

The gender pattern amongst victims of abuse is complex. Official statistics tend to suggest that boys and girls are almost equally likely to be investigated as possible victims of abuse and to be taken into care by social welfare agencies (Trocmé et al. 1994; Federal-Provincial Working Group 1994, 24, 106). It seems likely that boys and girls are equally subject to abuse simply by token of their status as children. Age, however, may mitigate some of the effect for boys. While some evidence suggests that older boys may be more subject to frequent, severe parental violence (Knudsen 1992, 58), other research suggests that boys are more likely to be victimized when they are younger and gradually outgrow this victimization pattern. Girls, in contrast, do not outgrow their powerlessness and are more likely to be abused as they mature into adolescence (Trocmé et al. 1994, 82). This pattern is consistent with a social context in which men, as a group, wield more power than women, as a group.

It is probable that patterns of female and male upbringing play a part in children's victimization. Interviews conducted by the Women's Research Centre in Vancouver with seventeen adult female survivors of child sexual abuse certainly suggest gender is relevant. In some cases, offending fathers played the stereotypic, patriarchal role of domineering authoritarian and used male privilege and violence to control and exploit their families. In other cases, even if survivors saw their mothers as dominant in the family, it appears that their fathers were the ultimate authority and they were a key consideration in family matters (1989, 39–40). Offending fathers who presented themselves as "wimps" who were dominated and abused by their wives often used this ruse to secure the allegiance of "Daddy's little girl," turning daughters against their mothers while obscuring the father's own responsibility (41). There are many relevant gender roles that need not assume uniform or stereotypic shapes to be important in abuse situations. Sexual offenders may run the gamut from macho men to shy, sensitive types, but their masculinity and its prerogatives remain pertinent. Conversely, whether victims are tomboys, wimps, or little ladies, learned concepts of masculinity and femininity may be an important aspect of their victimization. The Women's Research Centre study found, for example, that most abuse survivors were brought up to be "proper young ladies" with all the trappings of traditional femininity—passive, conforming, dependent, entertaining, and accommodating (47). Such gender socialization may produce potential victims.

There also appear to be gender differences in the effects experienced by children who have been exposed to violence. Some studies have shown that girls are more likely to internalize their emotions and become depressed and withdrawn. Boys generally tend to externalize through increased aggression in their interactions with others. Another study indicates that both sexes exhibit aggressive behaviour but address it to different parties: girls to boys and men; boys to their mothers and other females. Yet others have shown that severity and the amount of violence have differing effects on male and female children: for girls, the amount of violence and aggression from their mothers predicts behaviour problems more than just the amount of violence to which they have been exposed. Regardless of gender, severity of violence was found to be more predictive of psychological problems in one study; and it has been suggested that boys model their fathers' violent behaviour towards women (Hayes, Trocmé, and Jenney 2006, 206–207). (See Chapter 5 for further discussion.)

THE IMPACT OF CLASS, RACE, AND ETHNICITY

It has become commonplace to point out that all children—regardless of race, gender, and social class—are vulnerable to child abuse (Wallace 1996, 33; Van Stolk 1978, 34; Segal 1995). Daily reading of any city newspaper will certainly confirm that this is true. However, it is important to make two key points. First, research repeatedly indicates that economic deprivation increases the possibility of child abuse. Though there is often a complex interplay with other factors, such as violence in the father's or mother's family of origin, ongoing marital violence, social isolation, and so on, the family's economic plight plays a significant role. Secondly, the economic location of the family—its social class—determines whether or not family problems are scrutinized and labelled by social agencies. Middle- and upper-class families can afford privacy and private solutions; their respectability and social power make it less likely that they will be defined as neglectful or abusive. Poorer families more often seem to fit the stereo- type of neglectful or abusive parents and will more likely be in contact with social welfare agencies.

The report of the 2008 CIS indicates that in 91 per cent of substantiated cases of abuse, the children's primary caregiver was a female, of which 45 per cent were between the ages of 31 and 40. Caregivers under 22 and over 50 were relatively rare (5 per cent and 4 per cent respectively). In 94 per cent of cases, the child's primary caregiver was the biological parent. Only 2 per cent of the caregivers were an adoptive parent or a parent's partner. The primary caregiver was identified by child welfare workers to have at least one risk fac- tor[36] in 78 per cent of cases, the most frequently noted of which was being a current victim of domestic violence at 46 per cent, having few social supports at 39 per cent, having mental health issues at 27 per cent, alcohol abuse at 21 per cent, and drug or solvent abuse at 17 per cent. Fifty-one per cent of the families in which child abuse had been substantiated relied on full-time employment, while 33 per cent received unemployment benefits, social assis- tance, or some other type of benefits. More than half of these families (55 per cent) lived in rented accommodations of which 44 per cent were private and 11 per cent were public housing. Almost one-third (31 per cent) of the children involved in substantiated investigations lived in purchased homes. Five per cent lived in housing controlled by Aboriginal bands. Almost half the families (48 per cent) had not moved in the preceding twelve months; another 20 per cent had moved once during that same time period. At least one household hazard[37] was found to be present in 12 per cent of these homes, while multiple home health hazards were identified in 6 per cent, and accessible drugs or drug paraphernalia were noted in another 5 per cent of these homes (Public Health Agency 2010, 39–42).

Despite the obligatory acknowledgement that families of all races and social classes engage in child abuse, research indicates that poorer families are much more likely to be labelled abusive. Using data from the National Longitudinal Survey of Children and Youth, Letourneau, Fedick, and Willms (2007) report that mothers of preschool-aged children who have been exposed to domestic violence frequently have less education and live in households with lower socio-economic status. Their results indicate that these mothers may compensate for their children's exposure to violence by being very attentive and sensitive in their relationships with them, which may contribute to their children's successful development in the long term.

Rhonda Lenton's survey of child discipline techniques amongst Toronto parents found that mothers and fathers struggling with low family income or unemployment were more likely to use violence in disciplining their children (1990).[38] American research follows the same pattern. Gelles and Sweet, for example, report from their national survey that "families earning less than twenty thousand dollars a year have the highest rates of child abuse," and families where the husband is unemployed have child abuse rates 62 per cent higher than other families (1992, 249, 251). Research continues to confirm that poverty (that is, living in poor neighbourhoods) is clearly associated with increased rates of neglect as well as physical and sexual abuse (Drake and Pandey 1996).

Almost by definition, poor families are most likely to be what middle-class social workers term "neglectful." However, as many analysts point out, the governmental solution is rarely, if ever, to eradicate poverty, but rather to push and pull these individual parents (mothers) into fulfilling their parental obligations.

Since poverty tends to follow certain racial and ethnic lines in Canada and the United States, and since poverty is strongly associated with family abuse, it is not surprising to find that there are some clear racial and ethnic patterns of abuse.[39]

In Canada, for example, child abuse charges have been rampant in many Aboriginal communities. In the sixties and seventies, tremendous numbers of Aboriginal children were taken into care by provincial authorities, and the legacy of this residential school experience is considered to be the primary factor contributing to such widespread violence and abuse in Aboriginal families. Children were torn from their families and put into institutions where they suffered abuse at the hands of strangers. They grew up with no experience of family life and no sense of the importance of family life in their communities; their understanding of parental roles was therefore lacking (Baskin 2006). According to some estimates, Aboriginal children comprised 35 to 40 per cent of children apprehended by child welfare authorities during the sixties and seventies. The result of the "sixties scoop" was the removal of almost an entire generation of children into white foster homes in Canada and elsewhere. For example, in the 400-member Spallumcheen Indian Band in British Columbia, an astonishing eighty children were removed and placed in foster or other care in the seventies (MacDonald 1995). Alcohol abuse, family violence, and significant family breakdown are much more prevalent in Aboriginal families, leading to higher rates of child abuse as well (Baskin 2006).

According to the 2008 CIS, Aboriginal children made up 22 per cent of substantiated maltreatment cases: 15 per cent were of First Nations status, 3 per cent were First Nations Non-Status, 2 per cent were Metis, 1 per cent were Inuit, and 1 per cent had other Aboriginal heritage (Public Health Agency 2010, 39).

Collin-Vezina, Dion, and Trocmé (2009) discuss twenty studies of prevalence rates of sexual abuse among mostly Aboriginal adults, indicating a range from a moderate 16 per cent to extremely high at 100 per cent. They conclude that, realistically, it is probable that 25–50 per cent of Aboriginal adults were sexually abused while minors. This is a higher percentage than is believed to exist among non-Aboriginal Canadians. The researchers caution that, because of the diversity of Aboriginal communities, the fact that some of these incidents took place up to fifty years prior to the study, and the fact that some of the incidents occurred in residential schools, accuracy is a serious problem. The 1998 and 2003 Canadian Incidence Studies on Reported Child Abuse and Neglect indicated that rates of child sexual abuse were low among both Aboriginal and non-Aboriginal communities, but this finding is possibly due to low reporting levels rather than few actual cases. In fact, the first two cycles of this study showed lower rates among Aboriginal children because there was much less investigation done by child protection agencies in Aboriginal communities—only neglect was higher. The 2008 cycle was constructed to overcome these limitations with a broader sampling technique (Collin-Vézina, Dion, and Trocmé 2009). Concerns of overrepresentation of Aboriginal children in the child welfare system led investigators in the 2008 cycle to ensure documentation of Aboriginal heritage. They found that Aboriginal children were identified in substantiated investigations of maltreatment four times more than non-Aboriginal children (Public Health Agency 2010, 39).

Many immigrants and refugees in Canada face numerous barriers and forms of discrimination. Their status in this country contributes to fears and anxieties to which other Canadians are not subject, and which may play a part in the occurrence of child abuse in their families and their desire to keep it hidden, possibly preventing them from seeking assistance. According to Alaggia and Maiter (2006), immigrant parents may come to the attention of child welfare agencies more frequently because of their use of physical discipline with young children as well as teens. Parental styles and values may be responsible for immigrant and refugee parents using physical discipline with adolescents that Canadians may find less than acceptable; for instance, immigrant parents may want their teens to socialize primarily with other teens from the ethnic group, to dress and act more modestly than a typical Canadian teenager, and to respect the authority of their elders. In short, immigrant parents may wish to curtail the activities of their adolescents far more than other Canadian parents, and may encounter what they would consider greater rebelliousness in their offspring (116–17). The lack of culturally- and linguistically-specific agencies probably makes these families less likely to seek help due to fear that they will be misunderstood and possibly jeopardize their personal or community status in Canadian society.

Visible minority and Aboriginal children are investigated by child protection services 1.77 times more frequently than children from the general population. Asian children are more often reported and substantiated by investigation for physical abuse. Black and Aboriginal children are more likely to be reported and substantiated for neglect. Risk factors relating to child vulnerability, parental characteristics, and housing may be significant for Aboriginal children but not necessarily for Asian and Black children; therefore, these factors alone cannot account for the higher reporting and substantiation rates. Data from the U.S. indicates similar overrepresentations. This situation may be due, in part, to racist attitudes of social workers in their decision whether or not to substantiate a case, or systemic racism contributing to negative judgments about how certain families are forced to live and how these conditions may undermine their parenting (Lavergne et al. 2008).

102

THE IMPACT OF OTHER FACTORS

Like women, children with disabilities are more likely to suffer maltreatment. However, the definition of disability is as problematic as that of abuse, and there are distinct differences between learning disabilities, behavioural disabilities, and physical disabilities. According to Sobsey and Sobon (2006), research has indicated that children who suffer from disabilities "are probably two to four times as common among maltreated children than other children" and about one-quarter of abused children have diagnosed disabilities. It also appears that children with behavioural disabilities are more likely to be abused than children with other types of disabilities (62). The National Clearinghouse on Family Violence Overview Paper on Child Sexual Abuse (2006) states that children with disabilities are more likely to be sexually abused as well.

A review of seven surveys from a number of regions in the United States and Canada, although different in terms of sampling methods, wording, and measures of sexual orientation, revealed similar results: sexual minority teens in almost all of them were more likely to report sexual and physical abuse. Although all girls were more likely to report having been physically abused than boys, bisexual and lesbian girls reported higher levels of abuse than heterosexual girls. One in five (up to one in three) gay and bisexual boys reported physical abuse as opposed to one in eight heterosexual boys (Saewyc et al. 2006). Belonging to a sexual minority is thus another layer or sector of vulnerability for youth, exposing them to increased likelihood of victimization.

ECONOMIC COSTS AND CONSEQUENCES

The costs of child abuse to Canadian society are multiple, including judicial, social, educational, health, employment, and personal costs. Bowlus, McKenna, Day, and Wright (2003, v) estimate that in 1998 child abuse cost the Canadian public $15,705,910,047—a staggering figure. As a result of the emotional and psychological effects of abuse, young victims are more likely to fail and repeat grades. They often have difficult relationships with their peers and teachers. They may be disciplined in school more than non-abused children. The result is that children who have been abused often drop out of school, which ultimately makes it more difficult for them to obtain gainful employment and earn a good living. Many abused children run away from home and end up living on the streets, often engaging in high-risk behaviours such as prostitution and drug abuse. Teens who have been physically or sexually abused are twice as likely to get pregnant; if they have suffered both types of abuse, they are four times as likely (Bowlus et al. 2003, 24). Risky behaviours and inability to earn a decent living can contribute to illegal activity, leading to possible involvement with the criminal justice system and incarceration. Difficulty holding a job or having a child can mean the need to rely on social assistance. Ill physical and mental health as people try to cope with what has been done to them may result in self-medicating behaviours, like smoking and consumption of alcohol. Depression and anxiety may lead to suicide. According to the World Health Organization (2007), the costs to the United States amount to $94 billion per year, and to Australia approximately $520 million in 2000–2001 for child protection and supported placement alone. In short, the damage caused to children by abuse leads to high costs for all of us. We depend on the future generations to shoulder the responsibility for maintaining and advancing our society when we are no longer able to do so. What will happen to all of us if those future generations are so damaged by maltreatment in their families that they cannot?

CONCLUSIONS

We may never know the real prevalence or full extent of child abuse for many reasons. Some victims may not wish to label what was done to them by loved and trusted adults as child abuse. Some may not wish to talk about their experiences. The memories of some may have become distorted over the years—memories are faulty, at best. Humiliation and embarrassment may keep people from reporting.

Nevertheless, child abuse is not an inevitable, natural human constant. Its appearance in any society corresponds to historical and societal circumstances.[40] In the past, social beliefs and values were conducive to various expressions of what today is termed abuse, including infanticide, child prostitution, and child labour. Even today, the legacy of these social patterns persists in the deeply felt belief of many parents that their children are their property and that they have the right to do with them whatever they wish. In this sense, child abuse is a social construction based on both historical traditions and current beliefs and values.

Child abuse and neglect are also products of economic conditions. As we've seen, poor parents are by definition at greater risk of being unable to provide adequate food, shelter, clothing, and so on. By prevailing North American standards of abuse, many Third World parents are guilty of neglect. Further, it seems likely that economic pressures exacerbate the frustrations and anxieties of parenting and increase the likelihood that forms of child abuse other than neglect will occur. As one study noted, "Poverty reduces a family's capacity to respond to stress and contributes to the dislocation and disintegration of families" (Aitken and Mitchell 1995, 29).

Given the extensive documentation of the relationships between lower-income families and child abuse, changes in the economy must be considered significant indicators of future trends. In this regard, current high rates of unemployment, increasing rates of child poverty, and reductions in social welfare support for the poor are all ominous signs of what is to come. In particular, dramatic increases in poverty among the young and mother-headed families, along with the highest rates of child poverty recorded in decades, all suggest that a future increase in child abuse rates in Canada is likely (Aitken and Mitchell 1995).

Any discussion of child abuse must also acknowledge the global dimensions of the issue. The plight of abused and battered children is far from a local or national problem, and success in solving violence against children must ultimately be judged on an international scale. Unfortunately, growing public awareness of child abuse in North America and around the world has meant halting progress at best, and future indications are decidedly grim.

In sum, no matter whether you look around locally, nationally, or internationally, there is much to be done and enough work for everyone who is willing to fight for the right of children to have a childhood. In this context, it is important to recall Alice Miller's plea for friendly and supportive "witnesses" for children, "witnesses who could be of help to the suffering children. By witnesses I mean people who are not afraid to stand up for children assertively and protect them from adults' abuse of power" (1981, xiii). Every day, in Canada and around the world, children are dying for want of such witnesses.

105

4

ABUSE IN OTHER FAMILY RELATIONSHIPS

Ryan is a rising star in an extremely macho sport. He is also gay. No one knows this except his lover, Josh. Ryan is terrified that someone will find out about his sexual orientation and he will lose everything he has worked so hard to achieve—especially his relationship with his father, who coaches him. He spent most of his youth denying his homosexuality, forcing himself to be celibate, but when he met Josh, a handsome retail sales clerk in a high-end men's clothing store, it was love at first sight. He and Josh have had a clandestine relationship for two years, but now Josh wants more and he has become abusive, withholding sex, taunting and belittling Ryan, threatening to out him to everyone unless he gives Josh money and does his bidding. Ryan has been tormented into actually striking Josh a couple of times, but his remorse and horror at hitting what he considers a defence-less man and the love of his life has hobbled him. He forces himself to accept Josh's treatment, convincing himself that it is his fault that Josh has become abusive toward him. Truthfully, he hates himself for being gay. As well, because Josh is the only other person who knows about his homosexuality, Ryan dares not lose Josh because then he would have absolutely no one to talk to and with whom to reveal his true self.

One of the most significant changes in Canadian society has been the revision of national legislation that extended the right to legal marriage to same-sex couples in 2005. This revision was unprecedented in the Americas, both North and South. Canada has become one of the very few nations of the world to extend this kind of equality to homosexual and lesbian couples.

The negative side of this bold move is that family violence in same-sex couples has also "come out of the closet" in a sense, becoming part of the research agenda. Violence between same-sex couples is just as disturbing and tragic as between opposite-sex couples. The existence of abuse of intimate partners among lesbian couples has also become a troubling issue for feminist theorists, who have long held that violence in intimate relationships is male violence against women.

Elder abuse continues to be a significant area of concern to researchers, social service professionals and workers, and advocates as well. There has recently been an advertising campaign consisting of television commercials to raise awareness of this serious social issue. Sibling, adolescent, and parent abuse, however, remain under-researched areas.

SAME-SEX COUPLE ABUSE

If violence among heterosexual couples is hidden and difficult to study, then trying to ascertain accurate prevalence and incidence rates among a population that has historically been hidden and wary of scrutiny poses an even greater challenge. Violence between intimate partners of the same sex, particularly lesbians, has posed something of a conundrum for feminists who have long held that intimate partner violence is a gender-neutral euphemism for male battering of women.

Common explanations advanced for understanding the abuse of women in heterosexual relationships do not apply, as lesbians inhabit a very different social reality. Although both hetero- and homosexual women are frequently marginalized by race, ethnicity, and class, lesbians are often faced with a hostility and animosity that is unknown to straight women. According to Gillis and Diamond (2006, 130–33), feminists have tended to romanticize lesbian relationships as being a form of resistance to patriarchal power structures. Unfortunately, this has led to an inability to adequately account for violence between lesbian partners.

Claire Renzetti's (1992) pioneering national study on lesbian abuse on one hundred self-identified victims (as cited in Peterman and Dixon 2003) identified three types of abusive relationships: situational battering, chronic battering, and emotional or psychological battering. Situational battering arose out of specific situations and only occurred once or twice; this was the least common form of abuse. Chronic battering is more frequent and escalates over time. Battering is not physical in the emotionally or psychologically abusive relationship, though emotional or psychological abuse often accompanies physical battering. Eighty-seven per cent of Renzetti's subjects reported that they had been both physically and psychologically battered. Battering was similar to that in heterosexual relationships except in those aspects specifically relating to the position of homosexuality in society; that is, because it is still socially stigmatized among many groups, the threat of exposure of the victim's sexuality to friends, family, community, employers, or church is a form of abuse. "This is even more of a problem for bisexuals, who run the risk of being unwillingly exposed to both the heterosexual and the homosexual communities" (Peterman and Dixon 2003, "Types of Abuse," para. 1).

Janice Ristock, another leading researcher into lesbian partner abuse, argues that a structural approach that "identifies marginalized women as being more vulnerable to violence because of other aspects of their social location" (2005, 66) is a better way to analyze violent relationships because it opens a space for theorizing women's violence against women. Elsewhere, she states that an optimal approach to understanding lesbian abuse is to consider contextual factors surrounding abusive relationships: social contexts, such as homophobia, creating the invisibility and social isolation of lesbians; and the normalization of violence, such as the experience of abuse in previous relationships or the use of drugs and/or alcohol (2002, 57). These contexts may increase not only the risk of being victimized but also of being the victimizer, although they do not *cause* the abuse.

Ristock further states that, although the definition of lesbian partner abuse is similar to that of heterosexual partner abuse, it differs in that it includes the element of homophobia as a controlling tactic. In other words, lesbian partner abuse involves patterned violence or coercive behaviours that are meant to control the thoughts, beliefs, or conduct of the other partner or punish her for attempting to resist that control (2002, 8). Societal homophobia fuels the abuser's threat to "out" the partner's sexual orientation to others, such as family members or employers, and instills the fear that discrimination and social hostility will make it unlikely that there will be assistance available to the abused partner. Such a threat can force a woman to stay with her abusive partner. There may also be a sense of danger in disclosing to anyone that she is being abused for fear of being exposed to hostility or outed by the confidante.

The Domestic Abuse Intervention Project developed the Power and Control Wheel with a category known as HIV-Related Abuse. This type of abuse may be used whether it is the abuser or the victim who is HIV-positive. In the case of the victim, the abuser may threaten to tell others about his or her HIV-status, withhold medications or medical care, or threaten violence that may complicate the victim's status. The abuser may use his or her HIV-status to make the victim feel guilty or threaten to infect the victim (Gillis and Diamond 2006, 135).

Ristock's study reveals that physical size or strength and social power do not predict which partner will be the abuser in a lesbian relationship. She states, "Several women who identified as butch in this study reported being victimized by their smaller femme partner. They spoke of the added difficulties they face of not being believed or being shamed because of the assumption made on the basis of their butch identity or appearance that they must be the one who is abusive" (2002, 50). Many of the subjects admitted that they experienced multiple forms of abuse, although emotional abuse seems to be the dominant type, consisting of manipulation, lying, jealousy, isolation, and sleep deprivation, among other things. Stalking was another form of emotional abuse reported by eight women (almost 8 per cent). The vast majority of women admitted that verbal abuse accompanied the emotional abuse. Physical abuse was both directed at the victim and at objects in the room or, in a few cases, at pets. Eighteen per cent of the abused lesbians reported that their injuries from physical abuse had included broken bones, knife wounds, head trauma, and bruises. Some of this serious abuse had involved weapons such as guns and knives, or included strangling, choking, or beating. Some of the women also reported sexual abuse.

Although it is extremely difficult at this stage to estimate prevalence rates of lesbian abuse, some studies have suggested that rates equal or exceed those of heterosexual couples. Peterman and Dixon state that, according to the National Coalition Against Domestic Violence, domestic violence has occurred in about 25 to 33 per cent of female same-sex relationships (2003, para. 1). Tjaden, Thoennes, and Allison (1999, "Experiences with Intimate Partner Violence," para. 2–4) report that same-sex female partners reported less physical and sexual violence in their intimate relationships (11.4 per cent) than did opposite-sex female partners, (20.3 per cent). On the other hand, 15.4 per cent of same-sex male partners reported being raped or physically assaulted by their intimate partners, while only 7.7 per cent of opposite-sex male partners reported that their female partners had similarly violated them. Thus, for both same-sex and opposite-sex victims, having a male intimate partner exposed them to a greater likelihood of abuse.

The experience of being abused in an intimate relationship is compounded by the problems faced by being a lesbian in a predominantly heterosexual and heterosexist (that is, the belief that it is normal and natural to be heterosexual) society. Abused lesbians may not wish to admit being abused because they fear worsening the public image of lesbians or homosexuals in general. Since lesbians tend to associate with other lesbians and their friends are largely drawn from that community, an abused lesbian may find it difficult to confide in any of her friends because they may side with her abuser and abandon her. If part of the abuse is being isolated from friends and family, victims may have only their batterers to console them after an episode of battering. Going to a women's shelter for assistance and safety may be fruitless, as the batterer may also appear at the same shelter posing as a victim (Peterman and Dixon 2003).

A number of myths exist about intimate abuse among male same-sex partners. For example, the predominant model of masculinity may lead the public to believe that men who find themselves victimized by their gay male partners do not require assistance; that men cannot truly be victims. There is also the idea that the abuser is always the bigger of the two men, and that men are naturally violent so they can easily fight back and defend themselves. The public may also erroneously perceive violence to be sexually arousing for these men (Kirkland 2004). The perpetuation of such

110

myths could mean that gay men are doubly victimized and unable to access badly needed social resources to help them deal with the issue of violence in their intimate relationships.

Physical abuse among gay male couples has been most commonly studied. Unfortunately, the variability in methodologies makes it difficult to compare these studies, with prevalence rates varying from 14 to 62 per cent (as cited in Bartholomew et al. 2008; Kirkland 2004 reports 20 per cent). In addition, most studies have used small samples with self-selected subjects, so generalizability to the entire male same-sex couple population is questionable. Some studies have revealed that the violence among male same-sex couples is bidirectional, meaning that perpetrators may also be victims and vice versa. Bidirectionality may be as high as 57 per cent in cases where physical abuse was reported. The focus on the most obvious form of abuse obscures the fact that abuse may not involve any type of physical force (Kirkland 2004, 5).

Island and Letellier (1991), pioneering researchers in male same-sex relationship abuse, suggested that bidirectionality was uncommon and that violence in intimate same-sex relationships adhered to the traditional, distinct victim-perpetrator model. This stance may be partially due to a reluctance to undermine possible aid for gay male victims of abuse, which may result from the impression that the situation is not a type of family violence but rather mutual male violence (as cited in Bartholomew et al. 2008; see also Peterman and Dixon 2003). Bartholomew et al. state, "Not considering the potential bidirectionality of abuse, however, may give an incomplete picture of abusive gay relationships. As well, the assumption that victims and perpetrators are distinct individuals could lead to exaggerated prevalence estimates" (2008, "Bidirectional Partner Abuse," para. 2). Abuse may also be more serious in relationships where bidirectional violence is present.

In their study, conducted in Vancouver, BC, Bartholomew et al. (2008) found that the majority of physical abuse involved relatively minor acts of violence in relationships that had since ended. Ten per cent of their sample reported that a partner had used force or threats against them to engage in sexual relations. Due to inconsistency between victim and perpetrator reports, with the former being much higher than the latter, the researchers speculate that the perpetration reports are unreliable. Their results indicate that psychological and physical abuse tend to occur simultaneously, and furthermore that psychological abuse in a relationship is predictive of the development of physical violence. Rates of sexual victimization were seven times higher among men who had also experienced physical abuse than among those who had not. Bartholomew et al. conclude, "[t]hus, when partner abuse escalates, it may tend to follow a trajectory from psychological to physical to sexual abuse" (2008, "Levels of Abuse in Male Same-Sex Relationships," para. 5).

Bartholomew et al. (2008) observe that reported injury rates among same-sex couples were much higher than those typically reported among heterosexual couples. Therefore, gay men are more likely to suffer injuries in abusive relationships. As men, perpetrators' natural size and strength, as well as their socialization, make them more likely to inflict injuries on their partners. In terms of directionality, Bartholomew et al. state, "The majority of men reporting any abuse in a same-sex relationship reported that they had both inflicted and sustained abusive acts" (2008, "Directionality of Abuse in Gay Relationships," para. 1). Their study reveals that the highest levels of bidirectionality were reported in the current relationship and that the levels of abuse were similar. They suggest that, because the partners are of the same sex, inhibitions against retaliation are lower than in heterosexual relationships where bidirectionality is present. Their somewhat tentative conclusion from this study is that male same-sex intimate violence does not generally follow the traditional pattern of one partner as perpetrator, the other as victim.

In the same study, Bartholomew, Regan, Oram, and White (2008a) examined various factors to ascertain their correlation to same-sex intimate violence. They first compared factors that have been associated with heterosexual intimate violence: demographic variables, childhood history of family violence, substance abuse, and attachment orientation (2008a, "Do Correlates of Heterosexual Partner Abuse Also Apply to Male Same-sex Partner Abuse?", para. 1–7). They note that predictor variables of heterosexual partner abuse are also associated with same-sex partner abuse in similar ways, with the exception of age. Violence by mothers was more consistently associated with partner abuse, possibly due to a greater tendency of gay men to be close with their mothers and therefore have a stronger reaction to their abusive behaviours. Predictor variables that specifically related to homosexual men had stronger associations with same-sex partner abuse. For example, HIV-positive men were more likely to experience psychological abuse in bidirectional relationships. Interestingly, outness, rather than being in the closet, was associated with victimization. This association may be due to the greater opportunity of out men to have more experience with same-sex relationships. The authors note that internalized homophobia was the only predictor variable associated with all forms of partner abuse. (Bartholomew et al. 2008a, "Do Variables of Particular Relevance to Gay Relationships Predict Partner Abuse?", para. 4). Low self-esteem and self-hatred are likely at the heart of this variable.

SIBLING ABUSE

The phenomenon of sibling abuse is a fascinating one, since in one way, it is the most commonly acknowledged form of violence ("sibling rivalry"), yet in another, it is the most ignored. Parents freely admit that their children do not get along with one another and often engage in various forms of aggression, but these behaviours are not labelled as "violence" or included under the umbrella term "family violence." In fact, social norms encourage aggression among siblings to the point where parents believe that it is an inevitable part of growing up. Furthermore, some even view such conflict as "a good training ground for successful management of aggressive behaviour in the real world" (Gelles and Cornell 1990, 85). Therefore, parents are far less likely to attempt to curtail it.

Not only do parents have a difficult time seeing that "sibling rivalry" may be in actuality sibling abuse, but they also may not believe their children's accounts of suffering at the hands of siblings—or, worse yet, blame the children themselves for whatever these siblings do to them. This tendency to blame the victims implies that these children "deserve" such treatment, something that can be extremely damaging to the child's self-esteem and detrimental to family relations as a whole, especially when the abuse is of a sexual nature (Wiehe 1990).

The behaviours entailed by sibling abuse are seen to be far more innocent than similar behaviours directed at, for example, small children by parents, or wives by husbands. In other words, the same actions performed by husbands, parents, or caregivers against wives, children, or elders would not be tolerated. Yet because these actions are carried out by siblings, or "equals," they are more likely to be accepted, albeit with some reservation. This acceptance may relate to the notions of "equality" prevalent in our society, which are seen to somehow mitigate unpleasant conditions. That is, as long as people are of comparable status, this "equality" somehow makes their actions more tolerable.

Until recently, social scientists have also failed to devote serious attention to sibling violence, largely due to parents' widespread acceptance of it and their belief that such behaviour is necessary for children to learn how to handle themselves. Researchers have even contributed to this position by outlining five "positive" elements of sibling aggression, which include "benefits" such as sibling reassurance when parents are unavailable, acquisition of conflict management skills, and the promotion of feelings of loyalty (Goodwin and Roscoe 1990).

The Experience

In a 1977 study of sibling abuse, the most difficult problem encountered by researchers was getting parents to record anything but the most extreme cases of violence. This implies that the findings do not necessarily reveal the true frequency of sibling abuse (Steinmetz 1977, 44), nor do they allow researchers to state with any confidence whether sibling violence is increasing, decreasing, or remaining at the same level (Gelles and Cornell 1990, 87). Another interesting finding of the 1977 study was that parents were often used as a resource by the sibling in the weaker position, but that parents themselves believed conflicts were better resolved among the siblings than through their intervention (Steinmetz 1977, 44). This may also reflect the belief that, because such conflict occurs among "equals" or peers, it is not to be taken seriously; because siblings are members of a loving, supportive family unit, conflict among them is not believed to be truly hurtful or abusive. But the reality is that sibling conflict can be hurtful and that conflict may erupt among a certain age group.

Wishing to test this notion that child-on-child violence is not as serious as other types of violence, Finkelhor, Turner, and Ormrod (2006) analyzed data from the U.S. Developmental Victimization Survey, which assessed the experiences of a nationally representative sample of children from the ages of two to seventeen. They found that sibling violence usually yielded fewer injuries than peer violence, and involved fewer objects and assailants. However, it was more likely than peer violence to be chronic, particularly for younger children; and chronicity was associated with increased trauma symptoms. The researchers argue that their findings suggest that sibling violence among children is far from benign.

There is research to support that normalization of violence between siblings by parents significantly contributes to the severity and frequency of sibling abuse. It may lead to other risk factors and may promote aggressive behaviour rather than providing an outlet for it. Some studies indicate that child abuse by parents and sibling abuse are linked, as children imitate their parents' actions. Families in crisis or parents who are unavailable to meet their children's needs may also contribute to the risk of sibling violence. Moreover, when parents label some children, "good" and others "bad," they increase competition between children, who then fight over available family resources, including emotions. If siblings are interested in the same things, competition between them is heightened (as cited in Kiselica and Morrill-Richards 2007).

Research suggests that the number of conflicts and their causes among siblings differs according to age group or stage of life. Conflict is much more frequent in families with young children (eight years and younger) as opposed to those with teenagers (fourteen years and older), perhaps because, as children age, they spend less time with one another and more time outside the home. Young children tend to fight over possessions such as "toys, games, or the attention of adults." Adolescents (categorized as aged eight to fourteen years) engage in conflict over personal space, while teenagers tend to fight about "responsibilities, obligations, and social grace" (Steinmetz 1977, 51, 56). Use of physical force as a resolution for conflict decreases as the ages of the children increase, because older children are better able to articulate their complaints and thus are able to resolve conflict through discussion.

Goodwin and Roscoe (1990, 454) cite research that reveals that sibling violence may be a better predictor of violence in adulthood than violence

115

between parents. Sibling violence provides the children with practical opportunities to carry out abusive behaviour rather than simply witnessing it. One study surveyed American junior high school students (mean age 12.3 years) about their experiences as victims and perpetrators of aggression toward siblings. The findings revealed that 88 per cent of males and 94 per cent of females identified themselves as victims, while 85 per cent of males and 96 per cent of females stated that they had been perpetrators. The violent behaviour they experienced included shoving and kicking. These findings indicate levels of violence among siblings much higher than those reported by adults and parents, possibly indicating the lack of serious attention to the problem given by adults and parents. The findings also suggest that females are more violent than males—statistics that contradict findings that show girls are less violent than boys (Straus, Gelles, and Steinmetz 1980, 88–89). However, we can assume that other factors play a role when children self-report. For example, boys may be less likely to view certain behaviours as violent or aggressive, while girls may be more inclined to describe some of their behaviour as aggressive. Therefore, gender socialization could account for the higher figure of girls reporting being the perpetrators of sibling abuse.

In a similar study, American high school students (mean age 16.9 years) were surveyed concerning violence involving their closest-aged siblings over the previous twelve months (Goodwin and Roscoe 1990). The researchers found that the major source of sibling conflict was over possessions and verbal exchanges. Females were more likely to cite jealousy and preferential treatment by parents as sources of conflict. More males threatened to harm their siblings, while more females were teased. In terms of actual physical violence, 65 per cent of females as opposed to 64 per cent of males reported being perpetrators, while 64 per cent of females and 66 per cent of males stated that they had been victims. A higher number of males reported using a mild form of physical force as a way of resolving conflicts with siblings than females, who tended to use verbal methods, although such methods included shouting.

The findings of this report support the argument that as children age, they learn to use language as a way to resolve conflict rather than resorting to physical aggression. However, the level of physical violence at this age, when adolescents are big enough to inflict serious damage on one another, indicates that sibling aggression is still a significant problem. The fact that males used physical force more often than females may indicate social norms that encourage aggression in males as part of their masculine socialization.

In Vernon Wiehe's (1990) study of 150 self-identified victims of sibling abuse, most stated that the perpetrator of the physical abuse was male. Since 89 per cent of the respondents were female, it would appear from these reports that it is mostly brothers who abuse. Wiehe's analysis is that power in America is gender-related, with males believing that they should have power and that females should be placed into powerless positions. If a brother feels powerless, he may abuse his sister to make himself feel powerful in relation to her. The feeling of power that he gets from abusing his sister is a reinforcement for perpetrating such acts in the future. Wiehe also notes that, when it comes to sexual abuse in particular, it is not only families of low socio-economic status in which siblings victimize one another. In other words, contrary to certain myths, siblings of middle- and upper-class families are as likely to sexually abuse one another as those from lower-class families.

In Wiehe's study, the respondents described their responses to physical abuse as screaming and crying for help, separating themselves from their abuser and hiding, abusing a younger sibling in order to reject the role of victim and identify with the aggressor, and telling on the perpetrator to parents (which often resulted in the victim being blamed). Similar responses were experienced in cases of emotional abuse where fighting back was a typical form of resistance. However, very few victims of sexual abuse fought back. These victims pretended to be sleeping or simply submitted. This passivity may be because victims were generally younger and smaller than their abusers. Also, they may not have been aware of what the abuser was doing. Often secrecy and threats were involved, effectively silencing the victim.

Parents may not be made aware of sexual abuse because the victim may not be able to articulate what she or he is experiencing or may not perceive it as abuse. Fear of retaliation from the abuser is another reason victims often do not report sexual abuse to parents; or they may blame themselves for the abuse, thinking that, if they did not stop it themselves, they were somehow granting "permission" to the abuser. The atmosphere in the home may not allow for reporting such abuse; such subjects may be taboo (Wiehe 1990).[41]

There has been virtually no major research done on sibling abuse in Canada to date, with the exception of one study conducted by DeKeseredy and Ellis (1994). Their survey relied on a non-random sample of 215 undergraduate students and thirty-four interviews with children from six to eleven years old who have learning disabilities. Representativeness is problematic in this study due to both their method of sampling and the fact that self-reporting was involved; however, the study should be considered a pioneering effort by Canadian researchers to shed light on the issue. They asked respondents to report on conflict between themselves and their siblings and to specify whether they had experienced harm or had inflicted it upon siblings. Their findings show that 47.8 per cent of the undergraduates and 100 per cent of the children with learning disabilities had been victims of sibling abuse (as cited in Baker 1996).

According to Ellis and DeKeseredy, the Canadian study should not be compared with the American findings by Steinmetz (1977) and Straus, Gelles, and Steinmetz (1980) because different measures and samples were used, and the definitions of sibling violence were dissimilar. Because enough of the most basic components diverged, the findings were incompatible. This divergence in research in the two countries demonstrates a prevailing problem in family violence research as a whole: without standardized procedures and definitions, establishing a comprehensive portrait of the dimensions of family violence as a whole is very difficult.

Naming the Issue

The sibling bond is perhaps one of the most important in any individual's life. It is also one of the longest relationships anyone has in a lifetime (Tindale et al. 1994). The way that sibling interaction unfolds in a family may have an enormous effect on how individuals interact with others throughout the remainder of their lives. As a result, the matter of sibling abuse is a significant one. Unfortunately, it has not enjoyed a great deal of legitimacy in the public consciousness or even among academics, judging from the small number of studies that have been done. This is particularly true for Canada.

Wallace (1996) states, "[S]ibling abuse is any form of physical, mental, or sexual abuse inflicted by one child in a family unit on another" (101–102). Such a definition is useful because it encompasses children who may not be related by blood and those who may or may not reside in the home on a full-time basis. It also involves children in particular, rather than including those siblings who are over the age of eighteen.

Like other forms of abuse within the family, sibling abuse can be categorized into three types: physical, emotional, and sexual (Wallace 1996, 102). It should be noted that these various types of abuse often occur together. Seventy-one per cent of respondents in Wiehe's (1990) study stated that they had suffered all three. Physical abuse involves striking, kicking, punching, or using objects as weapons. Emotional abuse consists of name-calling, ridicule, degradation, exacerbating a fear, destroying personal possessions, or the torture or destruction of a pet. Emotional abuse is very difficult to identify due to the lack of physical evidence and because legal standards may not be clear enough to establish distinct boundaries regarding what constitutes emotional abuse (Wiehe 1990). The characteristics of sexual abuse distinguish between childhood curiosity and abuse. Some of the divergences involve differences in age and types of activities. Power and control are usually the hallmarks of abusive sexual behaviour between siblings, both of which are absent in cases of childhood exploration. One researcher has argued that sibling sexual abuse is a more serious form of adolescent sexual abuse due to the accessibility of the victim and the privacy of the family, which shrouds the activities of family members in secrecy (Wallace 1996, 102–103). Also, sibling sexual abuse tends to be compounded by shame on the part of both the victim and the perpetrator (Wiehe 1990).

Wiehe (1990) includes prolonged tickling as a form of abuse employed by siblings. Although tickling is not usually considered a form of abuse, there are instances when it ceases to be harmless fun and becomes torment. These instances occur when the one who is being tickled wants the behaviour to stop or is genuinely unwilling to participate, but the perpetrator ignores her or his wishes and fails to respect the integrity of the victim. Victims may be forcibly restrained or held down. The tickling may even become painful. This kind of behaviour may be particularly prone to dismissal by parents as "just playing." Such dismissal invalidates the victim's experience and may be more detrimental in the long run.

Sibling abuse can also be perpetrated by one child against another or it may take the form of serial abuse, which involves a perpetrator violating one sibling after another. Research on serial abuse is inconclusive partially because it is so difficult to conduct such studies and to interpret findings. Serial sibling abuse does not pertain only to sexual abuse; it may pertain to other forms of abuse as well (Wallace 1996).

PARENT ABUSE

The thought that children could abuse their parents is so far beyond the pale for most of us that we would quite likely dismiss such a notion as outlandish rather than give it serious consideration. Children are considered to be powerless in the family hierarchy; it is believed that parents are the ones with all the power. Yet child-to-parent abuse is very real.

How is it possible for parents to become the victims of abuse? As Gelles and Cornell (1990) point out, it has been argued that violence is a means of control or power for anyone, and that it is always present as a resource whenever anyone believes it should be used. It is perhaps just a cultural prejudice of ours that we believe the dominant are more likely to use violence as a resource than the subordinate.

Parent abuse is any kind of behaviour that is "deliberately harmful" and used to control parents (Cottrell 2001). It is estimated that 5 to 18 per cent of families experience parent abuse, but a more precise figure is difficult to establish. The type of violence is usually physical, but verbal and emotional abuse have also been noted (Crichton-Hill, Evans, and Meadows 2006). Verbal abuse is often a precursor to physical violence. Financial abuse by adolescents may occur because parents feel social pressure to provide their children with material possessions; abusive teens may use this sense of "obligation and inadequacy" against their parents to force them into spending more than they can afford (Cottrell 2001).

Researchers have argued that these abusers are children generally between the ages of ten and twenty-four; they are usually dependent upon their parents and live with them in the same home. Such a definition distinguishes this type of violence from that perpetrated against the elderly by their children; in this case, the "children" are quite young rather than middle-aged (see Wilson 1996).

Early reports estimated that "almost 10 per cent of children between the ages of three and eighteen have attacked their parents" (Wilson 1996, 102). Cottrell (2001) reports that parents stated their children began to display abusive behaviour toward them between the ages of twelve and fourteen, although there may have been indications earlier. Parents probably find it easier to dismiss the abusive behaviour of young children but "[t]eenagers' greater physical size may make them more threatening, and parents then begin to identify the child's behaviour as abusive" (Cottrell 2001, 7).

Using data gathered for the 1975 National Family Violence Survey employing the Conflict Tactics Scale, Ulman and Straus (2003) state that rates of violence against parents by their children were very high. Mothers were most commonly targeted and preschool-aged children were the most frequent perpetrators. From age ten to seventeen, the prevalence of child-to-parent abuse is 10 per cent. The rate of violence declines with the age of the child, possibly because they gain more control the older they get. On the other hand, the bigger and stronger the child becomes with age, the more capable of severe acts of violence she or he becomes.

Since parent abuse by children is so hard to fathom, understanding what kind of children would do such a thing may be even more difficult. Wilson (1996; see also Gelles and Cornell 1990) reports on some of the demographic traits that have been associated with abuse of parents in the literature. Gender has been found to be relevant in some research, while in other research the rate of violence by males and females has been relatively similar. Australian researchers Stewart, Jackson, Wilkes, and Mannix (2006) found that the majority of perpetrators of violence against mothers were males between 13 and 18 years of age. It would appear that visible minority adolescents are less likely to abuse their parents than Caucasians. Some researchers have posited that the discrepancy may be due to stricter discipline and less tolerance for insubordination among minority parents, or possibly due to stronger religious ties among some minority groups, which may mitigate the amount of violence they are likely to display to family members. Age is also a factor; older children are more violent toward parents than younger children. Several studies have shown that the peak age for aggression among adolescents is 15 to 17 years of age; others have found a peak age of 17 to 18 for females but none for males. However, it has been asserted that, as males age, they are less likely to display violence toward their mothers and more likely to display violence toward their fathers. Stewart et al. (2006) found that aggression appeared around the ages of 13 to 15. Size and strength of the adolescent has no bearing on whether she or he will perpetrate abusive behaviour toward her or his parents (see also Gelles and Cornell 1990).

Abusive teens often display other socially deviant behaviour, such as drug or alcohol abuse, or criminal activity such as shoplifting and prostitution. Sometimes they have been abused themselves or witnessed abuse in their home environment (Cottrell 2001). According to Ulman and Straus, parent-to-child violence by either the mother or father and parent-to-parent violence were associated with an increased probability of child-to-parent abuse. Mothers were more likely to be victimized when there was violence between either or both parents, but in the case of fathers, victimization only occurred when the mother was violent toward him (2003, 56; see also Stewart et al. 2006). A possible explanation may be that when children see their father being abused by their mother, their father appears more vulnerable and, therefore, a more feasible victim for them. The researchers believe that these data provide yet another reason why corporal punishment should not be used by parents.

Although the research is somewhat contradictory about the kind of family where parent abuse occurs, there are some common variables. One example is the presence of other forms of violence in the family. Cottrell's (2001) research indicates that single parenthood may have a connection as well. The average age of parents experiencing abuse was forty-four. Mothers and stepmothers, in single or two-parent homes, were most likely to be abused. They are usually the primary caregivers and spend more time with their children; however, they are also more likely to be busy with household duties and less able to spend leisure time with the children. Teens also absorb cultural messages that denigrate and devalue women, another probable reason they target their mothers for abuse (Cottrell 2003; Ulman and Straus 2003; Stewart et al. 2006).

Some studies have indicated that family relationships are distant and "disengaged" where parent abuse takes place; others have found that family relationships are overly involved and abusive adolescents are looking for a way to distance themselves when they abuse their parents. Still other studies have shown that adolescents abuse their parents when the spousal bond is not strong. Possibly, when the spousal bond is relatively weak, parents do not present a united front to their children, so a potentially abusive child may believe that she or he can successfully commit violence against one or both parents. There are researchers who assert that adolescents abuse parents when the family has become chaotic, the result of parents abdicating their control over matters; these adolescents are attempting to restore order to the family by taking control (see Wilson 1996; Gelles and Cornell 1990).

Adolescents who abuse their parents usually have little interest in school and have frequently experienced truancy or expulsion. They tend to have low self-esteem. Often they have been involved with some facet of law enforcement or social services, and have experienced violence in their homes. Their emotional needs may be better served by their friends, who are more likely to have deviant or delinquent values and who may be assaulting their own parents. Substance abuse is often prevalent among these adolescents, and some studies have found that alcohol use is correlated with parent abuse (see Wilson 1996; also Gelles and Cornell 1990).

Abuse may also be a response to the issue of independence/dependence. Adolescents are at a stage in their lives where they are receiving all kinds of familial and societal messages about appropriate behaviours. They are expected to take certain responsibilities, but they are restricted from taking others. They may be unhappy with the responsibilities that are being forced on them and frustrated because they are barred from taking on the responsibilities they would choose themselves. For example, adolescents have to deal with burgeoning sexual desires; they are told that these are appropriate and that they must deal with them, but conversely, it is not socially sanctioned for them to participate in the practices that would most effectively satisfy such desires. In other words, adolescents are becoming sexual beings, but they are not supposed to have sex because they are considered too young to properly deal with the consequences of sexual involvement.

Cottrell (2001) argues that there is no definitive explanation for why children abuse their parents, but there are a number of factors that contribute to the problem. One of these is a lack of parental authority in the home. Parents fear that their teens will not love them if they enforce rules and standards of behaviour; they want to be friends with their children. Teens do not feel safe when their parents refuse to take control of the family, which causes them to act out against their parents. When the family structure changes, often due to divorce, they may abuse the parent with whom they reside just to vent, and because the parent is available. Teens may feel alienated from their parents and crave their attention; abusing their parents is a way of acting out their frustration and anger. However, sometimes an adolescent's mental illness or some other medical condition is at the root of the abuse.

Parent abuse is hard to detect, partly because of the reluctance of victims to report it to authorities. They experience despair and isolation because they have lost control of their teens and their homelife; they feel that there is no support for them in the community. They cannot trust their own children. They often have to turn to prescription drugs to help them cope with the abuse. Focusing their attention and resources on the abusive teen may cause them to neglect their other children's needs; their relationship with these children may then suffer as well (Cottrell 2001). Many parents deny that their adolescents are abusing them because of their desire to protect their children, but also because they may be ashamed to admit that their children are violent toward them. They may fear that they will be blamed for their own victimization, or that they will be seen as "bad" parents. It is frequently not until the abusive behaviour is so severe that it can no longer be denied that parents will admit that it is happening to them. Parents may also fear that their adolescents will be taken away from them and that their family will break up if such behaviour is detected by authorities (Wilson 1996; Gelles and Cornell 1990).

The last form of abuse to be investigated—that perpetrated against elderly people—is another matter entirely. Although much work still needs to be done to establish a comprehensive body of knowledge, Canadians have made substantial contributions to the understanding of violence against senior citizens.

ELDER ABUSE

The conceptualization of elder abuse as a social problem evolved in the eighties in the wake of the "discoveries" of child and woman abuse. The first of the Baby Boom generation were reaching middle age. The ranks of the elder population would soon be swelling substantially as demographers realized Canada had an "aging" population, with growing numbers of older people and a shrinking birthrate. Projections indicated that at the dawn of the new millennium more than 10 per cent of Canada's population would be comprised of older adults, and by 2015 the proportion of older people would exceed that of people fifteen years of age and younger. Both men and women were living longer. Like the young, the elderly often have increased needs from family members and society in general, making them more vulnerable to abuse (Department of Justice Canada 2009; Harbison, McKinley, and Pettipas 2006). Also, in an urban, post-industrial society like Canada, there is no real role for elderly people. Most are out of the workforce, so they simply recede into the background of society (see Sev'er 2009; Litwin and Zaobi 2004). Academics and professionals working with elderly people began to realize that the government needed to pay attention to the situation and provide assistance to those suffering from abuse by creating policy to prevent and alleviate the possibility of it happening to others in the future.

Old age itself has become a social problem. In our youth-oriented, competitive culture, many people view the elderly as frail, unwell, and dependent; such a view generates a sense that there is a need to focus special attention on them (see Schlesinger 1988). Leroux and Petrunik (1990) state that being "elderly" has become a master status, dominating and obscuring all other statuses, and that people who are labelled with that master status are being segregated from the remainder of society. This is similar to the case of "battered women" raised by Jones, who argues that these women lose all other facets of their identities when they are viewed as victims of abuse. When an individual becomes a "senior citizen," all other dimensions of her or his life fade into the background as the cultural baggage surrounding the status moves into the spotlight. The desire to care for senior citizens takes precedence over the recognition that old people are adults with full legal and social rights and privileges. Social policy has tended to be formulated on the basis of this well-meaning, but rather mis-guided, attempt to help the elderly.

There is a danger that thinking of senior citizens as dependent and need-ing care can lead to the assumption that they are not capable of legal and social competence. The consequence of such an assumption could be the development of experts and advocates who, with the best of intentions, may violate the rights and dignity of the elderly with intervention poli-cies that do not consider the wishes of the elderly themselves (Leroux and Petrunik 1990). An illustration of such a violation can be found in the similarities drawn by Steinmetz between elder and child abuse. To equate elder abuse with violence against children is to ignore the essential fact that senior citizens are adults, not children; they have full legal status and civil rights.

In some sense, we may think of this phenomenon of viewing aging as a social problem as creating a greater "market" for services relating to the elderly and, therefore, more room in which advocates of various types may focus their attention on them. Leroux and Petrunik (1990) effectively argue that changing social trends and the "professional agenda" of the individuals who work in the field are largely responsible for putting family violence, including elder abuse, on the social agenda.

However, older people themselves have contributed in significant ways to addressing the problem of elder abuse. The British Columbia Coalition to Eliminate Abuse of Seniors (BCCEAS) is an organization led by seniors that conducts advocacy, peer counselling, and other programs addressing abuse. Older people were instrumental in the design of, and fundraising for, a shelter for abused women and men in Calgary, Alberta. They have also worked to educate the general public and elderly individuals about abuse, the rights of seniors, and the importance of seeking assistance (Harbison, McKinley, and Pettipas 2006).

The federal government has made important inroads into addressing elder abuse and neglect through the Family Violence Initiative (FVI) led by The Public Health Agency of Canada, although it is largely provincial governments that have enacted specific laws dealing with elder abuse. FVI's goal is to reduce family violence in Canada, toward which its primary function is to coordinate fifteen departments, agencies, and Crown corporations and fund projects to raise awareness and educate the Canadian public on various types of abuse, including abuse against older people. At the community level, the domestic violence model for program delivery is one of the methods of dealing with the needs of abused and neglected elders. It involves crisis intervention, such as telephone hotlines, court orders, counselling services and shelters, and public education, particularly targeting seniors themselves. Like the domestic violence model, advocacy programs are geared to addressing the needs of individuals or groups. They are not intrusive or part of the formal delivery system (Podnieks 2008).

McDonald and Wigdor (1995) provide a brief history of the background of Canadian research. What they refer to as the "first phase," the period when elder abuse was brought to the attention of the Canadian public, came to an end in 1992. That year the American *Journal of Elder Abuse and Neglect* devoted an entire issue to showcasing the most recent work done by Canadian researchers in the field. The first prevalence studies (studies that attempt to establish the extent to which types of abuse are present within particular populations) in Canada took place in Quebec, Manitoba, Nova Scotia, Alberta, and Ontario, and came out in the early to mid-eighties. Podnieks et al. published their national survey in 1990. Current research in Canada explores interactive aspects of elder abuse and the development of theory (Podnieks 2008).

Early research suggested that the most likely victim of elder abuse is a very old woman who is dependent on her caregiver (see Steinmetz 1993). However, Pillemer (1993) suggests that it is not the elderly who are dependent on their caregivers in many cases, but the caregivers who are dependent on the elderly. Social and geographic isolation of both victims and their families is linked with elder abuse. Vulnerability and powerlessness of the victim are also significant factors. Both isolation and vulnerability/powerlessness are often associated with widowhood (more prevalent among women because they live longer than men and tend not to remarry) and health problems of a physical or mental nature. These victims are unable to care for themselves, often live with their abusers, and are unwilling to report abuse, fearing institutionalization because they have no alternative shelter. Living with someone else has also been noted (Pillemer and Finkelhor 1988) as a risk factor involved with abuse. Co-residents are often abusers of the elderly, whether these co-residents are adult children or spouses, though elderly people tend to reside with spouses more frequently than with adult children. In fact, Pillemer and Finkelhor's finding that the risk of abuse for elderly men was twice that for elderly women was linked to the fact that these men tended to be co-residing with spouses more often than elderly women. Elderly men do not usually outlive their spouses and, when they do, they are more likely to remarry.

Recent research also strongly suggests that gender is a significant factor in elder abuse. According to the Canadian Department of Justice (2009) the proportion of elderly women victimized by family members was almost twice that of elderly men (45 per cent versus 25 per cent). Older women were more likely than older men to be victimized by a spouse or ex-spouse (35 per cent versus 21 per cent). Older women are also more likely to be killed by a family member. Between 1996 and 2005, of solved homicides, 63 per cent of elderly female victims were killed by a member of their family, most often by a spouse (40 per cent) or an adult son (34 per cent) (see also Spangler and Brandl 2007). Interestingly, a survey of 3,001 Canadians, including 718 seniors sixty-five years of age and over in 2006 indicated that 67 per cent of subjects believed that older women were more likely to be abused than older men (Environics Research Group 2008). According to Ashley Carson, Executive Director of OWL—The Voice of Midlife and Older Women, an American advocacy organization—citing 2004 statistics, states that 66 per cent of elder abuse victims are women and 89 per cent of abuse occurred in a domestic setting. In addition, "OWL believes that the abuse of older women is an under-recognized crisis that is exacerbated by the stigma related to abuse and the many types of oppression that continue to affect women during their lives, making them more vulnerable to the abuse" (Carson 2009, 6).

Past history of abuse (such as having been abused by a male spouse), dependency, frustration/anger/despair, psychological or mental factors, and environmental and systemic factors are also cited as being associated with elder abuse. The last factor relates to abuse of elderly people who are institutionalized and refers to such variables as where the institution is located in relation to the older person's home community, inadequate training of caregivers, and high stress rates among staff (Department of Justice Canada 2009). Litwin and Zoabi (2004) studied 120 abused elderly Arab Israelis to examine the validity of four explanations for the rise of elder abuse in a population transitioning from a traditional society to a modern one. They found that modernization and social integration accounted for about 80 per cent of the abuse, with amount of social support and network composition being the strongest predictors from the collection of social integration variables. Low income was also a significant contributing factor. The researchers argue that traditional society was characterized as close-knit, involving mutual dependency between family and community; modern society, on the other hand, is based on a secular lifestyle where families are more independent and isolated from community, and family members are less likely to be bound by strict hierarchical status. In other words, modernization, with its lower level of social integration, means that elderly people no longer hold the same power and respect within their families, putting them at greater risk of abuse by children and grandchildren. Community ties are weakened, further reducing the social power of elderly people. Gender and age were not considered to be significant risk factors for abuse in this study.

Another important risk factor in victim profiles is a lack of support services. Victims have no one to turn to other than their abusers, so they are isolated, vulnerable, and powerless, or at least perceive themselves to be. They are frightened of being abandoned. Without friends, other family members, or community services to provide them with alternatives to their abusive situation, they end up being victimized. The same may be true for those victims who are institutionalized. If they have no one else to rely upon for alternative support, they may feel that they have little choice but to accept their victimization. Elder abuse is also strongly correlated with having a history of abuse, so victimization may be an established pattern in the older person's life (Gnaedinger 1989; National Clearinghouse 1986).

Unfortunately, at this time it is very difficult to determine the exact dimensions of abuse of elderly people in this country. Findings from various studies and sources are frequently inconsistent and contradictory, most likely due to definition and methodology. However, an overview of the *Family Violence in Canada: Statistical Profiles* indicates the following:

- In 2005: Older women were more likely to be victims of family violence than older men; common assault was the most frequent form (55 per cent) against both men and women; and male family members were more likely to be accused of committing assault (almost eight out of ten), about 33 per cent being adult children and 34 per cent being spouses;
- In 2006: Family violence was more likely among senior women than men (20 per cent higher); and physical assault was the most common form of violence by both male and female perpetrators, though slightly more common among females (76 per cent as opposed to 62 per cent);
- In 2007: Older women were more likely to be victimized by family members than were senior men (47 versus 36 per 100,000); seniors 85 years of age or older were less commonly victimized than were seniors between 75 and 84 years old (22 versus 34 per 100,000); seniors between 65 and 74 years of age had the highest frequency of family violence for older people (52 per 100,000); and adult children were the most common perpetrators (15 per 100,000) as opposed to spouses or ex-spouses (13 per 100,000);
- In 2008: The rate of police-reported family violence against seniors was 43 per 100,000 for those sixty-five years of age and over; elderly women were more often victims than elderly men (47 as opposed to 37 per 100,000); and adult children were most likely to commit violence against elderly people, with current and former spouses following closely behind (14 and 13 per 100,000 respectively); and,
- In 2009: Senior women were the most frequent victims of family violence (52 per 100,000 as opposed to 43 per 100,000 for men); spouses and adult children were the most common perpetrators of violence against senior women, while adult children were more likely to victimize senior men; and common assault accounted for just over half of police-reported family violence against elders.

Such an overview sketches out the broad parameters of elder abuse patterns in Canada. It is not surprising that common assault is the most frequently reported form of family violence against older people, since it is the type of violence most likely to prompt someone to call the police for assistance; also, common assault is a broad category under the *Criminal Code* and may be applied by police to many different acts committed against an elderly person. The *Profiles* also note that where common assault is mentioned reported injuries were generally minor.

Canada's 1999 *General Social Survey on Victimization* indicates that about 7 per cent of adults over sixty-five years of age reported having experienced some form of emotional or financial abuse by a spouse, adult child, or caregiver in the previous five years. The survey revealed that most abuse had been committed by spouses. Emotional abuse was more common than financial abuse. Physical and sexual abuse were reported by only a tiny minority of respondents (1 per cent). However, according to the 2004 *General Social Survey*, older adults are less likely to experience intimate partner violence than adults under sixty-five. They were also less likely to experience emotional or financial abuse (8 per cent of older adults, compared to 13 per cent for those aged 55 to 64 and 31 per cent for those aged 15 to 24) (Department of Justice Canada 2009).

Naming the Issue

Most studies of elder abuse begin with a discussion about the problem of the lack of universality in definitions. McDonald, Collins, and Dergal (2006) state that part of the problem has been due to the diversity of stakeholders; that is, lawyers, social workers, policy makers, and so on, all have their own points of view regarding the most salient aspects of elder abuse, which influence the way they conceptualize the problem. However, they go on to note that throughout the nineties, efforts were made to try to address this lack of consensus. Globalization has influenced research on elder abuse by raising important questions about ethnocultural differences and how these affect what is considered abusive. The methods and sampling procedures by which elder abuse has been studied have also been problematic, and for this reason, prevalence and incidence have been difficult to pinpoint with any accuracy.

Similar to other types of family violence, elder abuse takes the forms of physical, emotional, psychological, and verbal abuse. Under psychological abuse, Hudson (1988) adds that if an elder's room is not kept clean and tidy, bedclothes are not changed appropriately, or there are no curtains on the windows, the environment in which she or he must spend a good deal of time will not be conducive to good mental health. Verbal abuse includes "infantilization," where an elderly person is treated like an incompetent child (Hudson 1988). This is similar to what Podnieks (1992, 38) refers to as "paternalism": well-meaning professionals or family members intervene in an elder's life and make decisions for her or him because they believe they "know what is best" for the older person.

Financial abuse is not simply taking money from elderly people by theft, deceit, or manipulation; it may also involve the mishandling of an older person's finances or property, or misuse of power of attorney and guardianship (McDonald, Collins, and Dergal 2006). Like many forms of family violence perpetrated against older persons, financial abuse is an abuse of trust. It is also frequently accompanied by verbal and psychological abuse as perpetrators threaten, badger, and lie to their victims. A 2009 American study carried out by MetLife Mature Market Institute (MMMI) and others estimates that financial abuse of the elderly amounts to an annual loss of at least $2.6 billion (MMMI 2009, 7). Although this figure includes abuse by business and industry as well as neighbours, strangers, and others, family members made up 16.9 per cent of the perpetrators and non-agency caregivers made up a further 10.9 per cent. In addition, "[a]pproximately 60 per cent of substantiated Adult Protective Services (APS) cases of financial abuse involved an adult child compared to 47 per cent for all other forms of abuse" (MMMI 2009, 13). Grandchildren made up 9.2 per cent of perpetrators, while other relatives made up 9.7 per cent. It is unclear whether male or female relatives are more likely to financially abuse their elderly relatives, but it appears that abusive family members are often dependent upon their victims for their survival. Abusers may also be influenced by problems with alcohol or drugs, gambling, or anti-social behaviour disorders (MMMI 2009, 13).

Women seem to be more frequently victims of financial abuse than men, partially because they live longer (making them more vulnerable due to illness and cognitive impairment) but also because some women may not be accustomed to making financial decisions on their own and thus turn to a trusted family member for assistance. Men often become victims of the "sweetheart scam," which involves lonely and possibly depressed elderly men being "befriended" by younger women who insinuate themselves into the men's lives until they are in a trusted position and able to assert power in financial decision-making (MMMI 2009, 9–11). These women then take advantage of their positions of power and dupe the older men out of their money through, for example, refinancing their homes, insurance policies, and investment in risky ventures. The financial exploitation and abuse of the elderly is a significant problem partly because of the considerable resources controlled by older adults. The report states that in the U.S. people over 50 years of age own at least 70 per cent of the net worth of all households. In Canada, between 1984 and 1999, families headed by seniors sixty-five years of age and over experienced a 56 per cent increase in wealth, with the median income rising from $80,800 to $126,000. This is in direct contrast to the decline in median wealth experienced by families headed by someone fifty-five years old or younger. For single seniors, the rise in median wealth was 69.2 per cent during that period (Turcotte and Schellenberg 2007, 69).

Sexual abuse is also a reality for some seniors. A qualitative U.S. study by Ramsey-Klawsnik (2003) found that 100 out of 130 alleged cases of elder sexual abuse took place within the family, perpetrated by intimate partners such as marital or relationship partners (as cited in Ramsey-Klawsnik and Brandl 2009). Some of the intimate partners were from new relationships, but others were from long-standing relationships of fifty years or more. This type of abuse can include a variety of "hands-on" offences, such as rape and molestation, as well as "hands-off" behaviours, like voyeurism, exhibitionism, and "harmful genital practices," where intrusive and unnecessary procedures, including inserting fingers or objects into the vagina, are perpetrated by caregivers. Adult children and grandchildren were also cited as perpetrators of sexual abuse. Since sexuality is not usually associated with elderly people, especially elderly women, this type of elder abuse may be completely overlooked. Even if detected, elderly people may be unwilling to allow intervention, as they rely upon their abusers for their personal care and may wish to protect them (Ramsey-Klawsnik and Brandl 2009).

The elderly also often suffer from neglect. Neglect may be passive (without intent) or active (with intent); it can also be thought of as "abandonment." This form of abuse may involve withholding of food or personal hygiene (as in not bathing an elderly person or not allowing them to clean themselves) or withholding other kinds of assistance (National Clearinghouse 1986). Some seniors may also neglect or harm themselves. However, material or financial abuse is the most widespread form of abuse found in the literature on elder abuse. The Canadian study conducted by Podnieks et al. (1990) discovered that, in cases of material abuse (2.5 per cent of the sample), distant relatives or non-relatives were more likely to be the abusers than close relatives. With regard to physical abuse (found in 0.5 per cent of the sample), the majority of the abusers were spouses of the victims. More research needs to be done on elder abuse, using standardized definitions, measurement instruments, and sampling techniques to provide for maximum uniformity; in this way, we may be able to gain enough comparability among studies to enable us to provide more accurate profiles of abusers.

The issue of "medication abuse" is also raised in some of the literature as a type of neglect by caregivers and in institutions (McDonald, Collins, and Dergal 2006). For example, "[r]ecent studies indicate that as many as 28 per cent of hospitalizations and deaths in the elderly are related to medication misadventures" (Conry 2009, 29).

Characterization of the Elderly

Koch and Koch (1980) state that the elderly are often categorized as being "younger" or "older." Those considered to be "younger" senior citizens are between the ages of sixty-five and seventy-two; "older" senior citizens are those over seventy-two years of age (as cited in Gelles and Cornell 1990, 100).

The British terms "grannybashing" and "granslamming," found in some of the early material on elder abuse, highlight how stereotypes have prevailed in the field (for an example, see Schlesinger 1988). At that time, older women had been more likely to be dependent on their families because their traditional role as homemakers meant that they had small pensions when they entered old age. Generally, elderly women tended to be depicted as old, frail, sick, and dependent. The Baby Boom generation is quite likely going to change this depiction, as many of the women of this generation are the products of feminism and the significant societal changes that took place in the sixties, in which women shed many aspects of their old social role and became educated, career-oriented, and productive.

Podnieks (1992), in her interviews with elderly women who had been abused by their husbands, expected to find that they would express feelings of powerlessness or helplessness. Instead, she discovered that these women were actually hardy and resilient. Having these qualities meant that they were able to cope with their lives, including the abuse, because they felt that they were exercising control over their situation. They remained emotionally healthy in the face of stress because they were able to choose *how* to handle that stress. Some of the factors relating to their resilience examined by Podnieks were their sense of self, inner strength, and independence. In essence, we might say that they had rejected the label of "victim." Podnieks's findings are more interesting in light of the fact that, demographically, these women fit the stereotypical profile of abuse victims: they were older elderly, dependent, widowed, had a history of abuse, and were institutionalized. This study adds a fresh dimension to the stereotypical characterization of the elderly and demonstrates that being old or even dependent on another does not make elderly people powerless or helpless.

Living Arrangements and Caregiving

These days, many senior citizens are in a better position financially and are more likely to have the option of independent living. However, because of increased longevity and advances in medical technology, older people are more likely to live longer and require extended periods of care. When forced to live with their grown children, some elderly people may become angry and resentful, leading to strain in their relationships with their children. Children who must care for elderly parents may now have to take on obligations that are likely to last much longer than in previous years. Having fewer siblings may place the burden of care on only one or two children, giving them very little respite. Coupled with their other family obligations, such long-lasting and onerous caregiving relationships may put enormous strain on adult children (Duxbury and Higgins 1994). Conflict or even violence may result from these strains.

Spangler and Brandl (2007) argue that power and control dynamics are at the heart of the abuse of elderly women who have an ongoing relationship with their abusers, whether the relationship is a parent-child or spousal one. They suggest that abusers often have feelings of entitlement that bestows them with special status, exempting them from certain rules governing behaviour. They also believe that their desires and needs take precedence over those of everyone else. In combination, these two beliefs allow them to do whatever they think is necessary to achieve their goals against elderly victims. They may pressure parents or grandparents to refinance their homes in order to give them money. If power and control dynamics are not the issue, abusers may suffer from a physical or mental condition that causes them to be abusive. In other cases, abusers may simply be misguided and ill-equipped to properly care for their elderly relatives. Citing Wolf (2000), Spangler and Brandl state that there is growing evidence to indicate that caregiver stress and the dependency of elders do not contribute to the abuse of older people. Such a misconception may put abused elders in a dangerous position because intervention is then focused on helping the caregiver rather than the elderly victim. Victims may also continue to live with their abusers, led to believe that things will change once the abuser's stress has been reduced.

Caregiving responsibilities may lead to "role strain," making it difficult for caregivers to perform in other roles as well. Role strain is a term used to describe the experience of having multiple roles—each of which demands time, energy, and commitment—which create strain to the point that it interferes with the ability to perform all or any one of them. Caregivers who must care for children or elderly parents or both, and who work outside the home, display common problems such as absenteeism from work, lateness, and having to leave work early, all of which may threaten their jobs (Duxbury and Higgins 1994). Losing a job due to caregiving responsibilities could lead to more stress and possible violent repercussions for those who are dependent upon these caregivers. Since an estimated one-quarter of workers over forty had elder-care responsibilities in 1991, and demographic trends indicate that the number of elderly in the population will continue to grow, it is likely that many more people will suffer from role strain in the future (Duxbury and Higgins 1994, 32). The possible repercussions of such increased responsibilities and role strain could mean higher levels of various types of family violence.

Yet, despite all the difficulties involved in caregiving, in 2007 nearly 70 per cent of care to seniors sixty-five and over with long-term health problems was provided by close family members, 60 per cent of whom were adult children or children-in-law, likely between forty-five and fifty-four years of age. The majority of these caregivers were daughters or daughters-in-law (57 per cent). Fewer than one in ten caregivers is a spouse; however, this may be due to definitions. Many spouses may view what they do for their partner as something other than "caregiving"; their care may simply be considered part of their role as a spouse. Caregiving may be necessary even if the elderly person is institutionalized. The vast majority of caregivers consider that they are coping very well or at least generally managing. Fewer than 5 per cent of them indicated that they were not doing very well or not doing well at all. The caregivers having trouble coping were most likely to be married women of working age who were employed and had at least one child at home. It is probable that these caregivers are suffering from the aforementioned role strain (Cranswick and Dosman 2008).

Most, but not all, elderly people live with their families, with their spouses, or alone; only a small percentage of the elderly population lives in institutional settings, like nursing homes and senior citizens' homes (about 7 per cent, according to studies by McDonald, Collins, and Dergal 2006; Turcotte and Schellenburg 2007). Most elderly people prefer to live with family members, if at all possible, when they are unable to live independently. Canadian statistics indicate that a larger proportion of elderly people eighty-five years of age and over are living alone as of 2001 (34 per cent as opposed to 22 per cent in 1981). In addition, larger numbers of seniors, even those eighty-five years of age and older, are still living with spouses due to the increased life expectancy of men (Turcotte and Schellenburg 2007).

The preference for living alone or with family is likely due to the depersonalized environment of institutions and the scarcity of such accommodations. As a consequence, research on elder abuse in nursing homes has been scant. There have been no prevalence or incidence studies on the national level. An Ontario study in the nineties consisted of a random telephone survey of 804 registered nurses and 804 registered nursing assistants. Nearly half of the respondents stated that they had witnessed at least one incident of abuse, with verbal abuse being the most common (37 per cent). Surprisingly, physical abuse was also cited by 32 per cent of the respondents. Unfortunately, less than half of the reported cases were pursued (McDonald, Collins, and Dergal 2006).

In her research, Canadian researcher Gnaedinger (1989) found that 97 per cent of staff members in institutions were female. Of these, 10 per cent admitted to abusing elderly residents physically while 40 per cent admitted to psychological abuse. These results are apparently similar to those of a Quebec survey conducted by Belanger (1981, as cited in Gnaedinger 1989). It should be noted, however, that the sample is gender-biased because staff members in most institutions are, in fact, women. As a result, it is difficult to discern whether females are more responsible for institutional abuse than are males. Gnaedinger also discovered that residents sometimes abuse each other, particularly if they are mentally impaired.

Pillemer and Moore's study (1990) demonstrates the complexity of elder abuse, specifically with regard to an institutional setting, but its implications can be extrapolated to the non-institutional setting as well. Their findings indicate that almost half the staff had been insulted or sworn at ten or more times in the preceding year by elderly residents; 41 per cent had been physically assaulted in some way ten or more times; 70 per cent had been hit or had something thrown at them, of which 61 per cent had experienced this kind of assault ten or more times; and 47 per cent had been kicked or bitten during the preceding year. Therefore, according to Pillemer and Moore, there is evidence that working in an institution that cares for elderly residents is a very high-risk occupation in terms of experiencing violence on the job. The implications of these findings are that, in a non-institutional setting as well (that is, caring for an elderly person at home), caregivers may have to endure a certain amount of abuse from their elderly charges, increasing the stress level associated with caring for them.

The profile of the institutional caregiver is similar to that of an intimate caregiver in many ways, since the kind of care she or he gives to her or his charges will be affected by personal stressors and problems as well as attitudes towards the elderly (Hudson 1988). The institutional caregiver's stress may be further increased by a lack of adequate staff in the institution, low pay, difficult charges, and criticisms from supervisors. In some cases, staff members may be "damned if they do and damned if they don't"— when caregivers attempt to deal with abusive residents or handle the abuse, they themselves are often accused of being abusive (Goldstein and Blank 1988). This kind of circumstance can be very frustrating, particularly if the staff member has no intention of being abusive, and can create a very high level of stress.

In addition, Pillemer and Moore found that 81 per cent of the staff members they studied had witnessed at least one instance of psychological abuse, most commonly by a staff member angrily yelling at an elderly resident. Of physical assault witnessed, excessive restraining was most often observed, followed by pushing, shoving, and pinching. Ten per cent of respondents admitted to physically abusing a resident; again, the most common act of abuse consisted of restraining. Forty per cent reported psychologically abusing residents, with the majority of the abuse (33 per cent) consisting of angry yelling. The candor of respondents may be due to the way the questions were formulated, or it might reflect genuine concern on the part of respondents over their own and fellow staff members' behaviour. At any rate, Pillemer and Moore associate staff-patient conflict and staff burnout with physical abuse, and burnout and patient aggression with psychological abuse. Furthermore, younger staff members and those with more negative attitudes toward patients were more likely to psychologically abuse elderly residents. The implication of this study is that high stress levels for caregivers, which in the institutional setting are linked with low wages, low numbers of staff, and insufficient training to handle interpersonal conflict with elderly residents, are correlated with both physical and psychological abuse.

In the nineties, some Canadian institutions underwent protocol changes with respect to detection and prevention of abuse. Provincial laws were enacted in Alberta and Manitoba, for example, to make reporting of elder abuse mandatory in places such as hospitals, seniors' lodges, social care facilities, group homes, and nursing homes (McDonald, Collins, and Dergal 2006).

Detection of Abuse

Although according to available data the percentage of elders being abused appears to be rather small, in terms of raw numbers there are still many individuals enduring maltreatment. Furthermore, there is no way of knowing the dark figure—the number of cases that never come to the attention of officials.

Some researchers claim that abuse is difficult to detect when it comes to the elderly because they tend to be more isolated from society and less tied into social networks. Gelles and Cornell (1990) suggest that isolation makes the continuation of violence more likely, presumably because the abuse is easier to hide and is less subject to social control. They also state that because the elderly are confined to their homes and dependent upon their caregivers/abusers, they are far less likely to report being abused. In fact, it is generally a third party who reports elder abuse (see also Schlesinger 1988).

Gelles and Cornell (1990) suggest several other reasons for which elders may be unwilling to report being abused. One is embarrassment—it may be very difficult to admit that they raised a child who could abuse them. Another reason is that they may assume the blame for the violence they suffer. Their love for and loyalty to their abuser may be stronger than their desire to escape the behaviour. Similarly, senior citizens may be more concerned about the welfare of those who perpetrate violence against them than about themselves. They may also fear possible repercussions if they report abuse. Also, the alternative to abuse in their homes by their caregivers may be less appealing; that is, the elderly may prefer to suffer abuse than to be institutionalized. They may also resist being labelled victims. Finally, they may be unaware of whom they can turn to for assistance, or community support may be inadequate. The portrait of the elderly painted by Gelles and Cornell thus suggests that senior citizens are rather helpless and very much dependent on their caregivers.

Despite these difficulties, elder abuse can be detected. Emergency staff members in hospitals are often the ones who report elder abuse because they are in a position to see physical injuries and to detect other types of harm that may have been suffered. Mandatory reporting laws mean that these staff members are under an obligation to report suspected abuse. However, reporting may still be problematic due to unclear definitions of abuse, the fear of wrongful accusation suits, and the possible removal and subsequent institutionalization of the older person, even against her or his will. There is a very real possibility of trespassing on the rights of the victim in the case of abuse of the elderly. On the other hand, there is the very real concern that if incidents were not reported, vulnerable people would be left without protection, crimes would not be reported to the proper authorities, and public good would be sacrificed in the name of individual good. Mandatory reporting lightens some of the burden for professionals of making the decision to report (Gnaedinger 1989).

Two factors further complicate the detection of abuse: first, many elderly people in Canada do not speak either official language well enough to communicate their situation to a third party or even to know what their rights are; and second, in an institutional setting, nurses or other staff members may be reluctant to report friends or colleagues who may be responsible for the abuse. Even though the Canadian Nurses Association code of ethics requires members to report cases of abuse, personal feelings and fear of wrongful accusation may make reporting extremely difficult (Gnaedinger 1989).

Researchers have thus far discussed detection of abuse largely in generic terms. There has been very little work done on ethnic variation with regard to elder abuse and its detection, even in the United States. A study done by Anetzberger (1987, as cited in Tindale et al. 1994) on Appalachian communities in and around Tennessee attempts to deal with cultures in specific geographical locations. In this study, Anetzberger found that the primary factors leading to the incidence of abuse were isolation, living in a rural setting, being poor, and having little education. In addition, when parents had abused their children, there was a very great possibility of these children abusing their parents at a later stage. Also, there was an increased likelihood of a child abusing a parent if there was a long period of co-residency of the parent and child. However, these findings do not differ greatly from those of other studies.

CONCLUSIONS

The study of family violence has broadened over the past decade to include same-sex intimate partner abuse and expand our understanding of parent, sibling, and elder abuse. Nevertheless, more work needs to be done, as these forms of family violence, like the abuse of children and intimate partners in heterosexual relationships, are often hidden from public view and difficult to probe. Public agencies have provided some rudimentary knowledge by presenting statistics based on the numbers of people who use their services or come to their attention. However, as has been discussed in earlier chapters, it is believed that only a small percentage of victims of various types of abuse in family relationships—and likely only the most severe cases—come into contact with these agencies.

Therefore, it is still difficult to make generalized statements that would give a concise but comprehensive overview of forms of abuse discussed in this chapter. If readers find the sometimes conflicting findings of existing studies and their lack of conclusive information confusing and frustrating, it is understandable, but unavoidable at this time. What has been done to date is preliminary work only; it represents an attempt to establish the terrain of these types of violence. Hopefully coherence and consensus are on the horizon.

5

LOOKING FOR EXPLANATIONS: EXPLORING THEORETICAL PERSPECTIVES

Canadian society is filled with conflict and violence of various types. Family violence does not occur in a vacuum. Even though the actions take place between *individuals*, individuals learn how to behave and think in certain ways from the society in which they live. To put it another way, the social context in which people live shapes how and why they act. Family violence takes place within a social framework. As a result, we must examine the diverse social aspects that facilitate its occurrence and recurrence to fully comprehend its complex dimensions.

THE SOCIAL REASONS FOR VIOLENCE

Many aspects of Western society promote violence, but capitalism may be chief among them. Capitalism is a hierarchical structure based on the exploitation of workers; thus, it is inherently abusive. The culture of capitalism promotes a dog-eat-dog ethos and causes the social bond to deteriorate due to competition, self-interest, efficiency, and rationality. In this contemporary economic climate, where the proverbial "pie" for workers has become so much smaller, fewer people enjoy economic prosperity. As a result, they may suffer the violence of economic deprivation and marginalization. With the dismantling of the welfare state, more and more people are descending into poverty. This further breaks down the social bond, as those desperately clinging to what they have are fearful that those below them will try to take from them; a kind of mean-spiritedness takes over

143

and they become resentful of anyone receiving anything "for free." Those trapped in poverty may feel abandoned and betrayed by society and may not care if they harm others.

Economic conditions play a crucial role in family conflict and violence. "Economic conditions" does not refer simply the level of income of the family, although this is also a contributing factor. Rather, it refers to the economic conditions that prevail in contemporary Canadian society. The nineties were marked by severe recessions in this country, a fact that had an enormous impact on people's lives. The tragic events of September 11, 2001 also affected the Canadian economy, though not nearly as seriously as the deep recession of 2008 (Economy Watch n.d.; Makinen 2002). The loss of jobs throughout Canada due to downsizing and closures in industrial sectors has meant less stability and security in terms of an individual's employment and income.

Poverty is a widespread phenomenon in our society. Even those who work most of the year are not exempt from impoverishment. In fact, 27.7 per cent of poor families in 1990 were those termed the "working poor" (Ross 1992 as cited in Harman 1995, 239). People whose incomes remain above the poverty line but are still close to it are not necessarily in less dire financial straits, Harman argues, because "poverty lines" are arbitrary constructions (1995). Due to the recessions of the nineties, many middle-income families, traditionally considered beyond the problems generated by poverty, also found themselves experiencing economic hardship. Unemployment rates were on the rise, and downsizing meant the loss of many mid-range white collar jobs. The prevalence of single-parent, mother-headed families also meant higher numbers of families enduring financial difficulties, since women have historically earned less income than men and their work has tended to be part-time (Harman 1995; Duffy and Pupo 1992).

However, Yalnizyan (2010) predicts that, because we were not able to recover from the recessions of the previous decade, the brutal recession of 2008 may have caused more than one in seven Canadians to join the ranks of the poor. The inability to recover is also linked to major cutbacks in unemployment insurance and social assistance made by federal and provincial governments. The most significant increase in poverty will be among those between eighteen and sixty-four years of age who may still be working. Many children will accompany their parents in their decline into poverty. Yahnizyan also asserts that "[f]or the first time in decades, we may also see a sobering increase in the number of seniors coping with low income, a phenomenon which did not occur in previous recessions but has already reared its head in these new numbers" (2010, 3).

Poverty rates for working-age adults rose by 67 per cent in the nineties. They peaked in 1997 and began to decline thereafter; however, by 2008 they were starting to increase once again (Yalnizyan 2010, 4). Studies of family violence have repeatedly demonstrated a high correlation between abuse and neglect and low socio-economic status.

More women having to work to supplement family income may contribute to various types of family violence. Siblings unsupervised by adults may have greater opportunities to perpetrate abuse on one another. Children may abuse their mothers or fathers because they feel neglected when both parents are working long hours outside the home. Elderly people suffer some forms of abuse because caregivers are not home to look after their needs or are too tired to do so once they get home (Harman 1995; Wharf 1994).

Neo-conservative governments, with their emphasis on cutbacks to social services and their focus on deficit reduction, have eroded the social welfare state and deprived Canadian society of the "safety net" of earlier days. This erosion has made life more difficult and stressful for more and more people. Not only does this deprivation increase the number of people who live in impoverishment, but it may also, in the long run, create "impoverished people" in the sense that economic and social deprivations often lead to heightened conflict within the family and with other members of society. The social bond breaks down as people suffering from deprivation seek to gain something for themselves, often at the expense of others. Conflict is heightened as people struggle against one another for scarce resources in the zero-sum game of competition. Such conflict may lead to an escalation of violence, which damages adults and children alike in various ways. Damaged children grow up to be damaged adults. A vicious circle is created and perpetuated in this way. Therefore, violence in the family could continue for two reasons: impoverished social contexts and impoverished people within those contexts (see O'Neill 1994).

The social ethos of neo-conservatism also produces a higher level of competition among individuals and pushes them to believe that those unable to support themselves do not deserve to do so. This attitude serves to make those who are already suffering feel worse about themselves and their situation. Poverty becomes a moral issue. Self-esteem suffers; shame and anger grow. This dangerous cocktail of destructive emotions may contribute to family violence as well, as people turn to drugs or alcohol, their mental states deteriorate, and their intimate relationships become the dumping ground for all their negativity. For these reasons and others, family violence is a major social issue and one that affects all of us.

Conflict and violence are thus endemic to the Canadian social context. They are not peripheral or alien elements; they are, in fact, part of our everyday lives in some form. Most of us cannot fully escape them. The implication is that we have all internalized conflict and violence. Many people indicate that they believe that a life without conflict, including family life, is not possible—or even desirable. A certain level of conflict is considered to be healthy. Such an attitude may be attributed to a set of ideas in operation in Canadian society that promotes the acceptance of conflict, as discussed below. There are some ideas that have become so ingrained in Canadian society and the consciousness of individuals that they are rarely viewed as anything other than what might be termed "the natural order." (See Todd and Lundy 2006 for a detailed structural analysis.)

WAYS OF THINKING

There are two ways of thinking that enjoy dominant (or hegemonic) positions in Canadian society: liberal philosophy and patriarchy. These can be referred to as "structuring" ideas because they have been instrumental in the creation of social structures and form the basis of Canadian culture.

Liberal philosophy emerged in the eighteenth century as a defence for the development of industrial capitalism, which brought about the separation between private and public spheres as production moved into factories and away from the home (Lynn and O'Neill 1995, 287). Since then, Western societies have cherished the notion of a split between the "public" and the "private" spheres; that somehow human beings move from one world to another. It is believed that somehow these two worlds do not overlap or, indeed, that they are not one and the same. Feminists have strongly challenged such notions, stating that "the personal is political." Their argument is that such a division is not only arbitrary and artificial, it is also oppressive to women and children, who are often relegated to the private sphere.

Miller (1990) argues that the cherished image of the private sphere depends on an image of the public as being dangerous and full of treachery. As long as people believe that it is the street—the world outside of home, hearth, and family—where they will be mistreated and where they must always be on guard against predatory strangers, they will be more likely to view the family as being diametrically opposed. In other words, they will hold the opinion that the family is a sheltered sanctuary, a much-needed "port in the storm," where no harm can befall them. Miller notes that the rhetoric of the family is remarkably resilient and enjoys a great deal of authority as both "a natural and a moral order." The moral authority of the family thus influences how we view other spheres as well (1990, 264–65).

"What is the problem with that?" it may be asked. The problem is that such thinking may blind people to the reality of their experience. If they adhere to the myth of the family as haven, they may be more likely to ignore what is happening to them. When their partners slap them during the course of an argument, they tell themselves that they "provoked" the behaviour. Perhaps their partners have come home drunk and beaten them. In this case, they decide that alcohol was to blame for their partners' behaviour. Or they might explain the violence by saying that something had "come over" their partners, this was not "usual" behaviour, or that she or he was behaving "like a different person" (Miller 1990). These explanations are attempts to make sense of the anomaly of abuse within the haven of the family, where relationships are supposed to be loving and caring; the acceptance of such explanations ensures that the myth lives on. Miller (1990) describes this process as a redefinition of the act of violence so that it fits with this way of thinking. This is rather ironic; the action is redefined to fit the set of ideas rather than the set of ideas questioned as a result of the action. It demonstrates how powerful this way of thinking really is. It also implies how dangerous it is for those who are the victims of violence.

Of course, sometimes the people who experience abuse have little choice but to redefine it and continue to maintain an idealized picture of the family. These people are the children, who suffer everything from a spanking to broken bones, from insults to forced sexual activity. Because they are so dependent upon their parents, they very rarely have alternatives. Children are a "captive audience" because they can do little to prevent their abuse at the hands of their parents or other family members. In addition, because they may have nowhere and no one to turn to, they are often forced to deal with the aftermath of their own emotions and their knowledge that they still want the love and attention of their abusers. Those who finally reach a point where they can no longer tolerate the violence sometimes take flight from their homes and families, preferring to live with the brutality of the streets rather than return to the hypocrisy and pain of their home life. At this point the myth of the family as a haven has at last disintegrated, unable to support the reality of the behaviour. Keeping the myth of the family alive means that ideas about family violence focus on certain individuals and particular families in the popular imagination. In a sense, it is a kind of tolerance. By adhering to the family myth, we are sticking our heads in the sand, ignoring the reality that violence in the family is a pervasive problem stemming from social causes, not psychological ones.

The development of this idea of the family as a haven can be traced back to the nineteenth century, when Protestant evangelical religions arose and redefined family roles (Bradbury 1996, 70–72). Wives were sentimentalized and made into the moral compass for all members of the middle-class families. Home and work were becoming increasingly separate from one another, even among the upper classes. This separation was in great contrast to earlier times, when the home was also the farm where the family worked to produce both subsistence and surplus, or when the home was also the craft shop where goods were made for sale. With industrialization and the rise of factories it became commonplace for people to leave their homes to go to work in another location. Middle-class wives were now increasingly charged with the responsibility of making the home a warm, cozy, and appealing place for their husbands. In addition, wives were to encourage their husbands' virtue and godliness. Legislation was enacted beginning in the 1850s to ensure that husbands bore the responsibility of supporting their wives after the marriage had broken down, even in the event of breakdown due to the husbands' abuse.

The idea that men and women should marry for love—and, by extension, that the family should be based on love—also grew in acceptance. People also came to believe that marital partners should be good companions. Previously, marriages had been based on necessity or economic considerations. Once again, however, the responsibility for nurturing the loving relationship was placed squarely on the woman's shoulders; if the marriage failed, the fault was with her. Working-class marriages were subject to the same changed notions, even though maintaining a loving marital relationship in the face of poor economic conditions was extremely difficult. Women of this class were frequently forced to remain in bad marriages because of low wages; it was rarely possible for women to survive on their own. The breakdown of working-class marriages was also quite public because a wife's only recourse, however rare, was to the courts and charities. Middle-class people then, as now, were capable of hiding their troubles in order to draw on greater family resources (Bradbury 1996, 73).

In tandem with the increasing significance of the family sphere, the myth of the family grew. This myth promotes a particular kind of family: the nuclear family. There is actually no consensus on what constitutes "the family," certainly in regards to the reality of family life in Canada. "The family" is a way of thinking charged with moral overtones, known as "familialism." Under this mode of thought, the family is often assumed to be a heterosexual couple with a male head of the household who enjoys power and authority over his wife and children (Luxton 1988). Lynn and O'Neill assert that children are considered to belong to their parents, and are subject to their parents' authority. In fact, they point out that often "[p]hysical abuse of children is not considered assault if done by parents" (1995, 277). The fact that loving relations are increasingly difficult to obtain outside of family relations as people move from place to place and job to job strengthens the idea of the family and makes people cling to the family more tenaciously than they might otherwise. Because this exclusivity and tenacity undermine the potential for community-based love and caring, the result is that the family becomes more prone to conflict and violence and, at the same time, more resistant to admitting to such problems (Luxton 1988).

Another element that contributes to the myth of the family is our determination to cling to the notion of privacy. Such intransigence is one reason family violence ends up being tolerated to some degree; however, it is also why it might arise. The argument is that the family is considered a private sphere, a place where public officials dare not trespass. People are afraid to interfere. Privacy is considered sacred. When this is coupled with the idea of the nuclear family, we have a dangerous situation. If men are supreme heads and women and children are their property and under their power and authority, and if we believe that public officials have no right to poke their nose into the family without invitation, then we have a situation where abusive relations can go on virtually unchecked. Social control—for example, through community disapproval—will be ineffectual to a great extent because it will not be able to reach inside the home. As a result, we must rely on individual self-control, a shaky proposition at best in light of the many stresses and strains of modern life.

Liberalism and democracy have fused together in Western thought to form a unified way of thinking. It is the foundation for the Canadian way of life, from the way that governments legislate to how men and women comprehend their day-to-day lives. This fused set of ideas has an enormous influence on the emergence of violence within the family context and on the manner in which family violence is treated both publicly and privately.

THE LIBERAL DEMOCRATIC PERSPECTIVE

Liberal philosophy accompanies capitalism. Many argue that liberal democracy *justifies* capitalism as an economic system. As a way of thinking, it has shaped our Canadian context in profound ways. Liberal democratic principles hold that people have choices and equality; they also emphasize the individual over society (Himelfarb and Richardson 1991, 81). We are imbued with notions of equality and freedom, and more importantly, the goodness and rightness of such notions, to the point where it becomes difficult to see the harm they may cause to ourselves and our social relations.

The ethos of competition is endemic to liberal democracy (see O'Neill 1994). It is premised on the notion that everyone is equal and thus has equal capacity to compete for scarce resources. "Scarce resources" is another idea fundamental to liberal democracy. It proposes that things that are most sought after are finite in nature—therefore, some people will enjoy them while others will not. People must compete with one another to obtain the things that they desire; if they do not, they must not expect to have them. This is referred to as "zero-sum" competition: what one individual acquires is at the expense of others. People must take what they desire before someone takes it from them. It is easily apparent how this type of ethos decreases the importance of social ties and social responsibility.

What may not be quite so evident is how such an ethos may influence family ties. As another type of social tie, the belief in zero-sum competition for scarce resources has the same effect on family relations. It is unrealistic to think that people learn a set of social values regarding how they should behave in the public sphere but are somehow able to shed these values the moment they walk into their homes and begin to interact with their families. Members of families must not only compete outside the family, they must also compete within it. In some instances, family ties may actually impair their ability to compete for scarce resources outside the unit, so the importance of such ties may diminish. For example, within the family, members may compete against one another for love, attention, approval, or material goods (as in sibling rivalry); and parents may struggle against each other to ensure that they are obtaining all to which they feel entitled. Such struggle and competition against kin and loved ones may decrease the sense of connection they feel toward each other. As self-interest gains priority over family bonds, family members may find it easier to engage in conflict and may resort to violence.

In addition, Kaufman (1987) asserts that the economic rationality that accompanies capitalism does violence to (male) workers, who become mere extensions of machines. Workers are often exposed to dangerous chemicals and substances, and often risk physical harm. Though not "violent" in conventional terms, this type of exposure is still an abuse against workers whose health may be severely damaged as a result. Dangerous jobs may result in the ultimate abuse: death of the worker. The logic of this argument is that, violated at their place of employment, men may internalize this violation; they then go on to violate others, including those they love.

Liberalism also presupposes that individuals are "disembodied, degendered, and defamilied" (O'Neill 1994, 41). In other words, individuals are regarded as atomistic units, without deep-seated ties to anyone or anything, who are somehow able to disengage themselves from their sense of being male or female. According to this assumption, human beings are free-floating, attaching themselves to someone or something only so long as it serves their interest, moving on when it no longer fulfills that function. This sort of ideational position contributes to the common belief that when family relations become abusive, the one being abused should simply leave. These ideas fly in the face of the reality that women, children, and the elderly have very little recourse to such an action. Even if these people—often the ones who are abused in situations of family violence—had the material resources to leave the family, they also have emotional ties that bind them to their abusers; or they have profound moral beliefs in gender roles, family life, and kinship ties that do not allow them to simply leave. It could be argued, then, that liberal democratic theory also presupposes that individuals are without feelings or desensitized.

Liberal democratic beliefs structure our society, our experiences, and perhaps most significantly, our thoughts. They engender a way of thinking that frames our view of society and how it operates, and that provides ways of understanding our experiences. When we believe our experience is underscored by the need to compete for finite resources that must be grasped quickly and decisively before someone else takes them from us, conflict becomes a way of life and a way of comprehension. When this sense of constant struggle is joined with notions of freedom of choice and equality of opportunity for all, then it is possible for family violence to become entrenched; that is, violence appears in relationships but it becomes trivialized as a matter of individual "choice" (of action and tolerance) and "equality" (in terms of who hits whom). In this way, people who remain in relationships characterized by violence do so because it is their "choice." Men who display violent behaviour are excused, to some extent, because there are cases where women are violent as well; this is construed as some form of "equality," which implies that violence is not a serious public issue. Entrenchment makes it difficult to envisage violence in the family as a social problem that concerns every member of society. It becomes hard to view family violence as an issue relating to social context rather than idiosyncratic tendencies. It becomes easier, however, to be insensitive to the pervasiveness of its harmful effects and simply retreat into a disgusted kind of blindness.

PATRIARCHY

Liberal democratic principles are shaped by patriarchy and, in turn, help to shape the way that patriarchy manifests itself in Canadian society. Patriarchy is indeed a way of thinking but, more significantly, it is a structure that pervades the social milieu. Many people are aware of the overt effects of patriarchy but they are frequently blind to its more insidious, covert aspects.

Patriarchy is so deeply engrained in Canadian society that it is readily overlooked. Not only does patriarchy mean that males are privileged and dominant, it also means that males occupy the upper levels of the public offices that control and deal with family violence. It is a hierarchical system that often puts women and children in the hands of men. According to many analysts, it is not possible to understand family violence without a comprehensive understanding of patriarchy as well.

Patriarchy, of course, has a long history—far too long to chronicle here.[42] Family violence has a similarly long history. Their histories are united in the long-standing moral obligation of men, as commanded by the church, to ensure that their wives and children behave themselves properly. Male violence may thus be legitimately employed to ensure such behaviour; it is the patriarch's Christian duty to "save their souls." In this way, violence against women and children was initially sanctioned by important social institutions and fortified by dominant ways of thinking (Lynn and O'Neill 1995).

Accompanying this sanction to control women and children through violence is the socially constructed definition of masculinity in terms of power and domination. Men are "supposed to" be the strong ones, the ones who go out into the social jungle and conquer the enemy (usually other men), thus protecting their dependent wives and children and providing for their needs. Pleck argues that "men's social identity is defined by the power they have over women and the power they can compete for against other men. But at another level, most men have very little power over their own lives" ([1974] 1995, 10). His position is based on the idea that masculinity has, over the years, become equated with the breadwinner role. This equation has meant substantively that, because men generally get little psychological return from the work that they do, they trade their job satisfaction for

153

satisfaction with their masculinity. Men gain a sense of privilege and power by having women wholly or partially dependent on them economically, and a sense of pride in not having to do "women's work" in the domestic sphere (that is, not having to do unpaid work). This portrait of hegemonic masculinity (which will later be discussed in greater detail) demonstrates that patriarchy is not just an attitude, but the structuring agent for ideas about gender. Under patriarchy, a particular way of being male is held up as being the definitive masculinity; only this way of being male is socially rewarded, while other ways are denigrated. The form of masculinity that enjoys hegemony is the one that fits the contemporary needs of the social order. At this historical moment, the social order requires unemotional, rational, competitive workers for corporations; and aggressive, obedient, hierarchically oriented soldiers for armies. Therefore, these are the qualities that are given priority in hegemonic masculinity.

Patriarchy also establishes a basis whereby men come to believe that they are the foundation of the family and, therefore, have a right to exercise their power over it. Violence is a byproduct of such a family system. Men are charged with the responsibility of maintaining the unit economically; hegemonic masculinity ensures that they measure their masculinity in this way. As a result, masculinity becomes a precarious situation that can be easily threatened (see Conway 1993).

Another unfortunate consequence of these hegemonic ideas about gender is that many men are reluctant to face the fact of family violence. Perpetrators—as well as some men who are not abusers themselves—deny responsibility, personally and collectively, for this brutalization (see Kuypers 1992). Their reluctance stems from at least two sources: first, because men are in charge of society due to patriarchy, the subject of family violence is extremely sensitive, and usually handled in a particular fashion. Shame plays a role in maintaining this silence and avoidance of responsibility. Second, boys also experience abuse in various forms from other males, and because being a victim is not consistent with the idealized masculine role, it is difficult for men to admit having endured violence and domination. However, women assist in the preservation of patriarchy, as well as men. Many women are just as reluctant to face the realities of violence in the family (Lynn and O'Neill 1995). The unwillingness of women may stem from similar sources: dependency upon men means that many women do not wish to examine too deeply the truth about men and violence for fear that they may have to face the possibility of being in danger in their own intimate relations. Also, those who are victims of abuse may be ashamed to admit that their family relations do not live up to the ideal.

There is also a myth in our society concerning control: people are expected to exercise control over themselves and their own destinies. If they fail to do so, they are often blamed for whatever happens to them. Such a characterization is common in cases of woman abuse, for example. The belief that we should be able to control ourselves and what happens to us may make it difficult for us to recognize the multi-dimensional nature of family violence. Alternatively, having the sense that we are in control of our lives may help us deal with almost any situation. In interviews with elderly woman who had been abused, Podnieks (1992) discovered that, even if they chose to remain in their abusive situations, feeling that they were in control of their lives and could make their own decisions was empowering. They felt a degree of satisfaction because they were able to choose their own destinies to some extent.

These are just some of the prevailing myths in Canadian society that are pertinent to family conflict and violence. Each one of them has an important role to play in setting the context for family violence; together they create powerful conditions for relationships between family members to lead to violence. Such myths are neither random nor purely arbitrary. Rather, they are rooted in reality as structures of power that privilege some individuals and situations over others. They are powerful forces; many people support some of them, even when they are contrary to their true interests, while attacking others that may serve them better. Myths also create foundations upon which identities are formed. Individuals internalize these myths as ideals, which help to form their motivations for behaviour and become justifications for their actions.

There has been a long history of violence in the family, violence that was largely tolerated due to the lack of power of women and children. This was true until the late sixties, when the balance of power began to shift with the rise of the civil rights and women's movements, and eventually the children's rights movement. As these groups made headway, their views gaining more and more acceptance in society, alternative ways of thinking became more prominent. Feminists are largely responsible for putting family violence on the public agenda and changing the consciousness of the general population. This shift has been accompanied by changes in definitions of family violence. Now spanking children, which was once considered normative, is debatably considered a form of child abuse. It has been defined by many as violence against children and, therefore, inexcusable as a form of discipline. One of the ways in which definitions are changed and promoted to the general population is through the various mass media.

THE ROLE OF THE MEDIA

The role of the media is central to the debate over ways of thinking because, for the most part, what is conveyed through the media is generally the most conservative of these ways of thinking—those that attempt to preserve the status quo. However, as groups with alternative ideas gain more power and power relations shift, they are more able to gain some access to media and, hence, to the public consciousness.

Furthermore, the mass media not only play an important role in the promotion of dominant myths but also in the conceptualization of "social problems." A social problem does not spring forth full-blown onto the centre stage of media reports. Rather, the media give the problem its shape and content.

There are many social-problems-in-the-making at any given time. Few of these, however, make it to the front page of the newspaper or the top of the news program on television or radio because members of the media can only highlight a limited number of them. Most receive intense, but short-lived coverage and then pass into the dreaded zone of old news. A few manage to remain in the spotlight for extended periods of time, constantly being redefined and recast over time. In order to remain in the public eye, these stories must promote easy identification for audiences.

Media characterizations of family violence tend to rely on "common family experience" to tap the emotional sensibilities of consumers. They take actions out of context, or truncate interactions so that consumers get only a fragment of the interaction and not the causative chain of events. Since the contexts tend to be private, media must rely on external sources, such as social workers, police officers, and court officials. The myth of journalism is that only the objective facts are presented, without any kind of subjective undertones. However, the exigencies of capitalism are such that only the most dramatic examples of abuse will be covered in the media, since they generate the most sales. This coverage makes it seem as if these extreme cases are the norm; the result is sensationalization of both the cases and the social problem itself. Furthermore, the media almost invariably point to "personal responsibility" of the individuals involved in family violence. That is, they tend to ignore or downplay social factors and strongly imply that abuse can be reduced to personal choice and culpability (Johnson 1989; Voumuakis and Ericson 1984).

There are programs on television that show how damaging family violence can be and the terrible toll it can take on human lives. However, in these instances as well, the media tend to preserve the status quo by presenting the most sensational cases as the basis for human interest stories. Once again, the tendency is to suggest that violence in the family is due to individual or family-specific pathologies, and that the victims are individuals or particular families rather than society as a whole. This once again trivializes family violence and makes it seem that it is not a social problem but a psychological or, at best, a kinship-relations problem. In this way, the media continue to divert the popular consciousness away from the larger social context of violence and the effects of violence on families. People continue to believe that family violence happens only to others, that it has nothing to do with the configuration of the family in our society, and that it does not relate to structured power differentials within social relationships.

The effect of the media is to segregate perpetrators in the popular imagination. Consequently, as in ancient times with lepers, those who are segregated appear to deserve it because there is something wrong with them (see Foucault 1979, Chapter 3). As a result, the general population does not feel it needs to take responsibility for family violence. It is "their" problem, "they're" sick or "they" need to be taken care of by psychiatrists, police, or prisons. It is not "our" problem. Family violence doesn't have anything to do with "us."

Thus, the role of the media is of enormous importance in terms of family conflict and violence. The media have the power to shape the issue and to shape the consciousness of Canadians. By sensationalizing and trivializing cases of abuse, the media create a segmented public vision of victims and perpetrators, conjuring up notions of an "us/them" polarization; they are then able to push "them" to the periphery of public consciousness and dismiss these people as pathological. In this way, the social nature of the act is ignored. Similarly, by taking acts of violence within the family out of context and out of their interactional sequence, the media are able to generate big "news" without disturbing the status quo vis-à-vis power relations.

THE INTERNET AND ITS INFLUENCE

No discussion of family life in the twenty-first century could be complete without some mention of the Internet and its influence on family relations. The Internet only became a household accessory in the nineties; however, by 1998, in the U.S. it was reported by Niccolai (1998) that 61 per cent of homes containing a personal computer were connected, representing a 30 per cent increase from a January 1998 market survey (as cited in Merkle and Richardson 2000, "Culture of the Internet and New Media Technology," para. 1). In 2002 more than 600 million people throughout the world had access to it (Manasian 2003, as cited in Bargh and McKenna 2004, 574). Statistics Canada (2009) reports that, although Internet use rose among all age groups between 2005 and 2007, 96 per cent of those between sixteen and twenty-four years of age went online as opposed to only 29 per cent of those sixty-five years of age and over.

Communication is one of the main reasons that people use the Internet. This is especially true since the birth of social networking sites, such as Facebook and Twitter. People use these sites to keep in touch with family, current friends, and acquaintances and to make new connections. They can find groups of people with common interests. Twitter allows an even closer following of people in their daily activities through "microblogging," which allows individuals' posts—or "tweets"—to be viewed by anyone and everyone unless the user restricts viewing. Apparently, 41 per cent of the tweets consist of "pointless babble," but 38 per cent of them are conversational, meaning that people can keep in touch with friends and relatives on a virtually moment-by-moment basis (Kelly 2009). Unfortunately, there also appears to be the potential for harassment and stalking. It is possible that a controlling, abusive husband could attempt to keep close tabs on his wife through monitoring his wife's tweets.

A study of Facebook states that by 2007 there were more than 21 million registered members generating 1.6 billion page views every day (Needham & Company 2007, as cited in Ellison, Steinfield, and Lampe 2007, 1144). In addition to the large number of members and viewings, "[t]he typical user spends about twenty minutes a day on the site, and two-thirds of users log in at least once a day" (Cassidy 2006; Needham & Company, 2007, as cited in Ellison, Steinfield, and Lampe 2007, 1144). Results of the study indicate that Facebook use is associated with "social capital," which refers to the resources accumulated by individuals and groups who have a network of relationships (Bourdieu and Wacquant 1992, as cited in Ellison, Steinfield, and Lampe 2007, 1145). There are two kinds of social capital: bridging, which represents weak ties between individuals who provide information and new perspectives; and bonding, representing tightly knit, emotionally close relationships. Facebook particularly facilitates an individual's bridging social capital. In other words, on Facebook individuals can "network"—making connections through other "friends" with people who may be a resource at some point, and maintaining those connections. Facebook can also be used to sustain familial contacts, which could be of assistance to those who are in abusive relationships. Parents tend to support their children's use of the Internet as an educational tool. There is also evidence to indicate that people are using the Internet not just for social networking and connecting with extended families, but perhaps more importantly, to share worries and seek advice for their problems (Meszaros 2004). Researchers and scholars are divided as to whether the influence of the Internet on families is positive or negative, and as yet, there is not enough research to provide a definitive answer.

DiMaggio, Hargittai, Newman, and Robinson (2001) point out that the relationship between technology and society has never been a unidirectional one, and that the agendas of powerful social actors shape the way that technology develops. The Internet is even more pliant because of its multi-dimensionality. Its interactive nature also affords individuals the opportunity to seek what they need from the Internet (Bargh and McKenna 2004). Tyler (2002) writes that the Internet often becomes another tool in an individual's social "toolkit," which is employed with other technologies, such as the telephone, along with face-to-face communication in her or his efforts to deal with personal issues. The socially anxious can initiate relationships in what is perceived as a safer environment affording anonymity. People can try out new identities on the Internet before adopting them in their actual lives. In this way, the Internet may be a powerful tool for an abuse victim seeking information about abuse and how to deal with the problem, as well as finding personal and social support that could help her or him to find solutions. The Internet may also be used to combat the kind of isolation that abusers tend to impose on their victims.

PSYCHOLOGICAL, SOCIOLOGICAL, AND FEMINIST THEORIES

While enormous strides have been made in researching the dimensions and patterns of family violence, theoretical explanations are still in the early stages of development. In the rest of this chapter, we outline the broad parameters of the three major approaches: psychological/social psychological, sociological, and feminist. While efforts will be made to identify the distinguishing characteristics of each of these approaches, there will be overlap between them. The same or similar arguments often appear in several different perspectives and frequently theorists (analysts) acknowledge the value of at least some aspect of a competing approach. Indeed, it is often difficult to fairly determine which category best represents the work discussed since there are certainly feminist psychologists and sociologists as well as feminists who employ psychological and sociological methodologies (Yllo 1993, 48). At the same time, there is also considerable disagreement and rancor between advocates of diverse perspectives as they struggle for recognition and dominance in identifying the roots of (and therefore the solutions to) family violence.

A diverse and rapidly expanding literature is emerging that attempts to explain violence in the family. Some of this literature has been developed by clinicians working with abusers and attempting to eliminate certain behaviours. Much has been articulated by feminist activists and researchers working with victims of abuse. Sociologists have also been developing their explanations in the rapidly growing literature on family violence. The following overview gives an introduction to some of the major theoretical approaches currently in use.

WHY DO MEN BATTER?

Psychological[43] and Social Psychological Explanations

Not surprisingly, much of the early thought on abusive males came from a psychological, or even a psychiatric, perspective. The emphasis was on explaining why these particular men were pathologically violent or prone to behaviour problems such as alcohol and drug addiction. The focus was on how their personalities differed from "normal" men and on disturbances in their early upbringing—domineering and rejecting mothers, distant and ineffectual fathers, and so on. The solution was some form of psychotherapeutic intervention.

More recent advances in social psychological theorizing about abusive men have placed more of the onus on social roots and connections. In this approach, however, abusers are still separated from "normal males." Donald G. Dutton, one of the leading authorities on the psychology of abusers, argues, for example, that "most men remain nonviolent toward intimate female partners over the course of their lifetime" (1995a, 17). He also suggests, as do other analysts, that batterers are not a homogeneous group and that some are indeed psychopathic (1995a, 25; 1995b, 120–60). These "psychopathic batterers" exhibit no pangs of remorse for their brutal attacks and are cool and composed in the midst of vicious and violent assaults. Indeed, these men are so psychologically flawed, their violence is generalized as anti-social behaviour and they are extremely difficult to treat. The relatively more common "cyclical abusers" are the focus of Dutton's work, and their violence, he argues, is treatable (1995a).

In Dutton's analysis, the batterer's violence toward his partner is traced back, in part, to having been shamed and rejected by his father. He writes that "if I had to pick a single parental action that generated abusiveness in men, I would say it's being shamed by their fathers" (1995a, 83). Ambivalent and angry mothers are also implicated. The abuser's mother, according to Dutton, mixes rejection and affection in a manner that leaves the adult child both drawn to and fearful of women (1995a, 106). The

161

solution is to create a therapeutic context in which abusers may understand and come to terms with these patterns of responding and relating, and create new behavioural alternatives. For example, by working on managing anger, the abuser learns to be more sensitive to his own feelings and desires and to articulate these feelings rather than suppress them. In group sessions, he charts his anger in a diary, examines each episode to discover the trigger, learns to recognize the physical reactions and inner dialogue ("the bitch tape") that escalate the anger, and learns to "talk down" the anger and soothe himself (1995a, 170).

This theoretical perspective and its therapeutic approaches are currently pre-eminent in efforts to understand the abuser's psychology and to provide appropriate counselling. It is important to distinguish this approach from others, but to also note that there are connections between them. The focus here is clearly on the individual male and on the personal/familial roots of his actions. In particular, the key premise is that his behaviour is not "normal" and only through counselling and therapy can it be brought into more normal parameters. However, this psychopathological framework does not completely ignore the socio-cultural environment that makes violent men more likely, establishes a social context (the privacy of the family) in which this violence may be displayed, and makes women (and children) the likely victims of this violence. In Dutton's work, for example, there is considerable recognition that abusers' actions are often at least partially rooted in "normal" social experiences and normal patterns of behaviour in Canadian society. For example, he notes that male gender socialization normally sets men up for emotional insensitivity and mother (woman)-blaming, which may become key ingredients in abusive episodes (1995a, 44, 88, 120–22). Dutton also points to alcohol as a socially acceptable way in which the abuser can suppress his uncomfortable feelings, and a socially legitimate rationale for "losing it" (54). He also acknowledges that society provides both "negative attitudes towards women" and "an acceptance of violence as a means of resolving violence" (121). Working from a social psychological perspective, Dutton and others often also incorporate a social learning approach, pointing out that abusers often grow up in a violent home, most frequently where the father abuses the mother (123).

Ultimately, however, Dutton and other psychologists argue that the focus must be primarily on the etiology of personal pathologies in the individual abuser. They seek to tease out the complex relationships between early childhood experiences and later acts of violence. They are quick to point out, for example, that most boys, regardless of male socialization patterns, do not become abusers; that even boys with violent male role models typically do not grow up to abuse their wives; and that females, despite their female socialization and societal subordination, do sometimes abuse their partners in lesbian relationships. The answers to these complexities, they argue, lie not so much in history, social institutions, and dominant ideologies as in the psyches of the abusers.

Sociological Theories

Sociological theories have several distinguishing characteristics. First, American sociologists have tended to approach the basic question "Why is there violence between intimates in families?" in gender-neutral terms. Secondly, since they examine the societal roots of abuse and the connections between family violence and social institutions, sociologists often explicitly reject the psychological and pathological model. Richard Gelles, who along with Murray Straus pioneered American research on family violence, points out, for example, that psychological defects (such as mental illness) and psychological explanations cannot account for 90 per cent of abusive family incidents (Gelles 1993, 41). Thirdly, some sociologists have distanced themselves from feminist analysis. Gelles, for example, acknowledges the value of feminist insights but argues that ultimately the framework must be rejected on the grounds that it focuses too narrowly on violence toward women and has little useful insight into child, elder, or sibling abuse, or abuse by women (1993, 42–43). Similarly, Canadian sociologist Mark Liddle argues that feminists, while making valuable contributions to our understanding of violence against women, are now bogged down by unclear conceptualizations of violence (and related terms) and a failure to examine the implications of the heterogeneity of masculinities; that is, that not all men are violent and not all men support violence against women (1989).

These distinctions between the sociological, psychological, and feminist perspectives appear to be particularly prominent in American sociology. Canadian sociologists, while rejecting psychological explanations, often

163

focus on gender analysis and explicitly identify themselves as working from a feminist perspective. As a result, the line between Canadian socio-logical and feminist theorizing is less clear.[44] However, Canadian work is often influenced by or responding to American sociological theories, and it is therefore important to outline some of the main developments in the United States.

In seeking to create explanations for intimate violence, sociologists have employed some of the basic theoretical orientations in sociology—social-ization, systems theory, conflict theory, subculture analysis, and so on. Most closely associated with social psychology and one of the most intui-tive explanations of wife abuse is the theory that abusers (and their victims) are socialized into violence in their family of origin. According to this *cycle of violence* or *social learning* approach, abusers learn from watching their fathers that violence is an appropriate and acceptable method of asserting their will in the home. Similarly, girls who witness abuse of their mothers may be learning to expect and accept the violence.

It is not surprising that this perspective has become popular. Unfortunately, it is at best only a partial explanation of violence against women in intimate relations. While it makes a great deal of intuitive sense, analysts must still account for two key research findings. First, as indicated in the Canadian Violence Against Women Survey (CVAWS), the majority of abusive men did not witness violence in their family of origin and secondly, the majority of men who did witness violence do not behave in a violent manner toward their wives (Johnson 1996, 177; see also Gelles and Cornell 1990, 76). The relationship between violence in childhood and adult use of violence is clearly a complex phenomenon that implicates institutions far beyond one's family.

Sociologists have gone beyond these social psychological perspectives and suggested that socialization into subcultural patterns of values helps explain some of the complexities and inconsistencies in wife abuse. For example, the frequently repeated finding that abusive men are more likely to come from the lower socio-economic ranks has led some analysts to argue that one key to understanding the batterer is the *patriarchal subculture of violence* amongst working-class males (Smith 1990a, 1990b; Hotaling and Sugarman 1986; Gelles 1993). Smith found that there was indeed a

relationship between wives' reports of their husbands' adherence to traditional patriarchal ideology, attitudes supportive of wife-beating, and actual
violence. For example, men who were violent toward their wives were more
likely to agree with this statement: "Sometimes it is important for a man to
show his wife/partner that he is head of the house." The men who endorsed
patriarchal and violent beliefs were also more likely to be unemployed and
poorly educated, so there is the possibility of a connection between lower-
class subcultural values and violent behaviour. Some analysts suggest that
since "lower-class" men experience limited power and authority in the
public domain, they are more likely to embrace values that legitimate their
control and primacy in the home (Messerschmidt 1993). However, this
relationship between social class, subcultural values, and violence is complex and far from fully understood, since many men (as evident in Smith's
research) who are poor, unemployed, and non-violent may still adhere to
traditional patriarchal ideas.

Canadian sociologists Lupri, Grandin, and Brinkerhoff recently re-
examined the proposed link between socio-economic status (SES) and
wife abuse. Using male self-reports from a representative national sample
of males eighteen years of age and older, their findings raised questions
about the notion that wife abuse is particularly common amongst working-
class men. In part, this reflects their methodological decision to focus on
psychological abuse as much as physical violence. Since they found psychological violence is higher amongst men who are better educated, it is
logical to assume that research based primarily or exclusively on physical
manifestations of abuse will generate an inaccurate picture of the SES patterns of violence. When an operational definition of violence that includes
physical, psychological, and sexual abuse is used, the results suggest that
chronic abuse is widespread and widely based throughout the social classes
(1994, 62, 67).[45]

Sex role theory is also used to locate violence against women in society.[46]
Feminist sociologists point out that prevailing notions of masculinity and
femininity generally mean that boys are brought up to be more aggressive, tough, competitive, and unemotional, while girls are encouraged to
be softer, more emotional, and more passive. These gendered patterns
of behaviour and emotionality tend to separate males and females and

165

set them up for patterns of conflict and violence (Mackie 1991, 231–32). Recent research into male socialization and masculinity suggests that it is not only the direct social messages supporting violence, aggression, or sexism that contribute to these patterns, but also the lack of clarity and security about male identity (Thorne-Finch 1992; Kuypers 1992).

In contrast to these individual-level theories, sociologists have also developed explanations that emphasize the institutional and societal levels of analysis. The general systems approach focuses on the family as a system of interrelated parts. This system is inherently subject to stresses and upset because of the intensity of the relationships as well as age and sex differences. Any number of probable factors, such as pregnancy, child rearing, relations with extended family, and family finances, are likely to generate marital conflict. From this perspective, violence is understood as one of several strategies available to family members as they seek to deal with upheavals within the family system (or, presumably, as imposed by other social institutions, such as the economy or the education system).

Problems result when some family members resort to violence as a strategy for coping with upheaval. For example, unemployed parents may find their parental authority challenged by their employed teenage children. One mechanism for re-establishing the family system's status quo would be to use physical violence to regain control over the children. If this strategy is successful—that is, if there is positive feedback—then it is likely to be repeated (Johnson 1996, 19–20; Gelles 1993).

This general systems approach is easily combined with resource theory, which states that those family members with considerable resources will have little need for violence to achieve dominance. However, when positive resources are absent or are removed, individuals may resort to other resources for power, such as physical violence (Gelles 1993). This theory is consistent with the view that levels of violence vary between social classes and various ethnic groups because of varying access to power resources (Johnson 1996, 18).

One of the other general trends in sociological thinking on woman abuse is elaboration on the typologies of batterers. American sociologists Finkelhor and Yllo (1995), for example, proposed three types of marital rape: battering rape, in which the husband rapes the wife as part of a larger pattern of physical violence and abuse; force-only rape, where there is little or no abuse, relative equality between the partners, and only as much force as necessary to force sex; and obsessive rapes, in which the male is bizarrely preoccupied with sex and pornography and the sex involves obsessive, sadistic practices (1985). More recently, Canadian sociologists Lupri, Grandin, and Brinkerhoff proposed from their research that there are three types of wife abusers: silent attackers, who use physical but not emotional or psychological violence; threateners, who use a variety of psychological aggression but not physical violence; and severe abusers, who use both psychological and physical violence against their spouses (1994, 58–59). These typologies are in their earliest stages of development, particularly in terms of explaining the social factors (social class, age, and so on) which may account for differences amongst violent men.[47] However, this line of analysis has important immediate implications. If abusers differ significantly from one another then it is unlikely that one course of remediation is useful for all. Since in each of the above examples (see also Dutton 1995a)[48] a significant minority of abusers are presented as characterized by severe psychiatric problems, it follows that psychiatric/psychological explanations (and treatments) are at least partially endorsed.

Sociological theory can be justifiably credited with generating a rich variety of explanations for violence against women. Many of these theories have been incorporated into feminist analyses and have created a "wider explanatory framework" for psychological and social psychological explanations; however, by their very nature, these complex, multi-dimensional explanations have not been particularly helpful in identifying either therapeutic or policy directions (Gelles 1993, 43). For these and other reasons, feminists have cultivated an alternative perspective.

Feminist Theories[49]

According to feminist analysis, in patriarchal societies, every social relationship is conditioned by the pervasive inequality between men and women. Feminists assert that the function and structure of every social institution—from family to religious to political—are embedded not only in differences between men and women but in the dominance of men as a group over women as a group. The economy, for example, is dependent on women's "free" reproductive and productive work in the home. If women refused to do the bulk of the work (housework, child care, emotional support), which daily and generationally prepares workers for employment, this economic system would grind to a halt. This inequality between men and women is understood as neither natural nor inevitable; it has evolved historically and currently serves the interests of many men as well as those with power in society (Yllo 1993, 54).[50] It is, however, susceptible to change and social action.

The feminist approach is also often distinguished by its methodological approaches. The research emphasis is on recording and accurately presenting the experiences of women. Often sociological (survey research) and psychological (clinical) research and theory are criticized for reinterpreting and re-victimizing battered women. As discussed in detail in preceding chapters, research that only tallies the number of physical blows or counts the number of victims fails to consider the effects on women, both as victims and as members of a society in which victimization of women is widespread. Similarly, research that relies on data about who hit whom and how often disregards the personal and societal context in which violence occurs (Johnson 1996). Feminist research is also constructed as advocacy work "for" women; that is, the goal is to work toward an end to both woman abuse and patriarchy, not simply an abstract advance in scientific knowledge (Bograd 1988).

Within these general parameters of feminist theory, there are significant divisions. Radical feminism, which has been deeply involved with the violence against women issue, emphasizes the role of patriarchy. From this vantage point, violence against women is embedded in every aspect of society and male-female interpersonal relations. Ending violence depends upon a societal transformation that will end male dominance. Socialist feminists, while in agreement with the need for a social revolution, emphasize the role of economic forces (notably capitalism) in disempowering women. As Coomaraswamy notes, for socialist feminists "violence is a result of economic exploitation and only secondarily a function of the male-female relationship" (1995, 19). Liberal feminists adopt a narrower view of the problem and advocate institutional (more shelters and so on) rather than systemic change. Lastly, ecofeminism links violence against women with the general patterns of exploitation and destruction of the natural order endemic to the military-industrial complex that currently dominates the world order (1995, 20). Each of these perspectives is an important aspect of contemporary feminist theory. Although we refer to feminism as a generic category, we recognize that within feminist theory there is a rich diversity of perspectives.

By the eighties, feminists—particularly radical feminists in the shelter movement—had developed their major theoretical initiative: the *power and control approach* to family violence (MacLeod 1994). According to this perspective, male violence in the family must be located in the larger context of male power both within the family and within the larger society. When men use violence, they do so knowing that they live in a society in which violence against women—in the form of sexual assault, sexual harassment, and wife battering—is part of the taken-for-granted reality that spans generations. They do so knowing that the societal response, including the criminal justice response, often blames the victim for the violence and frequently treats the victimizer with lenience.

However, women's response to male violence must also be located in these societal patterns of power and control. A woman does not react solely to the specific violent incident; she responds in the context of a lifetime of relevant experiences—a friend who has been sexually harassed at work, a cousin who was the victim of date rape, exposure to media images of male violence, and so on. His aggression and violence, along with her fear and hopelessness, cannot be understood outside the context of their gendered experiences of violence and power.

Domestic violence is a "control tactic" within the family. According to the Domestic Abuse Intervention Project of Duluth, Minnesota, physical and sexual violence can be conceptualized as a wheel in which the spokes (intimidation, isolation, emotional abuse, threatening or co-opting the children, economic abuse, coercion and threats, male privilege, minimizing, denying, and blaming) all serve to connect violence to its hub of power and control (Yllo 1993, 54–55). According to this feminist framework, men do not use violence because they disagree with their wives or because their wives are too demanding or because they are stressed; rather, men want to dominate and control women. Growing up and living under patriarchy,

169

men have been conditioned to believe that this is both right and appropriate. Physical and sexual violence are then used to achieve control over women.[51]

WHY DO ABUSED WOMEN STAY?

First and foremost, before addressing this issue, it should be noted that many feminists and social activists find this popular question inherently offensive. To them, it implies that somehow the victimized women are to blame for and should explain the violence. The implication is that by staying in the relationship after the first sign of psychological or physical violence, the woman herself is part of the problem, perhaps because she is abnormal (masochistic) or weak. Clearly, the popularity of this question is a classic example of victim-blaming.[52] Victims, aware of this public response, are inclined to blame themselves and to withdraw further. In very real terms, the question, if it implies a defect or weakness in women who stay in abusive relationships, serves to perpetuate the violence.

Furthermore, this line of inquiry is factually flawed because it assumes that, by leaving, the woman can end the violence and abuse. Almost half of abuse victims do leave. However, many discover that leaving, or even threatening to leave, escalates rather than ends the violence. The CVAWS reports that for about one-fifth of abused women the violence and intimidation continued after separation, and of those cases about one-third experienced an escalation in the abuse (Johnson 1996, 170). Indeed, evidence suggests that abused women who leave may be particularly at risk of lethal violence. Wilson and Daly report that married women who separated from their husbands had murder rates three times higher than women who were living with their husbands (1994, 7).[53]

With these facts in mind, we can examine the literature from the victim's perspective. Analysts have much to tell us about why women stay, and the answers are helpful not only in understanding the violence but also in articulating useful responses.

Psychological and Social Psychological Explanations

As with psychological and psychiatric approaches to the batterer, there are some analyses that explain the abuse of the victim in terms of the victim's self-esteem issues, dependency needs, depression, and anxiety. The notion that abused women are masochistic—that is, that they desire to be physically abused and derive pleasure from it—has enjoyed some popularity (Gelles and Cornell 1950, 72–74). However, these psychological assessments have been subject to thorough critique and are today less popular as explanations of abused women's actions (Caplan 1985).

One of the most prominent psychologists working in this area is Leonore Walker, who clearly treads the line between feminist and psychological perspectives. In the seventies, she first suggested that abused women's actions are conditioned by the particular psychological dynamic in abusive relationships. The relationship, she argued, tends to follow a *cycle of abuse* in which an episode of violence is followed by a honeymoon stage wherein the abuser apologizes for his violent behaviour and makes promises to reform. This period gradually (or quickly) gives way to a period of mounting tensions, which ultimately produces another violent episode. The cycle then repeats itself. The result, according to Walker, creates a psychological condition of *learned helplessness* in the abuse victims. Much like experimental animals who are subject to unpredictable patterns of reward and punishment, the women face an uncontrollable pattern of violence. As a result, victims become personally disorganized, depressed, and unable to effect change (Walker 1979, 1993).

The socio-psychological notion of *traumatic bonding* as developed by Painter and Dutton (1985) paints a similar picture. They argue that relationships between batterer and victim (or hostage/captor, abused child/ abusing parent) are characterized by two traits: a power imbalance and intermittent (perhaps cyclical) abuse. These kinds of relations produce a contradictory sense of helplessness and potency. The victim may feel powerless to leave the relationship yet may also feel that she is partly responsible for the violence, and that by changing her behaviour she may be able to control it. Together these psychological dimensions lock victim and victimizer together.

Some feminist activists are embracing these and other psychological perspectives on woman abuse. For example, Marilyn Goodman, who works in a Rhode Island shelter for women, rejects the "male-dominated society" approach as too simplistic and argues that a more psychological strategy is appropriate. She believes that when a woman is unable to leave an abuser or has a series of abusive relationships she must be recognized as having a problem of her own. While she is not responsible for the violence against her, Goodman argues that a dysfunctional childhood is likely to blame for the woman's vulnerability to violence. Needless to say, the solution she advocates entails considerable psychological counselling (1990).

Sociological Theories

Certainly, there are mainstream sociological approaches that have some applicability to the plight of women victims. For example, the CVWAS reported that the majority of women (70 per cent) who left their abusive spouses returned at least once. Their reasons are a testimony to the traditional *sex role socialization* as well as the economic inequalities between men and women. The most frequently reported reason for returning was for the sake of the children (31 per cent), followed by wanting to give the relationship another try (24 per cent), the husband promised to change (7 per cent), and lack of money or a place to go (9 per cent) (Johnson 1996, 189). It certainly appears that the ideologies of maternalism and romance are alive and well and are a potent combination when linked to economic inequities.

Feminist Theories

Feminists, despite their well-founded critique of this type of victim-blaming, have in fact provided considerable insight into the plight of abused women. As noted previously, they've drawn attention to the importance of recognizing the larger social context that conditions and informs women's responses to violence. Just as male violence is structured by societal patterns of male dominance, women act and react within the parameters constructed by their social realities. Rather than accepting socio-psychological explanations (such as the cycle of violence and learned helplessness), which explain women's staying in terms of psychiatric defects, weakness, or immaturity,[54] feminists argue that women often stay or leave based on a rational evaluation of economic factors, the prospects of escape, the possibilities of support, the availability of alternative shelter, and threats to other family members (Bowker 1993, 158–63). Thus, "[a] woman's decision to

172

stay appears to follow logically from power disparity and the cultural rules she has learned about marriage, the family and woman's role as traditionally defined" (Hoff 1990, 42; see also 32, 47).[55] This perspective is consistent with the experience of shelter workers, who find that abused women often do not experience an intermittent cycle of abuse, but that the abuse is constant. It is also more consistent with the feminist framework that is inclined to normalize rather than pathologize the violence and that focuses on the larger socio-cultural context of abuse.

As previously discussed, one of the more recent feminist theories likely to provide the most nuanced approach to understanding the complexity of violence against women is intersectionality. A type of feminist standpoint theory, intersectionality theorizes that the interaction between gender, race, and other categories of difference in individual women's lives, in conjunction with the social practices, cultural ideologies, and institutional arrangements of the societies in which they live, produces particular configurations of power in these women's lives. This configuration of power affects a woman's experience of violence. Intersectionality was conceived to bring the experiences of marginalized women onto the centre stage of research. It also emphasizes how different women's experiences of intimate violence can be. (For detailed discussions of intersectionality see Davis 2008; Knudsen 2006; Choo and Ferree 2010.)

Though heralded as "the most important contribution that women's studies has made so far" (McCall 2005, 1771, as cited in Davis 2008, 68), intersectionality is not without its critics.[56] Methodological difficulties abound with this theory due to its imprecise definition and, therefore, unclear guidelines as to how to use it when conducting research. Nevertheless, the strength of intersectionality may lie in its ability to not just uncover and articulate the experiences of marginalized women and intimate violence, but also to problematize and reveal the power structures in the very concepts and categories used to define this violence (Knudsen 2006).

Choo and Ferree (2010) argue that there are three "styles" of understanding intersectionality in practice. The group-centred approach focuses on social locations that produce particular standpoints. The process-centred style rejects the "locations" approach in favour of the notion that material and cultural relations among various social power structures produce particular standpoints—this is a more dynamic style of intersectionality. The system-centred approach, also known as "institutional interpenetration," focuses on the feedback effects among historically constructed systems to which other historically constructed systems must adapt. Choo and Ferree believe that this last style of intersectionality promotes a methodological orientation that is both relational and interactional. The strength of such an orientation is that "mainstream" processes are also viewed as part of the feedback system, adapting to other systems that are adapting to them.

Intersectionality may also address the differences amongst women in Canada—for example, women who cannot speak English or French, those who are poorly educated, or who are subject to racism—which have often meant more difficulty for some women to challenge their relative powerlessness and dependency in an abusive relationship and to locate external sources of support. For example, women in minority groups may be accustomed to experiencing the police as a hostile community presence. The economic vulnerability of single mothers is also heightened due to overt and covert discrimination in employment practices. Similarly, women who are geographically isolated may have greater difficulties ending the violence and escaping the relationship than urban women (Struthers 1994).

In particular, intersectionality could shed a great deal of light on Aboriginal women's experience of incest, which reflects both the impact of sexual victimization and relations among the specific power systems faced by Aboriginal Canadians. For example, they report, as do many adult survivors, that they feel guilty and shamed, vulnerable and fragmented. However, these feelings are intertwined with their experiences as Aboriginals. They grew up being devalued and belittled as "fat squaws" and "dirty Indians." Some, as a result, feel flawed from birth, believing that "they deserved to be abused." As children, they were aware of mainstream society's stereotypes of "dirty drunk Indians...all sluts and bitches." It is difficult to disentangle the impact of these experiences of "feeling worthless and undeserving of help" from the shame inflicted by the abuse itself; the two coexist and support one another (McEvoy and Daniluk 1995). Aboriginal women are also fearful that disclosure of violence will lead to further abuse, to their children being taken from them, and their partners being incarcerated (McGillivray and Comaskey 1999, as cited in Baskin 2006, 26). These feelings often lead to learned helplessness (Baskin 2006, 26). Understanding the abuse means examining the social and historical context in which it occurred, which would be facilitated by a methodological approach using the system-centred style of intersectionality.

An earlier—and similar—form of multi-dimensional analysis is the *feminist relational view of battering,* laid out by Virginia Goldner, Peggy Penn, Marcia Sheinberg, and Gillian Walker (1990). Their work seeks to integrate social learning, socio-political, and systemic levels of analysis; in other words, they strive to create an analytical framework that is useful at the individual, interpersonal, and societal levels. One of the leading American feminists in the field, Kersti Yllo, comments, "These researchers are trying to explore the full subjective experience of batterers and the women they abuse without losing sight of male dominance in relationships and in society" (1993, 57).

According to the relational view, the individual roots of violence are laid by socialization patterns that establish both the social and personal differences between men and women and the inequalities between them. In the process, the separation of men's and women's psychological and social worlds is established along with contradictory feelings about masculine and feminine identities. Men, for example, learn to repress their emotions ("big boys don't cry") yet still seek emotional connection through love and sexuality. A man who comes from a family with deeply traditional gender norms may experience conflict in seeking emotional connection with a woman while still clinging to his sense of manliness. In this context, male violence against female intimate partners may hold two contradictory elements: the man may use the violence not only to establish control over the woman (the power and control paradigm) but also to diminish his fears and contradictory feelings about emotional connections with the "other"— the woman. Violence may thus be both a rational response to control the woman and limit her power over him and a regressive, emotional response ("losing it") to panic over his masculine identity and gender insecurities.

The woman's role in the violent relationship is similarly constructed in the context of her female socialization. Her sense of self-worth and identity are likely moulded in terms of her ability to build and maintain the caregiver role (wife/mother). In other words, traditional socialization creates deeply personal structures in which dependency is central. When confronted with a controlling, abusive, and violent male, the woman will find it difficult to "reclaim...a sense of her independent subjectivity and establish... or re-establish...her capacity for agency in the world" (Goldner et al. 1990, 349). She will be subject not only to her own inner sense of her identity as a woman but also to the cultural messages that reinforce male dominance.

Gender socialization and gendered psychological structures are deeply embedded in societal structures that are constructed around and depend upon the gender schema of both difference and inequality. Indeed, the key social institutions (the economy, the family, the education system, and the military) are premised on gendered social realities (the division of labour, occupational segregation, and so on), and in this sense the social system itself rests firmly on a gendered foundation.

With these formulations, Goldner et al. (1990) are seeking to establish an analytical framework that does not pathologize or privatize the violence; that locates violence amidst the normal processes and power structures of our society; and that can move back and forth from the intimate, personal, and therapeutic to the public, structural, and social policy levels of analysis. Creating such a theoretical framework is crucial to developing appropriate therapeutic interventions, focused research questions, and viable public actions or policies.

WHY DO PARENTS ABUSE THEIR CHILDREN?[57]

Mainstream Theories and Models

As public awareness of and academic interest in child abuse have grown exponentially in the past two decades, so too have efforts to create explanations for abusive parents. Theoretical frameworks have tended to develop in response to two distinct interpretations of the question: Why do parents abuse their children? Many mainstream analysts have developed theoretical formulations that target the implied question: Why do *certain* parents abuse their children? In this body of work, the emphasis has been on explaining the patterns of abuse; in particular, the greater reported rates of abuse in poor, single-parent, and minority families. Other theorists, however, have tackled a much more challenging and broadly framed issue: Why does our culture condone any violence and abuse against children? Rather than focusing on specific groups of families, these analysts question the normative patterns of child rearing in our society and call into question basic, cherished values. Typically working from a feminist or cultural perspective, their work is amongst the most contentious and unsettling to emerge from the family violence literature.

As with wife abuse, early theorizing drew heavily on a psychoanalytic or psychological perspective. Many analysts applied a psychopathological explanation to child abuse, arguing, for example, that abusers were suffering from depression, poor impulse control, or some other mental disorder. However, the deluge of research in the past two decades has firmly established that psychological illness is of limited utility in explaining most violence against children; indeed, research has failed to document any consistent relationship between a specific psychological disorder and a particular type or expression of abuse. Most analysts today appear to agree that psychopathology explains a very small proportion (4 to 10 per cent) of all maltreatment of children (Lenton 1990, 159; Gelles and Cornell 1990, 112). Consequently, theorizing has tended to move away from this individualistic approach.

Again, one of the most popular approaches has been the *social learning theory* (Swift 1995, 96).[58] According to this perspective, children who grow up in a violent household learn to model the rage and violence that they have witnessed (Tower 1996, 71). These childhood lessons include not only the use or non-use of violence in interpersonal relationships but also the justifications for violence. As Alice Miller comments, "The way we were treated as small children is the way we treat ourselves the rest of our life. And we often impose our most agonizing suffering on others" (Miller 1983, 133).

While the social learning perspective is appealing, it does have its weaknesses. Specifically, some abusive parents (along with wife abusers or elder abusers) have not been abused as children, and many victims of abuse do not grow up to be adults who use physical violence either in their marital or parental roles.[59] There are, in all probability, as many exceptions as there are one-to-one relationships.[60]

The social learning approach is strongly related to the *social-situational model* of child abuse. From this perspective, there are two main elements in child abuse situations: One concerns the societal norms and values regarding violence, child discipline, and child rearing that are learned at home. These social norms and values then intersect with the second element: structural stress. Various families throughout society will be subject to diverse stresses such as economic deprivation, illness, or divorce. According to this perspective, families subject to considerable stresses—such as poor families coping with marital and addiction problems—and living in a culture that legitimizes disciplinary violence against children would be at greatly increased risk of child abuse.

The social-situational approach does allow for more complexity than social learning perspectives and seems to explain some of the variations amongst families in terms of reported abuse. However, the conceptualization of stress is difficult; not all families or even most families on welfare physically abuse their children, and while we tend not to hear as much about middle- and upper-class child abuse, we know from numerous celebrity cases that it exists.[61] One of the groundbreaking personal accounts of incest in Canada, Sylvia Fraser's *My Father's House*, locates the violence in a relatively comfortable middle-class world (1987). Perhaps stress, in the form of economic problems, marital difficulties, or addiction, does figure in instances of child abuse amongst the middle-class and the well-off. However, such an amorphous concept provides little insight as to why severe abuse appears in some families subjected to stress and not in others.

James Garbarino's *ecological model* seeks to address precisely this complex interrelationship of factors that result in child abuse.[62] Just as any organism must constantly adapt to numerous aspects of its environment, the family develops in the midst of a complex of neighbourhood/community, institutional, and societal/historical relationships. As C. Wright Mills pointed out forty years ago, the individual must be viewed in a societal (the complex interplay of institutions such as the economy and the state) and historical (the legacy of beliefs, values, and power structures that characterize our society) context. To recognize this interplay between the individual level of analysis and the societal level, we must understand that many seemingly extraneous factors—an argument in the office, a sermon at church—may influence the ongoing development of our family life. Larger social events—a declaration of war, changes in economic policy—are likely to have an even greater impact on the day-to-day development of our family (Garbarino 1977).

Garbarino does not, however, suggest that all these influences are equally relevant to family violence. Rather he targets two *necessary* factors: ideological support for the use of physical force against children and inadequate social support systems for the family (1977, 728). If the family emerges in a social context that both legitimates the use of force in disciplining children and provides little support for the family, child abuse is likely. For example, if there are few quality daycare centres, if kinship connections are weak, if parents are less educated, if social services are scarce or short-term, or if neighbourhoods are victims of social decay, high-risk (poor, stressed) families are at greater risk of child abuse. At the individual level, various *sufficient* factors such as parents under marital stress, struggling with addictions, or dealing with an unwanted child may tip the balance in the creation of an abusive situation. However, in the absence of the *necessary* conditions noted above, these difficulties will not produce child abuse.

Garbarino's work has been particularly important because it explicitly challenges the psychopathological approach and suggests that research must incorporate the complex interplay between individual, institutional, and societal elements. This line of analysis is consistent with policy and practice that attacks the ideological foundations of abuse, fosters community and neighbourhood development, and calls for improved social services for the impoverished.

Feminist and Other Approaches

Each of the preceding perspectives, however helpful, appears to focus on variations in child abuse rates among different segments of the population—particularly, why are poor and lower-class, Aboriginal, or minority families more likely to abuse their children? As discussed previously, the research on this point remains problematic. Even nationally representative surveys based on self-reports, such as Gelles and Straus (1986), tend to define "severe abuse" in a largely class-specific fashion; that is, as "physical violence." The research record does seem to document that working-class

179

families are often more likely to spank and physically discipline their children. They, along with minority families, are also more likely to be reported for neglect by social welfare agencies. However, as with patterns of wife abuse (Lupri, Grandin, and Brinkerhoff 1994), middle- and upper-class families may be more inclined to use psychological forms of abuse. As pointed out by victims of wife battering, the humiliation, shame, and denigration of psychological abuse may be at least as damaging as physical violence. Furthermore, numerous analysts have made the point that poorer families are more subject to the scrutiny of welfare workers than well-off families. Many middle- and upper-class forms of parental neglect—such as sending children to boarding schools and summer camps, or leaving them with an endless series of caregivers—are defined as socially legitimate actions. Mainstream theories may be seeking to explain differentials in child abuse that do not exist, are not significant, or are more complex than currently acknowledged.

Feminist theory takes a much more comprehensive perspective on the issue of child abuse and seeks to answer the question: Why does our society support the parental abuse and mistreatment of children at all?[63] As with wife/woman abuse, feminists identify patriarchy as the primary factor. Patriarchal social structures presuppose notions of hierarchy (superiority and inferiority), otherness (us and them), and power. Our first lessons in separating the world into dominant and subordinate parts (husband/wife; parent/child) are learned in the family, as are the earliest lessons about power and control (Firestone 1973). Contemporary notions about parental authority and rights are rooted in the historical rights of men to own, control, and discipline women and children. According to patriarchal tradition, fathers have consistently played the pivotal power role in the family. The adage "wait till your father gets home," with its implied threat that father will dispense final justice, speaks to both the power and control men have had in their families over the generations.

If starting from the position that patriarchy is key to the organization and content of family life, explanations of specific aspects of child abuse follow. Neglect, for example, is part of the construction of women's impoverishment. Since neglect and poverty are complexly interlocked, it is not surprising that women, who are more likely than men to be single parents and poor, are more likely to be charged with neglect. The latest poverty statistics reveal striking male/female inequalities. Throughout their adult lives, women are typically more likely than men to be poor (National Council of Welfare 1997, 34). Women's vulnerability to poverty is further heightened if they become single mothers.

Similarly, the physical and sexual abuse of children is conditioned by the male/female patterns discussed above. These forms of abuse are generated by the belief that children are the property of fathers and, secondarily, mothers. Given that men are conceptualized as the sexual actors and dominators under patriarchy, it is to be expected that men are most likely to undertake the sexual exploitation of children.[64] Girls' early socialization to be obedient, pleasing to others, and "attractive" sets them up for childhood sexual victimization.

Most feminist theorists do not, however, suggest that patriarchy translates into "the overwhelming majority of child abusers [being] male," as suggested by some analysts (Conway 1993, 81). While inequality between men and women sets the stage for child abuse, abuse does not necessarily or usually take the form of a threatened patriarch lashing out against challenges to his prerogatives. Rather, feminist analysis often acknowledges that mothers abuse their children, perhaps even as much as fathers (Washburne 1983, 291). However, the societal sources of fathers' and mothers' violence against children differ. While fathers "batter their children because they have power," women batter "because they have little power" (Cole 1988, 523). It follows that women's violence against their children must be understood as an outgrowth of the basic inequalities between men and women.

We live in a society where women are expected (even required) to have children;[65] and once a woman becomes a parent, it is she who is required to assume the primary caregiver role. This translates into educational, career, and occupational choices that are sculpted to fit mothering responsibilities; it also often means reduced career choices and opportunities, restricted economic independence, and limited pension funds. Despite these sacrifices, women still receive few social rewards for their efforts and little in the way of societal support for managing the process of parenting. Despite much commentary on changes in the family, the division of domestic work,

181

including child rearing, is still far from equally shared between the average husband and wife (Pupo 1997). It is this socially structured pattern of
personal frustration, overwork, and dependent vulnerability that sets many
women up to be abusive. Some, of course, are lashing out at their children
in response to their own victimization. Others, however, are expressing
their alienation and misery by lashing out at the only available victim with
less power than they have (Cole 1988; Washburne 1983; Gelles and Straus
1986, 247–48).

It follows from feminist analysis that the ultimate solutions to child
abuse hinge on nothing less than revolutionary social change. The social
order premised on inequalities between men and women and socially constructed male violence would need to be fundamentally altered. The change
would be so profound that it is difficult to conceive of "family life" without
the gendered inequalities currently taken for granted. Since the contemporary family is interrelated in complex ways to all other social institutions
and their patterns of gender inequality, no aspect of social existence would
be untouched. In the absence of such a transformation, feminist analysis
suggests that men and women, for differing reasons, are "quite likely" to
continue to abuse their children (Cole 1988, 530).

Feminist analysis does not stand alone in this general critique of our
social structure and its implications for violence against children. One of
the most influential criticisms has been the work of Alice Miller. Although
for over twenty years Miller practised psychoanalysis, since 1979 she has
developed a far-ranging sociological analysis of child rearing that challenges both psychoanalytic and mainstream approaches. Though she does
not base her work in feminist theory, she joins feminists in arguing that
child abuse is rooted in our historical traditions and endemic to our social
structure, and that normal, average parents are thus likely to mistreat their
children.

According to Miller, we are socialized into accepting a "poisonous peda-
gogy" in which we come to believe (despite contradictory experiences as
children) that as parents we have the right and responsibility to control
and dominate our children. Consider, for example, the embarrassment and
anger of parents whose young children are "acting up" and being disobedient in a public place. Children, for their part, are required to learn not

182

only to accept but to value domination by parents as being in their "best interests." In this process, children learn to repress their true feelings and submit. While the product of such "cruel" child rearing practices may be functional to any social order dependent on an obedient, repressed citizenry, it is hardly functional to the children themselves, who are forced to give up their vitality, curiosity, and exuberance. Further, Miller argues that such children will in all likelihood repeat the abusive pattern with their own offspring (Miller 1981, 1983). There is significant evidence in the various studies discussed in Chapter 3 to support Miller's position, as corporal punishment has been associated with the physical abuse of children.

It is, of course, broadly framed perspectives such as Miller's and feminists' that are the most challenging and, possibly, the most disheartening. These analyses suggest that the entire social order is in need of change. The task is certainly daunting and, many will argue, unnecessary. Advocates of social learning or psychological frameworks believe, for example, that counselling and treatment specifically targeting offenders will eventually resolve the child abuse issue. However, the evidence of the past two decades suggests that such narrowly conceptualized analyses cannot adequately account for the sheer volume of violence and abuse that is publicly reported. Many popular social commentators on family violence today argue that most families are dysfunctional. If this is an accurate assessment, the implication is that there must be something profoundly amiss in our society and our culture.

WHY ARE SAME-SEX PARTNERS, SIBLINGS, PARENTS, AND ELDERS ABUSED?

Although a number of theories have been advanced to explain violence in the family, these have limited value in accounting for sibling, same-sex partner, parent, and elder abuse. They do, however, offer some insight into why these types of abuse exist and advance interpretations at both the individual and societal levels of analysis. Many of the former explanations stem from the symbolic interactionist (or social psychological) paradigm, which deals with such things as socialization, role-playing, and personal interpretations.

183

Why Do Same-Sex Partners Abuse One Another?

Same-sex relationships and marriages are, unfortunately, at least as prone to be violent as heterosexual ones. The knowledge that lesbians can be abusive to their intimate partners has been a source of discomfort for some feminist theorists, although there is some recognition that patriarchal structures and ideas still exert influence on relationships between women. The fact that gays, lesbians, and transgendered individuals have generally grown up in heterosexual families contributes to same-sex partner abuse if violence was present.

Violence among same-sex partners, particularly lesbians, indicates how complex intimate violence is and how important the impact of social forces is on interactions between partners. Heterosexism and homophobia are cited as prime reasons behind same-sex violence and also why gay and lesbian victims tend not to report their abuse to authorities. Negative social perceptions of gays and lesbians put particular stress on their intimate relationships. Remaining closeted and the concomitant fear of exposure are likely to further stress a same-sex relationship. One or both partners being HIV-positive or having AIDS adds to the pressure on the individuals and on their relationship. Violence may then be a response to such stresses and pressure. However, since research on these intimate relationships is still in its infancy, any explanation at this point would be tentative.

Why Do Siblings Abuse One Another?

The foremost response to such a question is given through *social learning theory*: children have learned violence in their family. They may have witnessed violence between their parents, or they may have experienced violence at the hands of their parents, or both parent/parent and parent/ child relationships in their family might be characterized by abusive treatment. The violence children have experienced might even be something many people consider quite benign: spanking. In any case, through viewing and/or experiencing abusive relationships, children learn that family relations—which are supposedly loving relationships—may also be characterized by violence. Concomitantly, these children learn that an effective resolution for conflict involves hitting or verbally abusing the person with whom conflict is experienced. As a result, when siblings interact and their interactions produce conflict, the children may resort to violent behaviours.

Feminist issues of power and control go hand in hand with the notion of learned violence in the family. Studies have shown that generally it is one sibling who abuses another, not necessarily all siblings abusing each other equally. However, when one sibling is being abused by another, the victim may then go on to abuse someone else. There is also some suggestion in the literature that an abusive sibling may serially abuse others. At any rate, some studies have shown that a sibling becomes abusive to another in an effort to assert power and control over the sibling targeted for abuse. There may be jealousy between them; the abusing sibling may feel that the one she or he is victimizing is favoured by the parents. She or he cannot control the parents' emotions, and for that reason, the abuser may experience the desire to assert her or his authority over the favoured one in an attempt to gain a measure of control. Alternatively, it may be her or his own insecurity that drives a sibling to abuse another. The abuse, as a way of asserting power, may be a means of boosting low self-esteem (Wiehe 1990).

According to *sex role theory*, gender socialization may also play a role in sibling abuse. Since males are generally socialized to be the more powerful members of society, while females are generally taught to be submissive, a brother may abuse his sister, particularly when sexual abuse is involved, in order to actualize his socialization. In other words, he may try to act out the gender role he has been taught at the expense of his sister. This may be a form of rehearsal for anticipated adult relationships. He is learning to engage in dominance and control of women. He may also be mimicking the way he sees his father treating his mother.

In some cases, *social exchange/control theory* may apply: a sibling may abuse another, in effect, because she or he can get away with it. If parents have a benign view of sibling conflict and refuse to define abusive behaviour for what it is, the sibling may simply be allowed to get away with maltreatment of another.

To conclude, although there is no well-developed theory pertaining to sibling abuse, we can see that there are some at least tentative ways to explain such behaviour.

Why Do Children Abuse Their Parents?

Other violence in the family is often affiliated with parental abuse. Once again, *social learning theory* suggests that children learn abusive behaviour from their family and, in turn, use it against their own parents.

Exchange theory suggests that family life may become chaotic when parents do not assert their authority and take charge of the family. Overly permissive parents who do not set proper limits for their children fall into this category. Adolescents step in to fill the void and assert their own authority. They feel that someone must be in charge of the family, and since their parents are not doing so, they must take that role. Once again, we see the feminist issues of power and control in this explanation. Ineffective parenting means that children must fill the role of the parents, but because they are not yet equipped for the role—being emotionally immature and dependent—they lash out angrily at their parents for putting them in such an untenable position. The violence may even be a way, inappropriate as it may be, for adolescents to attempt to force their parents to respond and regain control over the family, although parents may paradoxically resist every effort (Wilson 1996).

Exchange theory may also help to understand the suggestion that parent abuse is a way for children to gain their independence from their parents (Wilson 1996). This may seem a rather extreme method for accomplishing this goal, but the kind of abuse employed must be taken into consideration before dismissing the explanation. An adolescent who is highly dependent on her or his parents may use verbal abuse or even mild forms of physical abuse to gain some distance from them. If conflict escalates between the child and her or his parents, more serious types of physical abuse against the parents may result. However, real independence cannot be achieved in this manner, as the adolescent is not developmentally mature enough to handle it; instead, the result is continuing emotional dependence. In any event, the adolescent may simply be attempting to break off the old exchange with her or his parents in order to establish a new, less dependent, more equal one.

A perhaps more serious problem is that when the adolescent resorts to such behaviour as a problem-solving mechanism, the cycle of violence and abuse is continued. The use of violence may lead the adolescent into further delinquency and future criminal involvement. For the family as a unit, an adolescent becoming abusive toward parents perpetuates domestic violence and continues the cycle of abuse (Wilson 1996).

Children may also abuse their parents due to a weakened parent/child bond (Wharf 1994). The bond may be weakened by parents working long hours and having little time left to devote their attention to the needs of their children. Children may become resentful toward parents because they feel neglected or irrelevant. On the other hand, if parents are not able to meet the material needs and desires of children due to low income, the children may feel angry and deprived, taking out their negative feelings on their parents. They may believe that their parents are not good enough because they cannot provide them with what other children have. Such scenarios are conflict-producing in themselves; coupled with a weakened bond between the parents and children, the outcome could be parent abuse.

These explanations seem to rely heavily on the notion of adolescent anger motivating the perpetrator to abuse her or his parents. They also suggest that the condition of adolescence is at the heart of parent abuse. The insights of *exchange theory* may be helpful in understanding why this would be the case; that is, the adolescent may be using violence to repair the inequality of the parent/adolescent relationship.

Why Do Elders Become Victims of Abuse?

There has been much more theoretical work done on this particular form of abuse, at least partly due to the fact that elder abuse, as a social issue, enjoys more legitimacy in the eyes of both the government and the public than do sibling, adolescent, or parent abuse. As a result, there is much more literature available in the area of elder abuse.

Theoretical explanations for why elders are abused may be grouped into four main paradigms: *symbolic interactionist, situational, exchange,* and *feminist* theories. It would appear that there is some overlap among these theories, especially in terms of the variables they consider, but there are distinctions among them that warrant examining them separately.

Symbolic interactionist theory is mainly concerned with how individuals learn certain behaviours and patterned interactions (Pittaway, Westhues, and Peressini 1995; Tindale et al. 1994; McDonald et al. 1991). It is also referred to by some researchers as "social learning theory" (Johnson 1996; Gelles and Cornell 1990; Schlesinger 1988), the "development framework" (National Clearinghouse 1986), or the "intergenerational transmission of violence theory." According to this theory, a caregiver may abuse an elder because the former was abused her-/himself. In other words, there is a history of abuse in the caregiver's family so she or he has learned to resolve conflict or to deal with the elderly person by using violent methods. It may be seen as a continuation of family patterns of interaction. The implication is that the abuser has internalized the use of violence as a method of dealing with other members of the family and will, therefore, almost automatically resort to this kind of behaviour. The onus is thus placed on the psychosocial characteristics of the abuser.

Also associated with *symbolic interactionism* are the means by which relationships are developed by family members and the explanations that are created through this interaction; that is, through the use of symbols, usually words. *Symbolic interactionist* theory allows for a different understanding of violence by each member of the family and the consequences of these disparate understandings as family members interact with one another (Tindale et al. 1994). For example, a well-known explanation of violence within the family is that it is a means by which loving, responsible parents discipline errant children in order to mould them into better citizens. Sibling rivalry is a phrase frequently used by parents to explain violence between their children, thus trivializing it as a behaviour common to and acceptable from brothers and sisters, in moderation. Similarly, verbal abuse from her husband may mean violence to a wife, but to him it is just teasing.

Another possible explanation for elder abuse that could be placed under the heading of *symbolic interactionism* is the *filial crisis approach,* which argues that elder abuse is a continuation of parent/child conflict. A weak attachment between parents and children means that a positive model for good relationships is missing. Adult children and their elderly parents may not be able to negotiate and exchange support in an appropriate manner; consequently, abuse of the elderly parent may result when the child is in the caregiving role. Open communication and a sense of balance in their exchanges may be absent due to the weak attachment between parents and children. Such a pattern may be passed on to subsequent generations as well, since the children will not have a positive model for family relations (Tindale et al. 1994).

Learned helplessness (Podnieks 1988) of the elderly person may also be included under this theoretical framework. The senior was perhaps abused at an earlier stage in her or his life and has learned to be a victim. One study has shown that 40 per cent of abused elderly people suffered abuse prior to age fifty-five (Pittaway et al. 1995). Other researchers have suggested that the elderly may develop traits such as being too demanding, wanting everything done their way, or displaying passive-aggressive behaviour because they are frustrated by their own dependency. These traits make them very difficult for their caregivers to deal with, and they may be at greater risk for abusive treatment as a result (Goldstein and Blank 1988).

To summarize the *symbolic interactionist* approach to explaining elder abuse: both abusers and victims enter the situation with internalized behaviours learned from previous relationships, including the use of violence as a way of resolving conflict; they interact with one another on the basis of social status such as age and gender, and on the basis of roles such as caregiver or spouse, and their interactions develop a pattern; they learn how to behave in those patterned interactions and they give meaning to those interactions based on their previous learning and the interactions themselves. Either or neither of them may characterize their situation as an abusive one, based on the meanings or explanations they have created; it may require a third party to identify the situation as being abusive. In any case, this approach implies that the root cause of the abuse is to be found in the individuals themselves. It is a more sociological alternative to psychological models that attribute the abuse to the pathology of the caregiver, which may include sociopathy, mental illness, or the abuse of a substance such as alcohol.

Situational theory, also known as "caregiver stress theory" (McDonald, Collins, and Dergal 2006; Podnieks 1988) and the "environmental framework" (National Clearinghouse 1986), considers the significance of stressors with which the caregiver must cope, implying that when these stressors become too great, the caregiver will be more likely to abuse the elder in her or his care. Being sandwiched between children and elderly parents or being older and perhaps in ill health is also considered stressful for the caregiver. Other stressors may consist of problems with alcohol, drug use, psychological difficulties, work responsibilities, financial concerns, unemployment or poverty, and social isolation, to name a few (Johnson 1996). Thus, stressors can be personal, internal, or external to the family. In any case, resorting to elder abuse as a way of countering stress is an inappropriate coping mechanism.

Such an explanation does not, however, lend any insight into why some caregivers who are faced with stressors do not abuse their elderly charges. It is a rather mechanistic explanation implying that there is either a threshold of stress beyond which caregivers will resort to violence or that stress somehow automatically predisposes a caregiver to become an abuser. Neither alternative offers any predictive power, however; that is, neither suggests *when* a caregiver will turn to abuse so that such a turning point could be avoided.

Exchange theory examines how power differentials in relationships based on rewards and punishment might precipitate abuse. Dependency is an important factor in elder abuse, according to this theory. Discussions of dependency dominate the literature on elder abuse, with most focusing on the dependency of the elder. The basic explanation is that the financial, physical, and emotional dependency of the senior on her or his caregiver results in a great deal of stress on the part of the caregiver. Unable to cope, the caregiver might lash out at the elder in her or his care (Pittaway, Westhues, and Peressini 1995; Tindale et al. 1994). Due to the unequal nature of the relationship, the caregiver may feel that she or he is reaping very little reward, while the elder is receiving more than her or his fair share. Dependency of the elder also means that the caregiver cannot easily terminate the relationship; that is, the dependency of the elder effectively renders the caregiver powerless. Therefore, abuse of the elder may be a way for the caregiver to balance the reward and punishment equation more in her or his own favour. A significant flaw in this theoretical explanation is that it is based on the ageist assumption that elders are automatically dependent and powerless (McDonald, Collins, and Dergal 2006, 438).

In fact, newer research suggests that it is not elder dependency that is significant in the abusive situation but *caregiver* dependency. The theoretical approach may still explain elder abuse in this case by asserting that the inequality of the exchange works to make the caregiver resentful of the power that the elder exerts over her or him because she or he is dependent for support on the elder; therefore, to restore balance in the power differential, the caregiver lashes out at the elder. Another term used for this type of theoretical approach is "web of dependencies" (Tindale et al. 1994).

Feminist theory is mainly concerned with gender inequality, citing the unequal distribution of social power as being at the root of elder abuse (Pittaway, Westhues, and Peressini 1995). When an entire social category of people (for example, women) is devalued, it is this group that is more likely to be the target of abuse. Some researchers hold that elder abuse, in many cases, is "spousal abuse grown old" (see Aronson, Thomewell, and Williams 1995). Men abuse women because they are socialized to see themselves as powerful and dominant, particularly over women. They believe that they have a right to control women and have no compunction about using violence to do so. Sometimes women retaliate, which may explain some of the findings of Pillemer and Finkelhor's (1988) study, in which men, who tend more than women to be married in their senior years, were more at risk of being victims of abuse. It is possible that the wives of these men were retaliating for violence they had suffered in their lives.

If the same ethos of societal devaluation and inequality is applied to senior citizens as a group, feminist theory explains elder abuse as a product of a society in which they are held in low esteem and denied services devoted to their care. Stereotypes about older people depicting them as making no contribution to society—characterizing them as incompetent, burdensome, infirm, or senile—are also thought to make it easier for caregivers to abuse them and ignore their needs (National Clearinghouse 1986).

To conclude: there are a number of theoretical paradigms that have been used in one way or another to attempt to explain the phenomenon of elder abuse; however, none of them addresses the problem in its entirety nor has the power to predict when elder abuse will occur. Part of the problem with these theories is the fact that none of them has been developed specifically in relation to elder abuse; they have all been borrowed and adapted from other disciplines and fields of study.

6

LOOKING FOR SOLUTIONS

As is evident throughout the preceding chapters, family violence continues to be a pervasive social problem. The cost to Canadian society is incalculable in terms of human suffering and lost or wasted talents and abilities. However, it is a problem that is now taken much more seriously than in the past, and there have been efforts on many levels to deal with it.

Evidence that men's attitudes are changing can be found in national polls taken in Canada and the United States, the former in 2002 and the latter in 2007. These polls indicate, for example, that almost two-thirds of Canadian men believe that men are not doing enough to address violence against women in this country, and that 87 per cent of men believe that funding women's groups and facilities that deal with woman abuse is a high or medium priority. In the U.S. more than two-thirds of fathers stated that they had spoken to their sons about the importance of violence-free relationships, and 57 per cent of men believe that they can make a difference in preventing violence and sexual assault in domestic relationships (National Clearinghouse on Family Violence 2010a).

An important contribution to raising men's consciousness about their own role in dealing with violence against women has come from the White Ribbon Campaign, co-founded by Dr. Michael Kaufman, a former professor at York University in Toronto, Ontario. According to The National Clearinghouse on Family Violence, the White Ribbon Campaign is "the largest effort in the world of men working to end violence against women.

In over sixty countries, campaigns are led by both men and women with a focus on educating men and boys. The campaign's white ribbon is a symbol of a man's pledge to never commit, condone or remain silent about violence against women" (2010a).[66] Its main efforts involve educating men and boys to raise awareness of violence against women and to teach males how to have healthy and equal relationships with females. The annual campaign in Canada runs from November 25 to December 6, the day commemorating the tragic shooting of fourteen young women in Montreal.

WOMAN ABUSE

Personal Interventions: Shelters, Counselling, and Related Strategies

Personal interventions, such as counselling and therapy for the victim or abuser, are tremendously attractive since they seem to respond so immediately to the needs of the individual. It is not surprising, then, that considerable efforts have been directed toward these kinds of solutions. Based on a psychological and socio-psychological understanding of the issue, therapists and counsellors have sought to heal the violence one individual at a time. However, such an approach is expensive and time-consuming, and many sociologists and feminists question whether such an approach can ever address the societal dimensions of family violence. Also problematic, and more troubling, is that this strategy addresses the problem after the fact. Nevertheless, it is difficult to ignore the personal plight of so many.

The first concerted response to the plight of abused women was to provide them with safe and secure shelters. In this way the women's movement hoped to ensure that all women, regardless of income, had somewhere to go and someone who cared. Initially, this meant finding a house that could accommodate a number of women, locating funding to sustain the shelters, and training volunteers. It was immediately apparent, however, that additional efforts would be required. For example, telephone crisis counselling for women who could not leave the abusive home but who needed support and information became a high priority. Women's security within the shelters also became an important consideration. While efforts were made to keep the location of shelters secret, this was not a successful strategy, and enraged men still showed up at the doors of some shelters; additional funding was needed to secure the premises with such additions as bullet-proof glass and television monitors. Counselling also became more sophisticated as efforts were made to respond not only to victims but to their children as well.[67]

Between April 1, 2007, and March 31, 2008, about 100,000 women and children across Canada were admitted to 569 shelters. This figure represents a relatively stable number of annual clients. Nearly 80 per cent of them were seeking refuge from family violence. Most of the violence was psychological/emotional or physical abuse and many of the women who were accompanied by their children were attempting to protect the children from witnessing violence against their mothers or being victims themselves. Most of the abusers were spouses or former spouses (Sauvé and Burns 2009). The 2005–2006 Canadian Transition Home Survey also indicated that there were a growing number of emergency-type shelters, which offer short-term housing and crisis intervention. This is in contrast to transition homes, or shelters, which allow clients to stay for longer periods of time (from one day to almost three months) and offer more services, such as counselling for women and children. Transition homes also engage in outreach to the community, providing services to those who are not resident within their facilities. Women escaping from violent home situations are more likely to choose transition homes rather than emergency shelters because of the additional services provided to help them cope with their situation. Women between twenty-five and thirty-four years of age are most likely to seek refuge in a shelter. On April 16, 2008 ("snapshot day" for the survey), 299 women and 148 children were turned away from both emergency and transition shelters due to lack of space (Sauvé and Burns 2009). In 2005–2006 the annual cost of operating shelters was about $317 million (Taylor-Butts 2007).

Most shelters do not accept male clients, although among those that do, the majority are emergency shelters. Despite media hype and the cultural consensus that husband abuse is rampant in our society, only a small fraction of men admitted to shelters are specifically fleeing from spousal abuse (about 3 per cent) (Sauvé and Burns 2009). Minaker and Snider (2006) state that their cursory search of programs for abused men in Edmonton,

Alberta, yielded few that actually provided services for male victims of intimate abuse. Instead, they observe that "[m]ost provide individual counselling support (for any problem, from depression to substance abuse), some are nothing more than personal answering machines, and many are listed multiple times" ("Claims making through Internet culture," para. 8). The Sexual Assault Centre of Edmonton apparently served primarily women, even though the centre was listed in the contemporary directory of services and programs for abused men published by the federal government. In addition, "[t]he males they do serve are primarily victims of child abuse, and most of them were victimized by other males" ("Claims making through Internet culture," para. 8).

The Transition Home Survey for 2007–2008 indicates that there were fewer readmissions for abused women at shelters specifically designed to address family violence. A quarter of the women who attended at shelters on snapshot day had been there before; however, this figure represents an 11 per cent decrease from 2006. This decrease may indicate that the programs offered by shelters have been effective in helping women to escape abusive situations, though it is difficult to say without conducting further research. Counselling tends to focus on empowering the woman, ensuring she is fully informed about community services and support systems, and supporting whatever decisions she makes. Based on feminist analysis, this approach seeks to re-establish the woman's sense of agency and control. Most shelter workers acknowledge that many women return to abusive situations; however, because leaving a violent relationship is often a long process, this is not interpreted as a failure. Perhaps next time she leaves, she will leave for good. As one counsellor comments, "If a woman is going back to the relationship, we've given her the tools to help herself and a lot more knowledge...A lot of women return" (Hanes, *Toronto Star*, 9 September 1994). In recent years, there has been an initiative to extend the counselling process so that the ultimate goal is not simply to encourage women to leave violent relationships and establish independent lives but to help "survivors" move on to become social advocates for abused women (Health Canada 1996).

Abusive men have also been offered counselling solutions. In 1978, Donald Dutton launched the first group therapy program in Canada for men convicted of wife assault. Since that time the number of such groups has grown, and counselling, with its strong psychological emphasis, has become intermingled with criminal justice approaches. The *2008 Directory of Canada's Treatment Programs for Men Who Abuse Their Partners* issued by the National Clearinghouse on Family Violence provides a comprehensive listing for all ten Canadian provinces and the Yukon and Northwest Territories. There are 161 facilities in the directory. Many of these facilities provide individual and/or group counselling as well as other methods of treatment. Some evaluate potential candidates in terms of whether the candidates are likely to benefit from the treatment being offered. Of those listed, 131 served mandatory clients (those referred by parole or probation officers), representing about 81 per cent of the total. Most of those that served mandatory clients also included voluntary clients among their clientele. Only 17 out of the 161, or about 10 per cent, served Aboriginal males, and there was one program that catered to same-sex couples located in Toronto, Ontario.

It is still not clear if the counselling approach is a reasonable and effective solution.[68] Some family violence therapists question whether the twelve- to sixteen-week group sessions are effective mechanisms for stopping years of violence.[69] Men who are charged with domestic assault may be compelled to attending counselling sessions, but it is not possible to ensure that they will actively work toward ending their violent behaviour. Abusive men may simply become better at controlling their violent impulses and using psychological abuse more effectively. Nevertheless, after years of court-ordered counselling and more acceptability for seeking such counselling, it may now be more of an option for some.

A recent study of abusive men indicates that men were more likely to seek assistance for their problems from a counsellor, family member, friend, and/or doctor. Over half the men stated that they felt the best person to help them was a counsellor. They also stated that they wanted a counsellor to help them before a friend, family member, doctor, or religious leader. When asked why they failed to seek assistance, the majority admitted that they did not know whom to contact. Thirty-eight per cent, however, stated that they were too embarrassed to approach anyone for help. A common trait among them was that they held traditional notions about masculinity, which prohibited them from admitting to having problems that may have contributed to their abusive behaviour—they were embarrassed and did not want to appear weak. The men informed the researchers that they would only be willing to seek assistance from someone who guaranteed them complete confidentiality (Campbell, Jaffe, and Kelly 2008). Therefore, although it appears that men may be more willing to use the services of a counsellor at this juncture, there are still significant barriers to their actually accessing such help to deal with their abusive behaviour.

Institutional Reforms: The Family Violence Initiative

According to the most recent performance report (National Clearinghouse on Family Violence 2010c), although initially launched in 1988 with $40 million in time-limited funding, the Family Violence Initiative (FVI) is in its third phase. Coordinated by the Public Health Agency of Canada, the FVI has been a long-term, ongoing federal program since 1996, annually committing $7 million to seven departments to supplement their funding. Among its many, varied efforts, it coordinates fifteen federal departments, agencies, and Crown corporations to collect national data, identify gaps, and fund the National Clearinghouse on Family Violence, which produces informational resources for the public. FVI has been responsible for many significant inroads in Canada and internationally in the battle against family violence.

The 2010 report also sets out a timeline of milestones in what is referred to as "Canada's Journey" toward violence-free families. The *Criminal Code* has been amended a number of times to strengthen laws aimed at various aspects of abuse. For instance, in 1997 Bill C-27 was introduced to make murder committed while stalking someone a first-degree offence. It also clarified that female genital mutilation is not permitted in this country. In 1999 Bill C-79 was passed to ensure that the safety of the victim is considered in any decisions pertaining to bail for the accused and to allow for publication bans to keep the identity of a victim or witness confidential. Important national research has been funded by FVI, commencing with the 1993 Violence Against Women Survey, followed by the annual *Family Violence in Canada: A Statistical Profile*, which began in 1999. Efforts to address violence in Aboriginal communities have been important contributions of the FVI. FVI also expanded the Shelter Enhancement Program in 1999 to include shelters and second-stage housing for youth. In 2002 family sponsorship of immigrants was changed so that someone convicted of a sexual or criminal offence against a relative is barred from sponsorship unless s/he has been pardoned or five years have passed since the completion of their sentence (Jamieson and Gomes 2010). These federal efforts, although important for their public recognition of family violence as a major social problem, have also been criticized, however. For instance, the annual statistical report on family violence has come under attack by feminists for using the gender-neutral Conflict Tactics Scale measurement, which makes it appear that women are equally, if not more, abusive toward their male partners than men are toward female partners.

Another important initiative undertaken by the federal government has been the establishment of courts specially designed to deal with domestic violence. One of the most significant differences between family violence and violence between strangers or non-intimates is the multi-dimensionality of the relationship between perpetrators and victims. In many cases, these individuals love one another and want to be reunited after the episode of violence. This reality makes prosecution much more difficult and requires a level of sensitivity that may not be necessary to the same extent in cases of violence between strangers or acquaintances. The four tenets of the Domestic Violence Court process are: early intervention, victim support, effective investigation and prosecution, and accountability of the offender.[70]

The first Domestic Violence Court opened in Winnipeg, Manitoba, in 1990. Since then, Domestic Violence Courts have also been created in Ontario (1997), the Yukon (2000), Alberta (2000), Saskatchewan (2003), New Brunswick (2007) and in Newfoundland and Labrador (2008/2009). These courts are meant to deal with the special circumstances of intimate violence and to be sensitive to the issues that accompany prosecution of current and former family members. There are differing models of specialized courts: some employ early intervention methods for low-risk offenders, while others use a therapeutic model. Most pursue vigorous prosecution of severe and repeat offenders (National Clearinghouse on Family Violence 2009a).

The Yukon court was meant to target the high rate of domestic violence in that territory and the victimization that Aboriginal people felt they experienced in the criminal justice system. Its introduction has led to fast-tracking of cases into courts within two weeks of the initial charge, a reduction in the number of victims who abandon or withdraw from the system, and a 15 per cent increase in the number of accused taking responsibility for their actions. Early guilty pleas increased by 43 per cent; re-assault rates after the first twelve months were only 9 per cent and, after the first fifteen months, 18 per cent (National Clearinghouse on Family Violence 2009a).

The Domestic Violence Court in Calgary, Alberta, partnered with HomeFront, a community collaboration of programs and services to reduce domestic violence, and to link victims and offenders with counselling and treatment programs. A 2004 study indicated that the number of offenders with new charges was reduced from 34 per cent to 12 per cent and the recidivism rate for those offenders who had completed HomeFront treatment was reduced to 5.7 per cent (National Clearinghouse on Family Violence 2009a). In Saskatchewan, the Regina and Battlefords domestic courts use the therapeutic model, which emphasizes healing, accountability, and victim support. An accused who pleads guilty and accepts responsibility is referred to a treatment program, while an accused who pleads not guilty is referred to another court for trial. The Saskatoon Domestic Violence Court, while also having a treatment component, is also equipped to deal with domestic violence trials and preliminary hearings. All three courts are committed to trying to change the long-term behaviour of offenders. They provide support for victims and families as soon after the offence as possible in order to increase victim safety. Victims are also given the opportunity to participate in decisions that affect the offenders (National Clearinghouse on Family Violence 2009a). The Moncton, New Brunswick, court is a partnership with community groups, government agencies, and departments that works to provide support for victims and families and intervention for offenders to reduce their likelihood of continuing to engage in domestic violence (National Clearinghouse on Family Violence 2009a). The dedication of specialized courts to the social problem of domestic violence demonstrates that the government takes this problem seriously. However, since the program is in its infancy and is not in force in all provinces and territories across Canada, it is too early to tell whether the courts will be effective in the battle against domestic violence in the long run or how they may eventually evolve.

In addition to specialized courts, many jurisdictions in Canada have taken a "pro-prosecution" position with respect to family violence charges. The idea is to ensure that more cases are resolved rather than stayed or withdrawn, and to involve victims in the legal process; these measures will hopefully reduce recidivism (Federal-Provincial-Territorial Working Group[71] 2003, as cited in Gannon and Brzozowski 2004, 53). The most common convictions in family violence cases are in the area of spousal abuse (35 per cent). The majority of these involve only one conviction—which is important because the number of convictions influences the severity of the sentence ultimately imposed on the offender. Four out of five single convictions are for common assault with an additional 12 per cent of convictions for major assault.[72] Convictions for major assault are more likely to be against female offenders—a surprising result considering that the vast majority of those accused of family violence are males, regardless of the type of violence. Male offenders were more likely to be convicted of common assault, while females were three times as likely to be convicted of major assault against their male partners (31 per cent and 10 per cent, respectively). It is suggested that women are more likely to use a weapon when they commit an act of family violence and/or that men wait until the violence is very serious before they consider contacting the police for assistance (Gannon and Brzozowski 2004).

Sentences are usually prison or probation, although a prison sentence is imposed less frequently than when the charge is against someone other than a spouse. This does not hold true for criminal harassment, where spouses who are convicted are more likely to be sentenced to incarceration. When sexual offences were involved, conditional sentences were meted out more frequently than other types of sanctions. Probation was the most common sentence for spousal violence other than criminal harassment, being passed in 72 per cent of cases.[73] Male spouses were almost three times more likely to be sentenced to incarceration than females, whether they were convicted of common assault, major assault, uttering threats, or criminal harassment. If ordered to be incarcerated, women also tend to get shorter sentences. Sixty-one per cent of convicted women received one month or less of incarceration, compared to 52 per cent of men. Female spouses convicted of violence against their husbands were more likely to be placed on probation and for shorter periods of time than male spouses who received probation. Male spouses who were estranged from their wives were more likely to get harsher sentences than current spouses. The highest rate of incarceration was imposed on younger men (Gannon and Brzozowski 2004).[74] From this brief overview, it appears that Domestic Violence Courts are attempting to punish offenders while trying not to be so harsh as to destroy the possibility of future family life between them and victims, if one exists. This may be indicative of the government's attempt to be sensitive to women's frequent desire to stop their partner's abuse, but not necessarily to have him jailed.

Victims are more involved in the court prosecution than in earlier times, although they are no longer free to withdraw charges or recant once charges have been laid against their abusers. Many people have criticized the fact that the government has stepped in to take charge of prosecution as disempowering female victims, but the advantage is that government officials are not emotionally involved in the situation and are not likely to be influenced by the perpetrator. The criminal justice system makes concession to this disempowerment with the use of Victim Impact Statements, in which a victim can provide to the court a personal statement outlining the abuse she suffered and its impact on her and her family's well-being. The statement may include the financial, physical, and emotional effects of the abuse. These statements are significant in that, once one has been prepared, the judge must take its contents into consideration when sentencing. In addition, the law now requires that a judge inquire of the Crown as to whether a victim has been informed of the opportunity to prepare an impact statement. Victim Impact Statements were advocated by the victims' rights movement to bring the victim and her experience back into the prosecution process (http://crcvc.ca). Research indicates that victims of abuse are more likely to co-operate with the prosecution of perpetrators if they have been contacted by the Victim/Witness Assistance Program. These programs are less intimidating to victims than are Crown Attorneys or police officers (Dawson and Dinovitzer 2001, as cited in Forrester 2009, 17).

One particularly contentious area of police reform has been the demand for "mandatory charging," which requires police to file charges against the abuser (when there is a reasonable basis to do so) in domestic violence situations. This initiative removes much of the police's discretion when called to domestic violence situations and also frequently runs counter to the wishes of the victim who might only want the violence to end or the abuser to be temporarily removed from the home (MacLeod and Picard 1989; Hannah-Moffat 1995). Immigrant women may suffer the most from the unintended consequences of the criminal justice system getting involved in their family relationships, including economic hardship, institutional surveillance, isolation from their communities, and breakup of the family, since these women are often sponsored by their husbands and, therefore, are utterly dependent on their abusers (Alaggia and Maiter 2006). Conflict resolution, such as family or community mediation, has been suggested as a preferred means of dealing with intimate violence in immigrant families, as they often better reflect methods in their countries of origin (Wachholz and Miedema 2000, 314). Implemented with the best of intentions, criminal justice responses without additional supports for the victims may create bigger problems for them and actually deter victims from reporting their abuse.

One of the consequences of mandatory charging policies in domestic violence cases and the shift to cultural acceptance of the theory of gender-neutrality is that of "dual arrest."[75] This is the practice where police officers attending at the scene of domestic disturbances respond to accusations of mutual violence by male or female partners by arresting both. As a result, more women are now being charged with domestic violence as well as more men. This raises the question of whether women are truly as violent as men or whether police officers are signalling their disapproval of a policy that removes their discretion to charge, which has historically been their prerogative. Instead of investigation into which of the parties is the primary aggressor and which is using violent actions as a defensive measure (which has commonly been the case in opposite-sex intimate violence, where the male is often the former and the female the latter), police officers may be "working to rule"—mechanically following through with the policy to send the message of how important their discretion in charging perpetrators really is. If that is the case, then they are guilty of inflicting further victimization on the victims of domestic abuse who refuse to be passive. Furthermore, there are significant differences between male and female arrestees. Males are more likely than females to have a history of intimate partner violence in terms of severity and consequences. They also tend to have extrafamilial criminal involvement. It seems that women are being unfairly treated under the "gender-blind" policy of mandatory arrest for domestic violence, since it is highly probable that most of the female arrestees are using defensive measures to protect themselves (Feder and Henning 2005). The implication of such a practice is that women may come to the conclusion that the criminal justice system is not a source of protection against their abusers and decline to call the police when they are attacked.

Support services in communities across Canada are more common, designed to assist victims and witnesses of crime. Thanks to the Internet, a simple search can provide numerous websites and broad access to information. Canadian Resource Centre for Victims of Crime (http://crcvc.ca) is one such website. The Ontario Ministry of the Attorney General, like other provincial and territorial websites in Canada, offers more localized information about victim services and provincial legislation regarding family violence. Ownership of a computer and the expense of having Internet service in one's home may be out of reach for some victims of family violence; however, local public libraries provide access to these resources completely free of charge.

Telephone crisis lines are also an important resource for victims of intimate abuse. The Broken Spirits Network, an Ontario directory for hotline numbers, can be invaluable for a victim seeking assistance and a human being to speak to (www.brokenspirits.com). The American company, Verizon Wireless, has established HopeLine from Verizon, which collects cell phones that are no longer being used by their owners and either refurbishes or recycles them. The refurbished phones are then provided to domestic violence organizations or local government and law enforcement agencies with three thousand minutes of wireless service for victims of domestic violence (http://aboutus.vzw.com/communityservice/hopeLine.html). There are some legal apps available for Smart Phones at present, but none of these apply specifically to family violence (www.canadianlawsite.ca).

203

As noted above, provincial and territorial governments in Canada have also pursued initiatives to confront the problem of family violence in their jurisdictions, recognizing that provincial health depends on the health of their citizens. Six provinces—Alberta, Manitoba, Nova Scotia, Newfoundland and Labrador, Prince Edward Island, and Saskatchewan—and all three territories have enacted legislation that specifically deals with family violence.

In 1995 Saskatchewan launched a particularly comprehensive and innovative effort with its *Victims of Domestic Violence Act*. The first legislation of its kind in Canada, the Act seeks to allow all victims of family violence—spouses, common-law spouses, children, seniors, disabled persons, and any person in a family-like relationship—three avenues of action: emergency intervention orders, victim assistance orders, and warrants of entry. For example, the legislation allows specially trained Justices of the Peace to award a victim exclusive possession of the home, direct police to remove the abuser from the home, or provide police accompaniment for a victim or abuser who wishes to remove personal items from the home. Warrants of entry can also be ordered that allow a designated person to enter a home to check on (and, if necessary, remove) a victim—for example, an abused elder or abused disabled woman. These legal initiatives were combined with extensive police education both on the new legislation and on the dynamics of family violence. Local shelters were involved in these educational efforts and much of the previous distrust between the police and shelter workers was eroded. Furthermore, Aboriginal groups were involved in both the consultation and implementation processes (MacLeod 1995a, 22–23; Turner 1995). This innovative legislation speaks strongly to both a commitment to end domestic violence and a willingness to explore avenues outside the traditional criminal justice approach.

Manitoba has also attempted to fundamentally alter its judicial system's response to family violence. Since 1990 family violence cases in Winnipeg—including spousal, child and elder abuse—have been heard in the Winnipeg Family Violence Court (FVC). The first of its kind in Canada, the court seeks to solve some of the problems found in other judicial systems by processing cases expeditiously (averaging three months from first appearance to disposition); involving victims/witnesses more fully in the court process so that they are less likely to recant or fail to appear; and by providing improved sentencing so that the victim is better protected and, where suitable, treatment and/or monitoring is mandated for the offender (Ursel 1995, 170). For example, the FVC includes two victim support programs—one for abused women and the other for child abuse victims and witnesses—so that victims are both supported and better represented in the judicial procedures. An early review of this initiative found that the court was successful in expeditiously processing cases as well as providing more consistent and appropriate sentencing. Rigorous prosecution results were more ambiguous in that there remains a problem with case attrition—that is, cases that were stayed because of lack of evidence or trials that resulted in verdicts of dismissal or discharge. However, given that the goals of the specialized court are not so much to "get a conviction" as to "not do harm" and "help to prevent violence," its successes are notable (MacLeod 1995a, 20).

In addition to the Domestic Violence Court pilot project in New Brunswick, numerous and various efforts are underway to assist community agencies, such as the Fredericton Sexual Assault Crisis Centre, in dealing with aspects of family violence. The province has also committed itself to addressing violence against Aboriginal women as a priority, developing a partnership with Gignoo House (www.thehealingjourney.ca)—its only Aboriginal transition house—in order to create a culturally sensitive toolkit (www2.gnb.ca/content/gnb/en/news/news_release.2010.11.1750.html).

The fact that Ontario, Quebec, and British Columbia do not number among those provinces is glaringly apparent. In Ontario, the *Domestic Violence Protection Act* was passed in 2000 but never proclaimed. It was intended to deal with physical violence or threats, stalking, and sexual abuse and allowed for emergency intervention orders that were to be available on a twenty-four-hour basis (Cross 2001). Quebec's laws with respect to spousal violence (defined in that province as pertaining solely to violence between couples—the term "family violence" is reserved for violence between other family members) are similar to those in other provinces: women who are subjected to violence by their partners may obtain an "810" (referring to s. 810 in the *Criminal Code*) by swearing out a document called an "information" (like a "charge") and appearing before a judge to obtain a peace bond. The informant (victim) has only to convince the judge that she has a bona fide reason to fear the defendant (perpetrator), not that the defendant actually committed an offence. Peace bonds are valid for twelve months. Breach of a peace bond is a criminal offence. If an offence has been committed, the victim may file a police complaint or the police may independently charge the offender (www.educaloi.qc.ca/en/loi/ married_and_civil_union_spouses/355/).

The biggest drawback to any peace bond or restraining order is that the offender must actually *breach* it in order to be apprehended by the police, which may mean that a woman is severely hurt or worse by the time the police can intervene. Ontario's emergency intervention order was supposed to be easier to enforce because it was to explicitly outline what behaviours by the alleged perpetrator were prohibited. It could also grant exclusive possession of the matrimonial or family home and other property to the victim, allowing her to remain in her home with her children safe from harassment, threats, or violence. Unfortunately, the proposed legislation was not without its shortcomings, such as the extra work required by the court system and the police to allow for twenty-four-hour services. In addi-tion, it did nothing to prevent violence (Cross 2001).

Some continue to question the fundamental wisdom of this whole approach. Toronto lawyer Clayton Ruby, for example, has raised the issue of whether jail time actually reduces the likelihood of reoffending and whether lengthier sentences are a greater deterrent to violence. He argues that no evidence suggests criminalization works to end the violence and that applying the criminal justice system to this issue is enormously expen-sive as well as ineffective. In his view, the ultimate solutions to woman abuse hinge on broader social changes that will ensure women a dignified, secure existence if and when they choose to leave their abusers (*Toronto Star*, 16 November 1996).

Yet, an early study of recidivism among offenders who had been pro-cessed through a Domestic Violence Court indicated that these offenders were "less likely to be reconvicted of a serious violent offence or of a spou-sal offence" and were also more likely to be sentenced to prison for their recidivism (Quann 2006, ii). One of the limitations of the study was that only a narrow number of variables were included due to the use of criminal records; it is possible that a broader range of factors might have been able to shed more light on the results. It is also possible that use of more current data might yield different results as public knowledge of the operation of such Domestic Violence Courts and the cultural influence of their existence could have an impact on recidivistic behaviour. More current studies on recidivism of offenders processed through Domestic Violence Courts should be done to track the effectiveness of this program.

Activists working outside the criminal justice system remain skeptical about this kind of institutional reform as a viable solution to woman abuse. It now appears that many of the reforms that feminists lobbied hard to achieve are not effective in protecting or empowering women, and feminists are at the forefront in challenging many of these policies.

Societal Changes: Feminist Initiatives

Since the earliest days of the modern women's movement, much feminist effort has been concrete and practical in nature. While feminist analysis would call for a social revolution in the structure and values of society, the day-to-day plight of women victims and their children called for shelters, support groups, counselling, reforms to the criminal justice system, and so forth. Many feminist activists devote their time and energy to precisely these kinds of efforts. However, while feminism has this decidedly practical and grounded dimension, it is also clear that feminist analysis emphasizes the need for substantive societal change. Since virtually every institutional arrangement is affected by gender inequalities, such change implicates every component of society. Possible steps toward achieving this degree of social transformation are, by definition, numerous.

Unfortunately, it appears that after all the years of progress toward feminist goals, setbacks have been experienced due to the agenda pursued by the federal and provincial governments, part of which has been the imposition of gender-neutrality on funded research and statistics. Bonisteel and Green (2005, 1) outline in detail the "shrinking space for feminist anti-violence advocacy and feminist civil society." They discuss the way that the federal government "significantly curtailed" feminist anti-violence activities in the nineties when it tightened restrictions on charitable organizations and created an "advocacy chill" (2005, 1). Along with the "culture of scarcity" promoted with its accompanying stripping of funding for the social safety net and the scrapping of the *Canada Assistance Plan Act* (CAP), corporate funding was able to make significant inroads into social and health services. Corporate involvement in terms of political policy-making became the norm for Canadian society. Corporatization, with its evaluation methods that are designed to measure profit, introduces these arguably foreign methods into the charitable services sector. According to Bonisteel and Green, charities were criticized for not "doing more with less" (2005, 2). They argue that these various aspects of curtailment have seriously impaired the ability of feminist anti-violence groups to advocate for broad social change. Revenue Canada pressed provincial governments to crack the whip on charitable organizations: non-profit status would be lost by any group, including women's shelters and rape crisis centres, that devoted more than 10 per cent of its funding to advocacy for its own clients. Funding cuts to women's groups that dared to criticize the government for its actions were threatened, notably by the Minister Responsible for Women's Issues for Ontario in 1996. Members of the Ontario Parliament accused her of waging ideological war on these groups (2005, 5). The voices of feminist anti-violence advocates were dramatically muted by these governmental actions.

The cuts in social spending and slashed contributions to the provinces by the federal government were referred to as the "Let-Them-Eat-Cake-Law" (Torjman 1995, as cited in Bonisteel and Green 2005, 8). Money that had been provided to feminist anti-violence groups was diverted by the federal government to their domestic violence courts and victim service programs, which took over most of the support that had been provided to that point by feminist grassroots and community-based organizations. As mentioned above, the shift also included a move away from a specifically woman-focused approach to a gender-neutral one. This diversion of money has led to underfunding for feminist anti-violence groups and a greater emphasis on their becoming financially independent. Unfortunately, this imposed starvation on these groups has meant that they have been forced to sit down at the same table with potential funders, which sometimes forces them to comply with conservative and bureaucratic terms and conditions they would not have considered in the past. When coupled with a lack of resources for their clientele, feminist anti-violence activists and their clients are thus far less likely to criticize the government and its agenda. These changes have meant that feminist anti-violence groups have had to become more hierarchical in their organization in order to look stronger and more stable to attract corporate funders and partnerships with other community organizations (Bonisteel and Green 2005).

The oppressive qualities of medicalization, which is the attribution of the effects of abuse and oppression to mental illness by psychiatrists and psychologists, are compounded by Canada's steady march toward health care privatization. Privatization of health care, like medicalization, individualizes the responsibility for health and security. In response to the cutbacks and undermining of feminist goals, feminist anti-violence activists have been at the forefront of public rallies and protests against government cuts and changes; they have analyzed and critiqued economic policies that have made it more difficult for governments to perpetuate the belief that family violence is an individual problem. In addition, they have built transnational coalitions trying to resist economic globalization. Transnational feminist analyses of the state have been particularly helpful in understanding how governments and their policies can undermine women's social equality (Morrow, Hankivsky, and Varcoe 2004, 372–74).

In response to increased recognition in feminist analysis of the differences amongst women, activists have sought to develop practical strategies that are sensitive and responsive to the needs of specific groups of women. For example, shelters produce public education material in a variety of languages so that immigrant and racial/ethnic minority women are included. Efforts are made to ensure that counsellors at shelters reflect a variety of racial, ethnic, and language groups or that translators are available. Counselling and support groups have also been developed that specifically target women who share a cultural background.

Aboriginal beliefs and practices have been particularly influential in feminist responses to violence. A body of research suggests that various forms of family violence are epidemic in some Aboriginal communities in Canada as well as in New Zealand and Australia. Although early responses tended to be traditional in that they proffered individual counselling, in recent years a much more comprehensive understanding of the problem has emerged and with it, more broadly framed social interventions. Currently, most family violence in Aboriginal communities is understood as embedded in five hundred years of colonization, economic marginalization, and racism. Violence against women and children, for example, is seen as rooted in the self-hatred cultivated by a history of oppression and cultural domination (LaRocque 1994).

From this analytical perspective, it follows that solutions must address the larger societal context. Individuals cannot be healed in the midst of ailing communities; rather, community supports and healing must go hand in hand with addressing the plight of victims and abusers. The specific actions are "healing circles" and "healing lodges" that seek to heal the community as a whole by "reclaiming ancestral values and traditions and striv[ing] to reintegrate the offender into a supportive community" (Gurr et al. 1996, 24, 27–29). Supported by friends and the larger community, including elders, victims speak to their abusers of the pain of victimization. The abusers are expected to listen respectfully, to acknowledge the harm they have done both to the individual and to the community as a whole. The focus is not on punishment, but on ending the violence and building the community. The abuser is supported in her or his efforts to acknowledge the abuse, to accept the shame, and to move on to healing and reintegration.

In this holistic approach, the individual is understood as located in the context of the family, the family in the context of the community, and the community in the context of the larger society (Gurr et al. 1996, 27). By bringing members of the community together and by locating the violence in the context of Aboriginal oppression and socio-economic problems such as poverty and welfare, advocates seek to combine the personal and the public through individual counselling and social change.

Using this approach as a basis, some feminists believe that restorative justice, which is "a movement within (and sometimes outside of) the criminal justice system, a victim-centered approach, with special relevance to marginalized populations" (van Wormer 2009, "What is Restorative Justice?", para. 1) is an appropriate method of dealing with intimate partner violence. This method is also reflective of the theory of intersectionality. There are four models of restorative justice: victim-offender conferencing, family group conferencing, healing circles, and community reparations. The strength of the victim-offender conferencing approach to the resolution of violence between intimate partners is that it recognizes that the parties involved are victim and perpetrator, not disputants. This recognition differentiates victim-offender conferencing from mediation. The goal is for the perpetrator to understand and empathize with the victim's experience of the violence. The victim, on the other hand, would have a choice as to how best to bring about healing of the situation. Restorative justice also recognizes that victims do not necessarily wish to end their relationship with the perpetrator—just the abuse. Nevertheless, this method would not work in a situation where the victim's life is in danger from the perpetrator (van Wormer 2009).

Other feminists reject the notion of bringing women and their assailants together for mediation or conferencing on the grounds that a history of violence and abuse makes it impossible for many women to confront their victimizers. Further, such efforts to bring victim and abuser together may jeopardize her safety. Precisely the same concerns have emerged around family group conferencing, and although efforts have been made to provide support for the victim and to ensure her or his protection, they have not satisfied some critics. Furthermore, it is not clear, outside of specific groups such as some Aboriginal communities, that there exists a supportive community or family group that can effectively implement and monitor the long-term outcome of the intervention. Currently, it seems likely that some Aboriginal responses to family violence will flourish in Aboriginal contexts, but it is not clear whether they can be effectively applied to many other communities (Stubbs 1995).

CHILD ABUSE

Personal Interventions: Counselling

Of course, considerable effort is currently directed toward providing counselling and treatment for adult survivors of abuse as well as for child victims. In this respect, much of what was previously discussed under wife abuse applies here. For example, children who accompany their mothers into shelters are typically provided with individual or group counselling. Children's discussion groups allow them to deal with issues such as identifying their feelings and building their self-esteem (Moore et al. 1989, 87–88; Pressman, Cameron, and Rothery 1989, 88–90). As with adult women who are battered, most therapy is provided on a crisis basis and there is little available beyond the family's stay in the shelter. As a result, whether or not children receive long-term therapy may depend on the family's resources and the accessibility of counselling in the community. While activists are calling for follow-up counselling and support groups for children who have left shelters, it appears unlikely that these services will proliferate in the current economic and political climate.

In the context of child abuse therapy, it should also be noted that there is an important ongoing debate amongst counsellors. Some, especially those working from a feminist position or working in the shelter movement, have adopted an *advocacy* position on counselling and insist on meeting with victims and perpetrators separately. As advocates for the victim, they require that the perpetrator accept responsibility for the violence prior to undertaking counselling with them. There are many rationales for this position. Most notably, it is believed that children may be at risk of re-victimization if their counselling is conducted in a family setting that includes the abuser. A significant aspect of that re-victimization would involve any perpetrator who refused to acknowledge responsibility for the abuse. Therapists working from the more traditional *family systems position* opt instead to treat the family as a unit. They want to address all the key players together, deal with the family dynamics between members, and, ideally, assist the family in moving beyond the abuse.

A third alternative, the *reconstructive position*, seeks to strike a middle ground by working through three stages. In the first stage, the victim and abuser receive individual counselling; in the second, the mother (if a non-abuser) and child are treated together and the nature of their relationship is addressed; and finally, conjoint family therapy with the abuser (assuming she or he takes responsibility for the violence) is attempted. Steps are taken to ensure the safety of the victim and to eliminate re-blaming the victim. The goal is to arrive at a point where the relationship issues between all family members are addressed (Rossman 1994).

Whichever position appears to be the more sensible, it is important to realize that therapists are addressing child abuse counselling from dramatically different perspectives. Feminist therapists, for example, emphasize the importance of addressing the needs of the child victim and often appear to be less concerned about reconstituting the family. In contrast, more mainstream counsellors are often more inclined to urge family members to move beyond the violence and re-establish their relationships as a family.

Institutional Solutions: Social Welfare and Criminal Justice

Currently, considerable efforts are being directed toward social welfare and criminal justice solutions to intrafamilial child abuse. In many respects, social welfare agencies, such as Children's Aid Societies (CAS), remain the first line of defence.[76] Typically, the CAS workers are the first to investigate suspected cases of child abuse. They may decide to call in the police for criminal investigation or, in some jurisdictions, police will typically accompany CAS workers as they contact the family.[77] The police may conclude, based on their investigation, that there is sufficient evidence to lay criminal charges. In the absence of a criminal charge, case workers may decide either that the case warrants no further investigation or that there should be further monitoring and exploration. In some cases, workers may conclude that the provision of support services to the family will help to prevent child abuse and they may arrange to provide such services as daycare, homemakers, or parenting skills counselling.

In some situations, greater intervention may be warranted. If workers decide the child is in need of protection, they will make arrangements for the removal of the child from the home. In some instances, parents will agree to the temporary, voluntary placement of the child with a friend or relative. If parents object to the child's removal, workers may apply to the court to apprehend the child. If the child appears in immediate danger, CAS workers are empowered to remove the child from the home without a warrant and with police assistance.

If at some point the case results in criminal charges, the offending parent(s) will be tried in criminal court. The court decides on the criminal charge to be laid and on the best solution for the child and the family. Judges typically seek to keep the family together. To this end, depending on the advice of the child welfare worker, they may order the child returned to the home under the continued supervision of family services. Alternatively, parents may temporarily lose custody of the child, who may be placed with friends or relatives, with a foster family, or in a group home. In cases

213

of severe abuse, the child is permanently removed from the custody of parent(s) and, depending on her or his age, placed for adoption (Federal-Provincial Working Group 1994; see also Vogl 1996).

While these basic structures of the social welfare and criminal justice systems have been in place for decades, the last decades of the twentieth century and the first years of the new millennium have witnessed upheavals and momentous reforms. These reforms have included the introduction of mandatory reporting, the creation of child abuse registers, changes to the *Criminal Code* and *Canada Evidence Act* to facilitate victim-witness testimony, extension of the time limits for laying child sexual abuse charges, and the establishment of Aboriginal-run child protection agencies.

Changes to the *Criminal Code* have created new offences relating specifically to child sexual assault, such as including female genital mutilation under the aggravated assault provision and amending provisions relating to child sex tourism. Luring children on the Internet; transmitting, making available, or exporting child pornography on the Internet; or intentionally accessing child pornography on the Internet have also been criminalized. Sentencing provisions have been strengthened as well (FVI Child Abuse Fact Sheet 2001). Breach of trust is an aggravating factor in the sentencing of an offender, possibly contributing to a more severe sentence (Gannon and Brzozowski 2004, 61).

The *Canada Evidence Act* has also been amended to allow children, depending on their age and the type of offence involved, to have a support person accompany them to court when they testify. Children can also no longer be cross-examined by the accused; they may be allowed to testify outside of the courtroom or behind a screen, or a videotape may be submitted as evidence rather than the child testifying in person (FVI Child Abuse Fact Sheet 2001).

The extension of time limits for laying abuse charges has made it easier for adults to come forward. Until recently, adult victims of child abuse were restricted by the statute of limitations in their recourse to the justice system. If abuse victims failed to initiate civil proceedings four years after the cause arose or within four years of reaching the age of majority (eighteen), they were forever denied this avenue of redress. Since many adult victims spent years coming to terms with their abuse, these restrictions were transparently unfair. In 1992, the Supreme Court of Canada relaxed these limitations and adult victims were able to come forward and seek justice many years after the original victimization (Vienneau, *Toronto Star*, 30 October 1992).[78]

One of the more significant efforts at institutional reform was the effort to create Aboriginal-run child welfare organizations. As a result, Aboriginal children are much less likely to be placed in non-Aboriginal foster or adoptive homes. For example, the Spallumcheen Band in British Columbia not only provides care for Aboriginal children but has also assumed responsibility for the supervision of their care in place of the provincial Ministry of Human Resources.

While the Spallumcheen Child Welfare program does not solve the larger issues of poverty and unemployment in the Aboriginal community and the lack of "self-sustaining economic resources," it is an important challenge to the previous approach to child neglect and abuse (MacDonald 1995). Although solutions vary from community to community and in many instances Aboriginal organizations work under agreements with the provincial or federal governments, Aboriginal children today often remain within or under the control of Aboriginal communities (Sinclair, Phillips, and Bala 1996).

In addition, there has been considerable effort within Aboriginal communities as well as Aboriginal groups in prisons to address the concerns and problems of adult victims of child abuse so that the cycle of violence is broken. Traditional healing methods are combined with increased awareness of cultural heritage and pride to provide a new foundation for adult life. Indeed, as with wife abuse, the Aboriginal communities have been amongst the most innovative in developing projects to provide community and educational interventions in child abuse along with counselling for victims (National Clearinghouse 1994).

Reforms to child welfare policies have included the implementation of risk assessment models, family preservation initiatives, strengthening of the "best interests of the child" principles, more emphasis on preventing child neglect, redesigning of permanency planning, and differential response models. In 2000 the Ontario *Child and Family Services Act* was revised, placing greater importance on investigation of children exposed to family violence. This increased emphasis resulted in the reported rate of exposure to family violence rising by 319 per cent between 2000 and 2005 (Fallon et al. 2005, as cited in Alaggia et al. 2007). It is also the most substantiated type of child maltreatment (Trocmé, Fallon, et al. 2005, as cited in Alaggia et al. 2007). However, the unintended consequence of the revision is that it places women who are being abused and unable to leave the family situation in an untenable position—if they report their own abuse, child protection workers may hold them responsible for not protecting their children from exposure. Immigrant and refugee women are especially vulnerable to this consequence as it is frequently much more difficult for them to leave an abusive family life. The worst consequence of such an emphasis is that the mother/victim becomes the focus of child protection workers, rather than the actual perpetrator and source of the violence; for the most part, the abuser avoids accountability for his actions. Some child protection workers report that they do not believe they have a mandate to intervene with the perpetrator, nor are they trained to deal with abusive partners. The result for abused women is that they have become the *sole* focus of the child protection system. Since 2005 the Children's Aid Societies of Ontario have implemented a model of differential response in which children exposed to family violence are evaluated and classified according to the level of risk they are experiencing in their home environment and referred accordingly. Low-risk cases are referred to voluntary community-based services, while high-risk cases are further investigated by child protection workers (Alaggia et al. 2007).[79]

The introduction of mandatory reporting has been a dramatic change in policy. Child protection laws in all jurisdictions except the Yukon (and throughout the United States) now require persons who suspect child abuse to report it to a child and family services authority. In some provinces, failure to report the abuse is a criminal offence that may result in a fine or imprisonment. In New Brunswick and Ontario, it is a criminal offence only for a professional (doctor, teacher, psychologist, and so on) to fail to report. That said, however, professionals are often reluctant to report suspected child abuse for various reasons.

Mandatory reporting has had its critics, who argue that it results in many unsubstantiated reports, increases the workload of already overburdened child protection workers, and wastes scarce resources that could and should be directed at real cases of child abuse and neglect. However, Mathews and Bross (2008) argue that mandatory reporting, despite its flaws, means that many more cases of abuse and neglect of children *will* come to the attention of authorities and children will get the assistance and protection they need. They demonstrate that countries that have mandatory reporting also have higher rates of substantiated cases of child abuse. For example, in the United States the rate of these cases per 1,000 children is 11.9 and in Canada the rate is 13.89, while in England and Western Australia, where mandatory reporting does not exist, the rates were 2.4 and 2.3, respectively. Annual child death rates in the U.S. fell from between 3,000 to 5,000 to about 1,100 after mandatory reporting laws were introduced. Countering arguments that self-reporting may be a superior method for uncovering child abuse, Mathews and Bross (2008) state that the rate of children reporting their abuse to an adult was only 0.5 per cent of substantiated cases in the U.S. in 2004 and 2 per cent in Canada in 2003. Parents are also not likely to come forward and admit that they are abusing their children or report such abuse even if they are not alleged perpetrators. In the U.S. in 2004 self-reporting of alleged perpetrators only made up 0.1 per cent of substantiated child abuse cases with 4 per cent for self-reporting of non-perpetrating parents, while in Canada in 2003 parents self-reporting made up 11 per cent of substantiated cases of child abuse and neglect. The majority of mandated reporters of substantiated abuse were professionals. Mathews and Bross (2008) argue that it is not mandatory reporting that causes problems but inadequate responses from child welfare workers. These workers lack the resources to properly follow up on reports, and policy is not sound enough to offer adequate guidance. They state that a liberal society must not ignore wrongs against children by adults and must ensure children's safety to the best of its ability.

Nevertheless, the system of mandatory reporting does not uncover all cases of child abuse and neglect, as some professionals, such as doctors, teachers, and other health professionals, who are mandated to report suspected child abuse sometimes fail to do so for a number of reasons. Some believe that they do not have enough training to properly identify the signs of abuse and fear reprisals. Others lack faith in the system of child protection. Mathews and Bross (2008) believe that child protection can be enhanced by retaining mandatory reporting and augmenting it with better education and training, and improving intake and screening methods.

Aboriginal-run child protection agencies may also have their short-comings. Critics complain that in some instances provincial child welfare organizations have simply vacated their responsibilities, providing little support, training, or guidance to Aboriginal organizations. The result, in some cases, has been an inadequate, poorly trained agency that cannot respond appropriately to the needs of the children it seeks to protect. Even in the late eighties there was documentation of extensive sexual abuse of children in some communities, and Aboriginal children continue to commit suicide at ten times the national average (Teichroeb 1997).

Finally, as with woman abuse, some advocates question whether the institutional approach itself is appropriate and worthwhile as a primary solution to child abuse. Dunsdon (1995), for example, points out that criminal proceedings may drain the family's resources and victimize the child further by removing the parent. The child may end up living in an unstable, unhappy, and impoverished home. Whatever the court disposition of the offending parent, she or he is likely to return to live with the child and, currently, is very unlikely to receive any counselling or rehabilitation while incarcerated. Alternatively, removing the child from the home and placing her or him in a series of foster homes is unlikely to dramatically improve the quality of the child's life.[80] Furthermore, decisions to remove children, which are currently made by social workers and judges, tend to be based on "majoritarian, white, middle-class norms and values" (1995, 451). Consequently, children may end up in care partly because their parents do not fit the appropriate stereotype, regardless of the children's relationship with the parent(s) or desire to remain in the home.

As a result of these various concerns, child protection remains at the centre of controversy. Many child welfare advocates have demanded new legislation that will clearly put the rights of children ahead of any concerns with keeping the family together (Pron, *Toronto Star*, 24 April 1997). Others urged greater powers for CAS workers both to investigate the possibility of abuse and to remove children they deem to be in danger. There has also been a growing demand that the child protection system be streamlined so that the movement of children through the system reaches appropriate resolutions more quickly, whether it be placement for adoption or return to the family (Welsh and Donovan 1997a, 1997b).

However, if the pitfalls of institutional solutions are to be avoided altogether, we must make societal changes that prevent violence against children. As most analysts agree, one critical first step toward challenging and changing societal attitudes is education.

Societal Changes: Education and the Internet

Not surprisingly, efforts at the societal level have frequently involved efforts to provide better public education on the nature, causes, and consequences of child abuse. Since child abuse often has long-term consequences on adult behaviour (addictive behaviours, generational family violence, interpersonal difficulties), information campaigns have targeted people in the workplace who may want to meet and discuss child abuse issues in order to better understand the effect of abuse on adult survivors.

As with almost everything else, the Internet provides the pathway by which vast amounts of information on child abuse and neglect and on existing services for adults and children are made available. Television ad campaigns advise children that there is help available if they are being abused—for example, Kids Help Phone is a hotline for kids to phone toll-free to talk to a counsellor; there is also a website. Cybertip.ca allows children to report sexual exploitation online or by telephone, including exploitation by way of pornography. There is so much information available now, thanks to the Internet, that it almost resembles the proverbial "embarrassment of riches." Lack of information may no longer be a barrier to exposure of child abuse and neglect; what may continue to be the biggest hurdle to reporting abuse is simply the fear of "letting the cat out of the bag" and losing control of what might happen once the secret is revealed.

In 2008 a charitable organization known as Child Advocacy Centre Niagara (www.cacniagara.org), modelled after such centres in the United States, became the first Canadian dedicated facility of its kind. Its mandate is to provide a safe environment for children to disclose their experiences of sexual and physical abuse and to lessen the trauma for the children having to repeat their stories to numerous professionals. A team of professionals, representing various child protection agencies, is available to assist children to provide details that could facilitate investigators in their task.

Some analysts, however, are critical of these incremental changes. Bishop (1991) argues, for example, that in-depth education is needed at all levels of society; it is ineffective and unrealistic to attempt to teach children to protect themselves. Rather, specific social reforms are needed, including a ban on the exploitation of children's sexuality in the marketplace and a ban on corporal punishment of children, including the elimination of arbitrary, degrading, and humiliating forms of discipline. In this context, the rights of children need to be asserted and community silence on child abuse outlawed.

Advocates of banning corporal punishment of children argue that allowing parental figures, under section 43 of the *Criminal Code*, to use physical force to correct children's behaviour provided that it is "reasonable" is tantamount to condoning physical child abuse. It is a violation of children's rights and is unconstitutional in light of the *Charter of Rights and Freedoms*. The Supreme Court of Canada on January 30, 2004, formally stated its disagreement with this argument in its decision in the case of *Canadian Foundation for Children, Youth, and the Law v. The Attorney General in Right of Canada*. As long as physical force is applied against a child "as part of a genuine effort to educate the child, poses no reasonable risk of harm that is more than transitory and trifling, and is reasonable under the circumstances" (2004, 60), parents will not be sanctioned under criminal law. The majority of the Honourable Justices attempted to mediate the turbulent waters between children's safety and the need for guidance and discipline from their parents. McGillivray and Durrant (2006) state that over sixty years of research assessing the effects of corporal punishment on children demonstrates that, even conservatively defined, it is detrimental in the short and long terms. Analyzing the criteria set out by the aforementioned decision using the data from the CIS 2003, Durrant, Trocmé, Fallon, Milne, and Black (2009) conclude that the Supreme Court of Canada's attempt to define reasonable force was not grounded in the reality of child maltreatment. The potential danger of corporal punishment is highlighted by the fact that "...three-quarters of child maltreatment incidents take place within a corrective context" (86). It is difficult to educate children and adults about child abuse when "reasonable" physical mal-treatment is still positively sanctioned by the highest court in the country for the purpose of "correction" and "education." Such ambiguity is not particularly instructive, especially in light of the evidence that belies the notions underpinning section 43.

The kind of changes urged by Bishop (1991) go far beyond education, implying the need for political action in the form of new policies, legislative proposals, and public debate. Other analysts also call for political action by challenging the role of poverty in Canadian life. As mentioned previously, it is apparent that poverty and economic marginalization are significant risk factors for child abuse and that neglect is often synonymous with being poor. Consequently, any economic policy that successfully addressed pov-erty rates would be the "single most effective way to promote child health and well-being." Specifically, higher minimum wage rates, guaranteed annual incomes, and significant child benefits along with "more equitable income, housing, child care, and job training provisions" would constitute a significant assault on poverty and poverty-generated ills such as family violence (Aitken and Mitchell 1995, 31; see also Watchel 1994; Tower 1996, 433–34; Callahan 1993).

Unfortunately, we may be living in a political era where much of the populace lacks the political will to undertake such systemic solutions and much policy appears to be moving in precisely the opposite direction as social welfare, medical coverage, employment insurance, disability insur-ance, child care, and family violence–related programs continue to be cut.

SAME-SEX COUPLE, ELDER, PARENT, AND SIBLING ABUSE

In searching for solutions to the various problems of family violence, a number of possible interventions have been suggested by professionals working in the field. Many of these involve dealing with the interactants of the abusive situation directly; for example, setting up shelters so that victims have somewhere to escape to when violence occurs, or passing legislation that enables police officers who attend at the scene of family violence to remove the perpetrator. Other types of interventions place more emphasis on the wider properties of family violence; in other words, on the social conditions that contribute to the creation of violent and abusive families. There are two such interventions. One consists of educational programs that are designed to teach people how to identify abusive behaviour when it happens to them or to someone else, either as perpetrator or victim. The other calls for community supports such as drop-in or care centres for teens or elderly people who need to escape the family setting temporarily to reduce the amount of stress they and their family members experience. Both types of interventions are necessary if we are to successfully deal with the problem of violence and abuse in families.[81]

Social policy needs to undergo a major overhaul in order to adequately address the various types of family violence. Any policy that focuses exclusively on cases of abuse, whether they are perpetrated against adults or children, and only deals with these cases as an individual phenomenon ignores the fact that poverty, or low income, is one of the most fundamental causes of family conflict and troubles. Individualization cannot adequately correct this problem. Social policy must be reformulated to deal with the underlying *social* causes of violence within the family. Without an appropriate economic base, one that is achieved without the cost of working extremely long hours under gruelling conditions, family relations cannot thrive. People's needs will not be met, and when this happens, people tend to suffer from anxiety and depression, and hostility builds. Relations become damaged by these negative feelings and result in damage to the people who experience them and those upon whom they vent these feelings. Damaged individuals cannot form the basis for a healthy society. Damage, like shame, is contagious and may affect entire populations. Social relations in general suffer. Therefore, social policy must deal with issues of greater economic security for families that are vulnerable. The social safety net cannot be yanked from under these families, because the probable outcome will be more violence and abuse, not only within the families themselves, but spread throughout society. Better income supplements, better wages and benefits, safer working conditions, lower-cost housing, and accessible day-care facilities are essential to the optimal functioning of families and society as a whole. Deficit-cutting cannot be employed as an excuse for the greater impoverishment of families because the cost of such cuts to the social safety net will have to be borne by the entire society and will simply be too high.

Gelles and Cornell (1990, 139) offer five policy steps that they believe would help to bring violence in families to an end. The first is to eliminate social norms that glorify and perpetuate violence. Some examples they offer are an end to spanking of children, which has been argued to teach children nothing but the appropriateness of hitting a loved one when the perpetrator believes that the situation justifies it. In this way, children learn that violence is a normal part of a loving relationship. Blending love and violence in an intimate setting can have tremendous repercussions throughout our society. Gelles and Cornell also assert that violence in the media should be curtailed. They argue that it is not necessary to show bloodied corpses strewn on streets in order to report the news, nor is it necessary or desirable to fill prime-time hours with various degrees of fighting, shooting, and killing, all in the guise of "entertainment" or "real-life drama." Even situation comedies, the staple of television fare, are rife with instances of verbal abuse and denigration of characters. These types of programs normalize different kinds of abuse by offering them up as scenes of everyday life to which most people can relate on some level. We begin to believe that this is what happens to everyone and that it is part of "human nature" to behave and treat others in such a manner. Violent scenes also pervade children's cartoons. Villains seeking to do harm to innocent people lurk around every corner while superheroes sometimes just barely manage to subdue them; however, there is a great deal of similarity between the good characters and the bad in terms of their behaviour. Children may get warped messages about what it means to be "good" and how violence may be incorporated into that role.

The second policy proposal offered by Gelles and Cornell is that "violence-provoking" stress should be eliminated from society. Poverty, social inequality, under- or unemployment, inadequate housing, lack of education, and poor nutrition are all factors that contribute to human misery and possibly overwhelming stress levels. People who suffer from these types of deprivation are often deeply angry over their situation and are not, therefore, likely to be well equipped to handle daily stressors. They may lash out with violence when their anger is aroused by a family member over something relatively insignificant, and may do much more damage than they intended.

As a third step toward creating social policy that will enable us to prevent violence, families must be integrated into a network of kin and community. It has been found that social isolation is a correlate of family violence. Whether the isolation precedes abuse or results from it is not clear, but that it is closely associated with violence is evident. To address this problem, we offer two ideas for communities to help families establish relationships outside the family and build a social bond. Neighbourhoods could organize committees to set up visiting programs; volunteers in these programs would then reach out to families in the area in a non-threatening way. Alternatively, neighbourhood parties could be held regularly, where everyone is invited to meet and mingle with their neighbours. While these suggestions might have a "Rockwellesque" ring to them, something that seems outdated in our cynical society, they may offer up possibilities of providing connections for increasingly socially alienated individuals and families. If the social bond were strengthened, there is a real chance that people may be able to overcome their tendencies to lash out at one another.

An important policy step in any program to decrease violence in families would be the removal of sexism and heterosexism from our social landscape. The power imbalance established by these forms of prejudice leads to social inequality and low valuation of entire social groups. In addition, heterosexism and sexism provide a model for other types of "-isms" that reinforce power inequities and result in similar low valuations of senior citizens, children, or ethnic minorities, among others. It has been argued that heterosexism, like other forms of oppression, make members of the oppressed group hate themselves and each other, thus contributing to a greater likelihood of them turning against one another.

The cycle of violence must be broken within particular families. Since violence is often transmitted from generation to generation, it is imperative to intervene and put an end to it. Parents must learn techniques to deal with children that do not lead to abuse and violence. Problem-solving and conflict resolution procedures could be taught to families. Neighbours could be encouraged to take children for a short period of time so that parents can reduce their stress levels. A community drop-in centre or Internet support might help to decrease stress and provide another outlet for overburdened family members.

Ethical issues must be taken into consideration any time intervention into an abusive family situation is contemplated. As Kryk (1995) notes, in our society we value self-determination but we also believe that society has an obligation to protect its citizens. We also cherish the notion that families themselves will safeguard their own members. Competing societal values make the decision to intervene an extremely difficult one and require that it be approached with caution.

Individual rights must not be unduly trespassed upon, regardless of how well-meaning professionals might be. Professionals must not arbitrarily decide to remove victims or perpetrators against the will of the parties involved. Alternatively, they must not attempt to keep victims or perpetrators from returning to their relationship if that is what they want. Despite frustration over repeated scenes of abuse between the same parties, professionals must at all times recall that people have the right to determine their own fates if they are legally and mentally competent to do so. Family relationships rarely involve *only* abuse and anger; there is usually love and loyalty as well. The intertwining of these emotions makes it hard for any individual, whether she or he is the victim or the perpetrator, to simply walk away from the relationship. Until she or he is ready to do so of her or his own volition, no professional, no matter how concerned or caring, should attempt to force her or him to leave the relationship. Such coercion could result in the possibility of greater damage to the victim.

Even when family relationships are marked by violence and abuse, intervention in the form of removal of either the victim or the perpetrator should not result in the destruction of these relationships if there is any possibility that they could be saved. Even temporary removal of abused children or elders may have a deleterious effect on their relations with other family members in addition to the abuser. No professional should cause harm with whatever decision she or he makes. Therefore, before removal is even suggested, there should be no doubt that the family relationship is already damaged beyond repair and that there is nothing to salvage. Of course, if the victim's life is threatened, then removal may be the only recourse. However, removal of the perpetrator might be a more beneficial response than removal of the victim, depending on the circumstances. This is particularly true in the case of children who are exposed to family violence; rather than focusing attention on the mother/victim of abuse, child protection workers must find a way to direct their attention toward the perpetrator and contribute to his rehabilitation and possible return to the family. This change in attention could, in fact, help to normalize family relations.

In the case of sibling abuse, for example, removal may pose a serious dilemma for professionals, since removal of siblings from the family may violate a number of rights. The rights of the parents may be violated if a professional steps in to remove a child abusing other siblings because it effectively destroys their parental role. It may be seen as a negative judgment of their parenting skills without strong enough justification. It may also stigmatize parents in the eyes of the community as well as their other children, possibly undermining their parental authority.

Also problematic is that removal may destroy the integrity of the family unit. Removal of a sibling from brothers and sisters assumes that the only relationship that exists among them is the abusive one. This is too narrow a definition of sibling relationships. It may destroy the other sibling relationships if the other children take sides for or against the abusive sibling. The relationship between the abusive sibling and the parents may also be severely damaged if the child believes that the parents did not fulfill their responsibilities in providing adequate guidance or discipline, or did not protect the abusive child from the authorities. The same may be true for the parent-child relationship with the remaining children, who may accuse their parents of the same failures.

The abusive child may suffer unduly in the sense of being socially stigmatized by the removal from the family unit, and also by being labelled an abuser. Removal fails to separate the behaviour from the person, reducing the child to a master status that denies the presence of other, positive qualities. It may isolate the child and exacerbate whatever factors may have contributed to the abusive behaviour in the first place. The child may also be placed in a facility in which other children with similar problems may reside, once again isolating the child from more positive influences and relationships. Furthermore, being removed from the family does not allow the abusive child to learn how to develop more positive relationships with siblings.

It cannot be stated strongly enough that intervention must be careful not to alienate individuals from the other members of their family or from others in their lives. Again, this prudence applies more to removal than to other, less intrusive types of intervention. Removing siblings, children, or elders from their home and family environment may sever their other relationships if, for example, other members of the family or relatives cannot maintain contact with the removed party. The individuals who are left behind may begin to feel ashamed that they did not stop the abuse or do something else to ameliorate the situation, which may have a corrosive effect on them or on their relationship with the removed party. Family relationships might break down as a result; consequently, the removed party will have less family support. Instead of removal, another option for intervention might consist of an outreach program that could provide the pertinent parties with an outlet for their anger and aggression or that might work in an advisory capacity to offer possible remedies for the abusive situation.

Harsh legislative measures (for example, removal, mandatory reporting, or prosecution) may thus exacerbate family violence rather than remedy it. The heightened emotions of both the victim and abuser, along with those of other family members, are exacerbated when these measures are taken. Some of the feelings likely to be heightened are stress; feeling overburdened with responsibilities; or low self-esteem stemming from the family conflict itself or due to poverty, unemployment, or problems with alcohol. These emotions may already be running high and could be pushed beyond control. Time spent in a detention centre may make an abuser more violent and more focused on seeking revenge; the same effect may result from a victim being placed in a shelter or foster home. Statistics demonstrate that a perpetrator's violence against a woman who leaves an abusive partner often escalates to the point of homicide. Thus, removal could be perceived by a perpetrator as an imposed separation and put a woman's life in greater danger, not less. An elderly person forced to go into an institution due to violence in the family may become bitter, angry, or depressed, creating further problems for that person in the institutional setting. In short, intrusive solutions, such as those connected with legislation, could potentially make the situation worse, inflicting more damage on the victim and family relationships in general. None of these hypothetical scenarios should rule out any sort of intervention or legal sanctions, however; they should simply serve to remind professionals and the general public about the need for sensitivity.

Victims' self-determination should be a priority. Victims should not be made to feel as if they have *less* control over their situation when a professional or advocate attempts to intervene on her or his behalf. Podnieks (1988) points to the accompanying loss of privacy as a factor that might contribute to loneliness and isolation of the victim. The professional must remain sensitive to the victim's desires at all times. This is especially true in light of Podnieks's (1992) finding that abused elderly women who felt in control of their lives and the decisions about their lives displayed the very positive quality of hardiness. Their self-esteem was preserved by their sense of self-determination.

The importance of self-determination should also be considered in pro-prosecution policies and Domestic Violence Courts. While victims have some input into the legal process through Victim Impact Statements, they no longer have exclusive decision-making power over whether the perpetrator will be prosecuted. This situation raises important ethical questions. Should the legal system, in its representation of society, go against the wishes of the victim in prosecuting the abuser? Who benefits from this prosecution? Is this truly an attempt to ameliorate conditions for victims, or is it simply a way to present the public with a seemingly more efficient legal system and the image of a government fulfilling its pledge to protect its citizens? In the absence of cynicism, it is still possible that the good intentions of professionals and advocates working in the multi-faceted and volatile field of family violence may lose sight of what their ultimate goal should be: helping families who are suffering from abuse.

Kryk (1995) outlines some ethical issues that pertain specifically to elder abuse. For example, the competence of the abused party must be taken into consideration. Is the victim in a position to make a reasonable decision concerning her or his own fate? Is she or he capable of caring for her or himself? What is best for the victim? This is a very delicate question. The professional contemplating intrusion into an abusive situation concerning a senior citizen should also look at the responsibilities, rights, and needs of caregivers. It is easy to charge caregivers with abuse and neglect, but it may be more difficult to do so once the professional has seriously considered the many constraints and demands facing the caregivers. If the abuser turns out to be mentally incapacitated, for example, should committal be recommended? What about the rights of the abuser? Also, when taking into account what is best for the victim, it may be found that what is best for her or his happiness is not necessarily best for her or his safety. In other words, the victim's happiness may be better ensured if she or he were to be left in the home with the abusive caregiver, even though the victim's safety would not be ensured. Should safety take precedence over happiness? How is the quality of life to be measured (that is, in terms of happiness or safety)? Similarly, if the victim's values commit her or him to the caregiver, even if said caregiver is violent and abusive, should the professional override these values and remove the victim or caregiver from the setting? Does that truly serve the needs of the victim? Should the victim's right to privacy be contravened to ensure safety? What if the victim is an abuser as well (as may often be the case when dealing with abuse involving adult, elderly, or same-sex partners)? All these questions present a conundrum, yet all must be seriously considered before intrusive solutions are contemplated. Ethical concerns also apply to intrusive interventions.

Legislation

On the federal level, provisions under the *Criminal Code of Canada* address the various types of abuses experienced by siblings, same-sex partners, parents, and elders. Sections 244 and 245.3 deal with physical assault. Sections 246.1 and 246.8 deal with sexual assault. Psychological or emotional abuse that consists of threats and intimidation is dealt with through sections 243.4 and 381. Neglect is covered by section 197 or section 247 if the neglect consists of forcible confinement (Gnaedinger 1989, 7). Material or financial abuse, which is virtually exclusive to elderly people, can be dealt with using section 304 (stopping mail with intent), section 324 (forgery), and sections 291 and 292 (theft by a person holding power of attorney).[82]

McDonald et al. (1991) argue that existing provisions under the *Criminal Code of Canada* offer limited usefulness in dealing with mistreatment of the elderly. Their limitation is due to the fact that they can only deal with provable cases of abuse and, therefore, do nothing to facilitate prevention. In other words, legislation is *reactive* rather than *proactive*. As with criminal law, laws that deal with governmental regulation of nursing homes and civil contracts place the onus of proof on the offended party, or victim, who must initiate the action and demonstrate to the court that she or he has been mistreated in some way. Such action requires knowledge of the system and the laws, as well as financial means to pay for legal advice and to retain a lawyer to carry out the suit. Use of existing criminal, regulatory, or civil legislation is always in reaction to an already perpetrated action. In addition, without adequate resources to deal with identified cases of elder abuse, adult protection programs do little to assist abused elders (McDonald, Collins, and Dergal 2006).

All provinces and territories in Canada, other than the Yukon, have enacted legislation to specifically deal with abuse of the elderly and other dependent adults (McDonald, Collins, and Dergal 2006). These laws are collectively known as "adult guardianship and adult protection legislation." Gordon (1995; see also McDonald et al. 1991; Gnaedinger 1989) provides an excellent overview of the evolution of this legislation, describing it as occurring in three waves of reform. With the exceptions of Newfoundland, New Brunswick, British Columbia, Quebec, and Nunavut, the provinces and territories all have statutes that deal specifically with domestic violence (McDonald, Collins, and Dergal 2006).

The drawback of adult protection legislation in most provinces (with the exception of Prince Edward Island) is that it is very much like *child* protection legislation. As has already been noted, elderly people are *not* children; they are full-fledged adults and have civil and legal rights that differ from those of children. Therefore, legislation that treats them *as if* they were children is both problematic and insulting.

Gordon (1995) states that the third-wave legislation incorporates the best features of the preceding two waves; however, he cautions that there are potentially three problem areas in this new legislation. One potential problem is the combination of guardianship and protection legislation. This combination may lead to more intrusive and more restrictive methods of dealing with abuse and neglect, such as court-ordered guardianship. One way to offset such a tendency is to have an advisory board oversee and periodically review guardianships and trusteeships. However, the cutbacks increasingly being made by provincial governments endanger advocacy services to elderly people.

The cutback situation comprises another of the potential problems. Ontario may be especially vulnerable since social advocacy is an integral part of the legal provisions for guardianship and protection of the elderly—provisions that rest on the assumption that, unless an elderly person objects, she or he can be ordered by the court to be placed under guardianship. If cutbacks result in the abolition or drastic reduction of advocacy services, seniors will not have anyone to object for them and may be placed under court-ordered guardianship against their will.

The third potential problem is that the power of professionals to intervene whenever they deem it necessary has been greatly reduced, which may result in an increase in abuse and neglect cases. That is, if elderly people have more control over their situation and are able to rely more on personal support networks, there may be more opportunity for members of their support network to abuse them or to continue to abuse them and less opportunity for detection by professionals who could offer assistance.

One of the very real problems with legislation aimed at prosecuting abusers is that there is often scant attention paid to their own victimization. In other words, if someone is abusing a partner or family member, but that person is either a past or current victim of abuse (even society in general), being prosecuted by the court system will do very little to remedy the dilemma posed by family violence. Although every individual is ultimately responsible for her or his behaviour, to punish someone who is already a victim for reproducing the behaviour that has made them into a victim is actually to punish them twice. Such double punishment can do very little to end abuse, and may simply become another facet of the abuse the victim/abuser has experienced. Victimization must be stopped at the source, or as close to the source as possible, in order to effectively deal with family violence.

This also applies to adolescents who come before the courts. When adolescents who have been violently mistreated by their parents come before the courts after ending up on the streets and/or committing criminal offences, officers of the court should be more attuned to the needs of these abuse victims—for example, they should be able to spot them as victims as well as perpetrators and understand how their needs may differ depending on their individual circumstances. The court should be more lenient with them and intervene to get help for them and their family rather than punish them. These cases should also have specific social workers to watch over adolescents to ensure that they are being dealt with fairly and having their needs met rather than just being processed. In addition, there should be less jail time and less general institutionalization of teens, since these methods are often more damaging than rehabilitative (Garbarino and Gilliam 1980).

There is an extensive debate among professionals regarding mandatory versus voluntary reporting (Bond et al. 1995). Among the arguments in favour of mandatory reporting are that it offers the ability to intervene at an earlier stage, is effective as a deterrent, and provides the opportunity to give assistance to those who might be unable to give consent. Those opposed contend that it is intrusive, creates problems with confidentiality, and may increase the number of unsubstantiated cases.

The provision of shelters for both victims and abusers may provide a recourse for abusive families. However, although there are shelters for battered women and hostels for men, it is generally found that elderly women and men do not fit into the shelter and hostel environments, nor do they feel comfortable with the often large age gap between themselves and the other residents. A Government of Canada publication (2008) indicates that there is one shelter in Calgary, Alberta, that is specifically for seniors, accommodating women with special needs and offering crisis counselling and cultural interpretation (77).[83] Older victims may also find that the services available in the shelter, such as counselling, may not be suited to their needs, while they may be lacking services to meet the special needs of elderly women, especially those with health problems or limitations due to their age. The same applies to men's hostels—elderly men may have special needs that cannot be accommodated in these places. Shelters for abused men, if they exist at all, are few and far between. Because of these problems with shelter, so many abused elderly people are afraid to report. They fear that they will be placed into an institution for lack of alternatives.

Potential or actual abusers could also be provided with shelters. Such a place could serve men who fear that they may be becoming abusive, as well as those who are already behaving in violent and abusive manners, giving them the opportunity to deal with their problems in a way that would be empowering. Rather than being jailed or forced into counselling, they would have the choice of going to these shelters instead; this may reduce the sense of being labelled and stigmatized and make them more positively disposed to change.

Shelters for children and adolescents fleeing from parental or sibling abuse may also be of some benefit, especially if accompanied by follow-up programs designed to assist victims and their families to recover from the effects of experiencing violence within the family. Even those siblings who do not personally experience abuse need to come to terms with what happened in their family. Group homes as a temporary or even permanent measure, or other types of alternative living options (Podnieks 1992), could also be developed to assist both abusers and victims. Such shelters could offer these individuals a separate space from the people and environments associated with the violence and abuse; distance may help to defuse the situation, giving the interactants a chance to examine their relationships and to explore alternative methods for interacting. For children or adolescents, group or alternative homes would give them a safe place to stay while they heal from the experience of abuse or, if they have been abusing their parents or siblings, to deal with their issues and be rehabilitated from abusive patterns. The staff could also serve as a liaison between them and their families, offering ways to reintegrate family relationships in a more positive manner.

Victims of same-sex violence require shelters that specifically address the needs of this group. Because perpetrators could follow their victims into a non-specific shelter, victims would not be safe. Their oppression and its manifestations are somewhat different than those of women who have been victimized by opposite-sex partners. Homosexual men may currently have the lowest degree of support services; therefore, shelters and services will need to be designed to accommodate the particular needs of these victims and perpetrators to adequately address same-sex intimate partner abuse.

Affordable housing in senior citizens' complexes could be another solution for elderly victims of abuse. Residences designed for seniors and their needs have become more common, but many of these appear to be geared to those elders in the higher socio-economic classes. Subsidized complexes catering to the various levels of care required by elderly people that still allow them privacy and some independence should be considered by governments rather than the established seniors' homes of the past.

Governments have recognized that the cost in human misery and the loss of human resources due to lives ravaged by violence and abuse are far higher than the cost of funding programs to create these services. Private corporations may be induced to contribute to such facilities where job or skills training at some level may be offered to younger people staying there. Their profile in the community would only be heightened if these corporations and businesses were seen to demonstrate their desire to be part of the community and lend their assistance. As well, perhaps shelters and group homes could be developed as small businesses by private individuals, subsidized by grants from governments to get started, possibly charging a small fee for room and board from those who can afford it and charging corporate sponsors for allowing them to place their products in these facilities. Government monitoring would, of course, be compulsory.

Education and the Internet

Education is a preventative measure against all forms of family violence and has the potential to reap the greatest rewards if people can be taught new ways of seeing, thinking, and interpreting. On the other hand, it is one of the most difficult measures because it requires ongoing and extensive work.

Victims of same-sex couple violence and parental abuse may be able to overcome their unwillingness to admit to their victimization if the general public is educated about the reality of the situations they face. Education and information can assist them to identify what is happening to them and to seek assistance from appropriate sources. The Internet and telephone hotlines can help these victims overcome their sense of stigma and free themselves from the shame that victims so frequently experience. One of the greatest hurdles to overcome for same-sex victims of intimate partner abuse is gender stereotyping—the feminist anti-violence movement needs to address its gender-based perspective if lesbians and gay men are to receive just and equal treatment for their victimization. This rethinking may be one of the greatest challenges to be faced by anti-violence groups in the future.

The Federal Elder Abuse Initiative has been established by the Canadian government to deal with elder abuse in all its forms, including neglect. It has launched an advertising campaign including television, Internet, and magazine advertisements to raise awareness and understanding of elder abuse in its myriad forms. However, the Government of Canada is just one of numerous organizations that present information on the Internet about elder abuse. There are many publications available in print and online dealing with this form of family violence. The federal government also announced support for sixteen projects across the country under the New Horizons for Seniors Program, which aims to reduce the incidence of elder abuse through such initiatives as the distribution of legal informa-tion and resources in PEI, developing workshops and awareness campaign kits for francophone minorities outside Quebec, and targeting Aboriginal seniors with educational resources in British Columbia. Ontario is invest-ing $900,000 annually to provide the Ontario Network for the Prevention of Elder Abuse (ONPEA) with funding stability to provide assistance for vic-tims of elder abuse throughout the province. ONPEA is one of the operators of the twenty-four-hour Senior Safety Line that offers support to victims in over 150 languages (National Clearinghouse on Family Violence 2009b).

According to the September 2010 Elder Abuse E-Bulletin, social media networks can also be used as a preventative method against elder abuse for victims and front-line workers. Recent research has shown that seniors are the fastest-growing group of Internet users. In 2007 45 per cent of those between 65 and 75 years of age and 21 per cent of those over 75 used the Internet, while 9 per cent of those between 55 and 64 years of age were blogging, uploading photographs, or part of discussion groups. Fifty-four per cent of people 55 and over who were Internet users had social network profiles. Social media networks present a forum within which people can "communicate, collaborate and share information." Those who work with the elderly can also share information and provide support and guidance for one another through these networks. For example, *Exploring the Space Between* is a blog for front-line workers, *CHNET-Works!* is a webinar (web-based conference system) for health professionals, and *USTREAM TV* is a live-streaming resource where presenters and hosts can participate in the same presentation from different locations. The Internet is such a powerful tool that it may open up all kinds of novel possibilities for victims and abusers alike to find informational resources and assistance for family violence. In addition, reluctance to seek help due to guilt or shame may be overcome by the relative anonymity offered by the Internet.

Friends or family members who are caregivers of the elderly need to learn about the special needs of their charges and how to handle them. Often, these caregivers assume they will simply know how to care for elders because they have affection for them or have raised children or given assistance in some other capacity. In addition, these caregivers need to learn how to handle stressful situations and ongoing stress, and to learn effective conflict resolution methods to help them deal with the problems they might encounter with the elderly. To that end, the National Initiative for the Care of the Elderly (NICE) was created. Through this initiative, a network of researchers and practitioners who are involved in the care of the elderly through various medical and health professions disseminate research and best practices relating to the care of senior citizens. This dissemination of information is intended to assist in detection, intervention, and prevention of elder abuse. It is also hoped that seniors will use this resource to become their own advocates against abuse (National Clearinghouse on Family Violence 2009b).

The same methods could be employed in other types of abuse. Parents and children of all ages could benefit from educational sessions at the local school in the evenings or during the regular school day for the children. Methods of non-violent conflict resolution and for handling anger appropriately would help children and parents cope with many of the frustrations endemic to family life so that violence does not become the only recourse. Parenting and family skills courses, as well as stress management courses, could be a part of every school curriculum in some form, and evening courses could be held for parents. Joint classes for parents and children/adolescents or siblings could also be held to deal with the family as a whole and to assist members in handling problems. They could also be a source of empowerment, helping victims to take steps to stop their abuse and helping abusers to find alternative ways of coping with stress and tension (Goodwin and Roscoe 1990).

In general, schools could help identify abuse victims, provide additional assistance, and help with prevention. For example, educators could inform

policy makers about the many issues surrounding abuse so they can institute more protective policies. Parent-teacher associations could provide
education in non-violent conflict resolution and other aspects of family
life to neighbourhood families or those with histories of abuse. And, most
importantly, schools could be more sensitive to students' learning needs
and provide more encouragement when students are having a tough time
(Garbarino and Gilliam 1980).

Raising public consciousness about the problems many families face
is essential. Educational programs should be launched to ensure that
Canadians become aware that social conditions, not just individual
pathologies, contribute to violence in families. Everyone should be made
aware of what constitutes an abusive situation, the many factors that can
precipitate violence in any family, ways to deal with an abusive situation,
and what services are available to families and individuals who are experiencing violence or neglect. Canadians should be aware of the fact that the
proportion of elderly people in the population is growing and that there are
particular factors that make them more vulnerable to abuse, such as physical and cognitive disabilities and isolation (One Voice 1995). They should
also be made to understand that many families, not just those that live in
low-income or impoverished homes, are suffering the effects of stress and
economic insecurity, and how these factors contribute to the impoverishment of family relations and members. In short, Canadians must be made
to realize that family violence is an issue that touches the lives of all people
who live in this country, not just those who experience it directly.

Community Support and Counselling Services

Without community support in various forms, education can do little to
ameliorate family violence. If people have nowhere to turn for relief and
advice when they find themselves caught up in an abusive or potentially
abusive situation, education is a waste of time and energy. The entire community, including friends and neighbours, as well as professionals and
agencies such as legal and medical services, must get involved in stopping
and preventing family violence (Garbarino and Gilliam 1980).

Support groups and both formal and informal counselling should be
made available to individuals who need them. Community centres for

teens, parents, and elders would offer people a non-threatening, non-stigmatizing place where they could go to get away from a volatile situation, seek camaraderie, and talk about their problems in complete confidentiality. Telephone hotlines are also helpful in this regard, as is the Internet. Peer counselling networks could also provide a welcome and safe forum in which victims of abuse can admit to their victimization and express their feelings about what they have gone through. Sometimes just being able to talk to someone and share experiences with them, having these experiences validated, can assist individuals in coping with and working through their problems (Beaulieu 1992; Schlesinger 1988; National Clearinghouse 1986). It can also help identify an abusive situation. In addition, resources like this would alleviate some of the social isolation many people experience.

Access to helping professionals, like social workers, medical/health care workers, and legal workers, could be another resource offered in a community centre. These professionals should all be trained to be sensitive and non-judgmental in their dealings with individuals experiencing violence, whether they are victims, abusers, or potential abusers. For example, caregivers of elderly people would benefit from a combined educational and counselling atmosphere with peers and professionals sensitive to the stresses of their lives (Podnieks 1988). For siblings who abuse or are likely to abuse, community-based strategies would be useful in providing alternatives. In other words, if children had somewhere to go to escape an escalating situation, they might be able to defuse it effectively before abuse ensues. If there were neighbourhood drop-in centres where children could go, where trained and sympathetic adults could supervise them and give them an outlet to vent their frustrations or give them activities to pursue to redirect their energies, perhaps children would feel less inclined to turn on their siblings. A non-threatening environment where they could go to get away temporarily from irritants in their homes might be enough to assist them in dealing with siblings in a more positive fashion. This kind of solution would be consistent with research findings that demonstrate that when children spend less time in the home with siblings, abuse decreases.

To resolve the problem of parent abuse, the best strategy might be training parents in parenting skills. Relevant skills would include firmness, supportiveness, additional problem-solving techniques, and more involvement in their adolescents' lives. Tackling the parents' own alcohol and drug abuse would help to strengthen the family system as a whole, which would, in turn, assist in improving interactions between parents and adolescents. An examination of the teen's peer group may also assist in assessing how deeply embedded in violent behaviours the adolescent is. A violent peer group would tend to reinforce abusive behaviour in the home (see Wilson 1996). Mediation may also assist in resolving issues between parents and their abusive teens (Cottrell 2001). Family therapy may be an optimal opportunity for dealing with all the aforementioned problems, as the therapist will have the opportunity to assess family interactions and structure and how they might contribute to adolescent violence against parents. This more holistic approach to therapy would probably be more beneficial than long-term individual therapy focusing on the abusive adolescent. The long-term goal for abused parents is to regain control over the relationship with their abusive children and begin to heal. Temporary removal of the child and focusing on themselves may be necessary for parents to gain inner strength and rebuild their sense of self-worth to allow them to cope with the situation. They need to have that strength and sense of worth to lay down a set of rules and enforce them with their abusive child. Support is also important for the parents to help them remain in control (Cottrell 2001).

Research

DeKeseredy (1996) suggests that better research is a key to the amelioration of abuse and to future prevention. He states that researchers must focus on using more representative samples and must develop better instruments and more precise and universal definitions of abuse before real progress can be made. Until researchers are in a position to assert that they are all studying the same thing—that what they are studying is, in fact, the problem that needs to be better understood, and that they are measuring it in comparable fashion—we will continue to have a contradictory body of literature that obfuscates more than illuminates the problem.

Research on family violence is a difficult endeavour. People are often concerned about their privacy. They are ashamed of talking about their experiences with violence and abuse. They fear that there will be negative repercussions for them if they reveal what is happening to them. People also have a very real concern for their family members, even those who are abusing them. Family relationships are highly complex and emotions are often intertwined. There may be abuse, but there also may be love. For all these reasons, as Tindale et al. (1994) recommend, researchers might do better to redirect their focus from the individuals involved and the abuse itself to the family relationships and the factors that affect family relations in order to better discern predictors and potential risk factors. They also propose that research be done on non-abusive families in order to see what the differences are in the way they relate to one another and to understand the factors that affect their relationships. In this way, researchers may be able to provide possible solutions to the social problem of family violence.

A brief overview of these solutions readily indicates that a great deal of both money and commitment are required from government and the citizenry of Canada. Neighbourhood or community task forces should be created to target specific problems and attend to their solutions (for example, care for teens, supervision, a place for teens to go after school, hot meals, homemaking services, and so on). Services should be for all families, not just abusive ones. Implementing them seems to be a formidable and daunting task. Yet, both funding and community involvement must be present. Until people realize that family violence is not just something that happens to others—whether they are poor, unemployed, addicted, or overstressed— but happens to all of us, and until people realize that violence affects all our lives by contributing to crime, human misery, and the impoverishment of generations of individuals, we will not be able to make a decisive move to end abuse.

7

ENDING FAMILY VIOLENCE

There have been a great many changes in the field of family violence since the original edition of this book in 1997. Our friend Mark's continuing story demonstrates what can happen to children who are victimized by their parents or exposed to their mothers' victimization by their fathers. As shown in the introduction, an individual damaged by family violence in his family of origin may go on to damage members of his own family. Mark's story also illustrates how the road to recovery for someone who has been victimized can be an arduous and volatile one. Successfully overcoming the legacy of family violence may be an extremely difficult goal to achieve, particularly without adequate support.

A review of the literature available since the first edition has revealed that the fundamental issues continue to be unresolved. Despite the proliferation of research, numerous journals devoted to and addressing the topic, institutes, and special divisions of agencies, there continues to be little agreement regarding definitions, measurement, causes, or solutions. Progress has been made in the sense that family violence has achieved legitimacy as a serious social problem. It is considered a public issue, has a prominent position on many research and funding agendas, and has generated its own industry in terms of professionals and advocates. The public has certainly become much more educated with regard to its various aspects. Yet, many of the original insights advanced by pioneers in the field, such as David Gil on child abuse, have largely been ignored in the literature and research, even though they remain pertinent. For instance, it has been noted that social problems such as poverty, a violent cultural milieu, inequality and power imbalances, sexism and ageism, and a lack of community support, among others, all contribute to family violence in some form. However, many theories about the causes of abuse still tend to psychologize and pathologize the phenomenon by implying or openly stating that personal traits of the victims and abusers, or their particular situations, are responsible for abusive behaviours. Sociological factors continue to be downplayed. Therefore, what we are left with is the impression that there are certain people who are waiting to abuse, certain others waiting to be abused, and certain situations that are abusive. The impression is that this is the beginning and end of the story.

The Government of Canada as well as provincial and territorial governments have embraced the serious nature of family violence and have enacted and amended legislation in an attempt to resolve it. There has also been funding advanced for research and advertising to educate the Canadian public on some of its various aspects—although not all. Same-sex couple, sibling, and parent abuse have not yet appeared on the general cultural horizon.

Yet, in some ways, government initiatives also represent a step backwards for violence against women, since the element of gender has been downplayed to make this form of family violence appear more neutral and reciprocal. The resounding endorsement of the feminist anti-violence movement given by the 1993 Violence Against Women Survey, with its revamped CTS, has now been somewhat watered down to give annual family violence statistical reports the appearance that there is gender symmetry in intimate partner violence. These statistical reports do point out that women suffer the most as victims of intimate partner violence, but they still tend to make it seem that men are as likely, if not slightly more likely, to be victims of violence at their female partners' hands. However, research on woman abuse is abundant and it continues to demonstrate that large numbers of women are physically, sexually, emotionally, and psychologically violated by their male partners. Sometimes the violence is severe enough to end in death. This research has become more diverse as researchers have expanded their horizons and explored how race, ethnicity, socio-economic status, marital status, pregnancy, alcohol use, and other factors interact—or intersect—with gender to make women's experiences of violence somewhat different. Through a more nuanced understanding of the way that intimate violence affects women, better services can be created to effectively deal with their suffering and help them to recover. But how do we reconcile these two "realities"?

The supposedly objective statistical reports referred to above, derived from the CTS, provide fuel to those who make the claim for "husband abuse," which they argue is as widespread and pervasive as violence against women but is being subverted by the feminist cause. This, they assert, is the reason that little or no public funding is being provided for support services for battered men. Nevertheless, despite the vehemence of these claims, there appears to be very little factual evidence to substantiate that husband abuse is as serious a social problem as woman abuse. Notably, only research employing the CTS yields gender symmetry in its findings. This suggests that the old research adage that you will find what you seek may be in operation with these studies. It is an unfortunate situation, however, for those men who do experience abuse and require assistance to deal with it, and whose legitimate claims may be lost in the clamour. Gay men in abusive relationships, for example, may find themselves caught in the middle of this scenario.

Those of us who are committed to stopping and preventing family violence may find that future progress in understanding its fullest dimensions may be impeded by methodologies that do little to reveal the truth behind this extremely complex phenomenon. The detailed discussions with respect to the CTS and the way that it purports to measure violence, as well as the different types of intimate partner violence categorized by Michael Johnson, help to illuminate the persisting challenges faced by researchers who aim to educate the public about the realities of abuse between intimate partners. The CTS continues to be endorsed by people who are considered to be experts in the field in both Canada and the United States; their main concessions to the substantial criticism from other respected family violence scholars and experts is that women do tend to be the victims of more serious types of violence and suffer more from the consequences. It is difficult to understand why such researchers continue to use the CTS when there is clearly a great deal of controversy over its utility; it leads one to question whether it is mostly due to methodological stubbornness or purely personal preference, rather than its service to the subject matter.

The data on same-sex intimate partner violence pertaining to lesbians further muddies the waters of the debates about whether women are as likely to be abusive as men. It appears that the rate of women perpetrating abuse against their female partners may be comparable to heterosexual men abusing women. Furthermore, in violent gay relationships, men are frequently the victims of their intimate partners. Since it is not clear at this point whether violence is consistently bidirectional in gay relationships, it is not possible to state definitively that men are as likely to be victims of abuse in intimate relationships if same-sex couples are included in the same analysis as opposite-sex ones. Nevertheless, there is real evidence to show that men can be victims as well, not just perpetrators of abuse. The findings to date regarding same-sex couples make the dynamics of intimate partner violence more complex and opaque than ever in some ways. Obviously, more research is needed. Unfortunately, of course, more research tends to reveal more complexity.

The federal and provincial governments' initiatives to attempt to curtail and prevent violence in families are to be applauded. The serious and debilitating effects of family violence are being taken seriously as significant social issues. However, the results of these initiatives have been mixed blessings. Few people would argue that the government should *not* be involved with intervention into, and prevention of, family violence; however, feminist anti-violence activists and many victims are dissatisfied by *how* the government has chosen to intervene. For instance, mandatory arrest policies have been problematic because they take discretionary power away from the police. Police may be retaliating against mandatory arrest policies by arresting both parties at the scene of a domestic dispute, even if the woman committed a violent act while defending herself from her male partner. Like pro-prosecution policies in Domestic Violence Courts, mandatory arrest policies eliminate any control the victim may have had in the past. The victim's role is reduced to input into sentencing through Victim Impact Statements.

In addition, government's position vis-à-vis gender neutrality is disturbing in light of so much research over the past decades unambiguously demonstrating that women are primarily the victims of family violence at every stage of life. The role of the abuser in a woman's life may change, but the sex of the abuser frequently does not. Women and girls are most often abused by the men in their lives. That government should ignore this reality or downplay it with a perverse stance of "fair play," with the suggestion that men's suffering at the hands of their female abusers is just as prevalent— even though there is insufficient evidence—is indecent.

Another disturbing aspect of government involvement in the field of family violence is its hamstringing of feminist anti-violence groups by withdrawing much-needed funding and resources, disallowing the importance of activism on behalf of their clients, and trying to force these groups into "lying down with their enemies." It appears that the government has co-opted feminist goals, reshaping them to fit its own agenda, and is trying to get rid of the competition.

One unanticipated development has been the explosion of Internet use over the past decade, which has become a heretofore unprecedented social force. In 1997 no one could have predicted how great the effect of the information highway would be, nor how much information and quasi-information there was to be found at the click of a mouse. Organizations, agencies, and individuals have created websites and pages providing information on how to detect various types of violence, how to identify yourself or someone you know as a victim, what you can do if you believe you or someone you know is being abused, and people you can contact for assistance. Facebook and Twitter and other social networking sites, as well as blogs, offer a unique way for victims to find support from others, or for abusers to monitor their victims.

Like government intervention, advocates want to take charge of victims. Other professionals, such as academics, lawyers, health and social services workers, want to control the definition, measurement, and parameters of family violence. Abusers want to control their victims; victims want to regain control over their own lives; the courts want to take charge of abusers. Control is the problem, yet the solutions all seek some form of control.

The approach to family violence to date has not been a holistic one, a fact that creates its own set of difficulties. Like the blind people positioned at various points on the elephant's body and trying to describe the whole thing, professionals in the field have tended to focus only on sections of the problem that coincide with their disciplines and approaches. Many policy analysts and advocates prefer to attempt solutions that attend to the problem on a case-by-case basis rather than a societal one. Not many are trying to see the "big picture" or working on how to deal with it. As daunting a task as this may be, without a more integrated approach to family violence, splintering is the best result that may be achieved.

Furthermore, the punitive nature of the whole system, which again takes an atomistic approach rather than a societal one, does not address the root causes of family violence. It merely places Band-Aids on the symptoms. It also ensures that the problem will continue to be dealt with on an individualistic basis rather than a systemic one. In effect, it becomes another part of the problem, as it creates subsets of difficulties for the people involved— often those it attempts to assist.

Feminists themselves have been accused of contributing to growing paranoia and over-reporting of abuse. They have been in the forefront of the family violence issue, having insisted that this matter, formerly considered part of the private domain, be put on the public agenda. Unfortunately, however, the feminist approach has not contributed greatly to the forging of a consensus on the matter among the various groups of professionals in the field. Their critical stance against patriarchal tendencies, often found in the approaches taker by other, non-feminist professionals tends to promote more infighting rather than consensus.

The necessity for more research highlights yet another problematic area. Under the current neo-conservative socio-political agenda, with the withdrawal of government spending and tax-cutting dominating its public agenda, looking for more funding to undertake large studies and stepping up the amount of research will be very difficult to accomplish. Yet, this cost-cutting ethos is generating more human misery and contributing to family violence itself. Welfare spending has been greatly reduced; good jobs are still being lost with new job creation tending to be at the lower end; wages are not increasing as much as expenses; and unions are fighting to hang on to their members. People's lives are becoming impoverished, but, more importantly, people themselves are becoming impoverished. Such a situation is highly likely to contribute to family violence and abuse.

Nonetheless, however tempting it may be to take a pessimistic stance on the future of the field of family violence, we must bear in mind that positive things are being done to tackle the problem. People are coming forward to reveal their personal experiences of abuse. Work is being done to demonstrate the scope of the problem and more people are being educated about it. There are many who are committed to ameliorating the situation and community-level work is being accomplished. Governments have gotten on board. All of us may eventually be empowered to take a stand and intervene whenever we are confronted by an abusive situation. Human agency is a powerful force and has the capacity to evoke great change.

Confronting family violence as individuals and as a society, whether we have personally experienced it or not, will hasten recovery for victims. Such recovery from family violence will benefit all of us, locally and globally, as members of our families and citizens of our country improve their lives, their sense of self, their productivity and creativity, and most of all, their joy in living. Such improvements can only raise the quality of all our lives. Unfortunately, in spite of all the impressive progress that has been made, we still have a great distance to cover before we can achieve this success.

And what of Mark? In the best of all worlds, the outcome would be that, truly remorseful for what he had done to Jen and their little boy, he agreed to plead guilty to his charge. Despite the Crown Attorney's request for the severest sentence, the judge recognized Mark's remorse as being sincere and gave him probation on condition that he participate in counselling. Jen's injuries were not as grave as they first appeared. She spent a few days in hospital and the doctors were able to save her pregnancy. She and her son went to a women's shelter where both of them received counselling. After a few weeks' wait, Mark was enrolled in an anger management course and counselling to help him deal with his childhood exposure to family violence. He began to visit with his son. He and Jen were able to start talking with one another and eventually to fully discuss what had happened. Their house sold with a little bit of money left over, so Mark and Jen decided to reconcile and start afresh. Mark continued to volunteer at the facility through which he had taken his counselling and anger management courses and was able to find employment through people that he met there. Mark and Jen's family was lucky enough to be able to overcome the legacy of family violence.

ENDNOTES

1 UNDERSTANDING FAMILY VIOLENCE FROM A SOCIETAL PERSPECTIVE

1   Adult Mark is a fictitious character, a composite of findings from research dealing with child victims and witnesses of family violence.

2   In recent years, there has been a debate over the use of the term "victim," arguing that it is too negative and passive. The term "survivor" has been promoted as being a much more positive and active portrayal of the people who have experienced various forms of family violence.

3   The term "feminist" is applied here to individuals who self-identify as feminists in their writings or whose work is included in collections described as feminist by their editors. It should be understood that the word "feminist" has come to have a diversity of meanings and to cover a complexity of perspectives and conflicts. Feminists certainly do not always agree with one another, nor do they necessarily embrace a standard point of view. (See Mandell 1995 for a discussion of various feminist theories.)

4   For more thumbnail sketches of this theory and its origins, see "Patricia Hill Collins" at www.uk.sagepub.com/upm-data/13299_Chapter_16_Web_Byte_Patricia _Hill_Collins. pdf and Kelly, Gonzalez-Guarda, and Taylor (2011, 64).

5   For other sociological perspectives on conflict, see Dahrendorf 1958, 1959; Collins 1975.

6   Katie Roiphe, Camille Paglia, and Christina Somers make up the unholy trinity referred to in the article and are/have been leading proponents of this type of "third wave" or post-feminist theorizing/diatribes.

2 INTIMATE PARTNER VIOLENCE OR WOMAN ABUSE?

7   For a much more in-depth examination of the ways in which various segments of Canadian society struggle to control prevailing definitions of violence against women and the solutions to this violence, see Gillian Walker's *Family Violence and the Women's Movement: The Conceptual Politics of Struggle* (1990).

8   The prevalence of common-law unions increased from 4 per cent to 16 per cent of the population between twenty-five and forty-nine years of age between 1981 and 2006 (Martin and Hou 2010, 70).

9   See Murphy and O'Leary 1989; O'Leary et al. 1989; O'Leary et al. 1994; Pan, Neidig, and O'Leary 1994 for more information on violence in dating relationships.

10 See Tjaden and Thoennes' report for National Institute of Justice Centers for Disease Control and Prevention for information about stalking in the United States, gathered from the National Violence Against Women Survey.

11 Such an increase does not necessarily indicate that stalking incidents went up by that amount, merely that reporting did.

12 Violent incidents may not be disputes or conflicts at all. Not infrequently, victims of wife abuse report that nothing had set the stage for the violence; it was completely unanticipated. For example, in a recent case in Toronto where a woman and live-in partner were set afire and almost killed by her ex-husband, she reported that their separation and divorce had seemed amicable and that her ex-husband's subsequent anger and violence were completely unexpected.

13 See Ferrel Christensen (1998) "Prostituted Science and Scholarship" on Fathers Canada for justice website, www.fathers.ca.

14 This annual report is free and accessible on the following website: www.statcan.gc.ca.

15 M. Johnson (2006) later changed the name of this type of violence to "situational couple violence" (SCV).

16 Johnson and Ferraro (2000) also point out that in the nineties a literature focusing on the international dimensions of woman abuse began to grow and to be recognized as a human rights issue rather than a family matter. Broader social issues such as terrorism, the effects of war, and internal conflict are being considered in relation to the abuse of women within intimate relationships. Such factors involve a conceptualization of "abuse" as being far more than who has pushed whom within the past twelve months (although the latter is still a serious concern). Another noteworthy accomplishment of research from the nineties is the large amount of information about violence in different types of intimate relationships, such as same-sex, dating and courtship, and cohabiting couples. More is known about lesbian couple violence than gay couple violence, probably due to the women's movement (Johnson and Ferraro 2000). (See Chapter 4 for a more detailed discussion of this type of intimate partner violence.)

17 Post-traumatic stress disorder (PTSD) is a category found in the *Diagnostic and Statistical Manual of Mental Disorders*, which catalogues psychological disorders and their symptoms. It first appeared as a diagnostic category in 1980 and has received considerable attention as an outcome of exposure to military combat—notably the

Vietnam War—or other violently traumatic events. Individuals afflicted with PTSD may experience difficulty concentrating, confused thinking, and poor judgment. For a detailed discussion of the criteria for diagnosis of PTSD, see Walker 1993, 138–44.

18 American research reveals that "wife abuse" is more common in African-American than white families. However, since race clearly intersects in a complex fashion with income, employment, and social status, the role, if any, of racial subcultures and racially distinct value systems is unclear.

19 It should be noted that not all reserves are equally subject to the problems of family violence. Some, such as Alkali Lake, have been able to make dramatic turnarounds in terms of community and spiritual revival, which result in dramatic reductions in family violence and addiction problems. Indeed, Aboriginal communities have been amongst the most innovative in addressing family violence issues (Gurr et al. 1996, 28).

20 While the CVAWS provides high-quality data, it does not solve all of the problems entailed in this type of research. As noted, being abused is a stigmatized and socially shameful situation which women respondents are being asked to admit to. It is to be expected that regardless of the use of only female interviewers, non-judgmental and supportive interviewing techniques, etc., some women will balk at admitting to victimization. If the woman being interviewed is married to or living with a man with high social status, she may have additional reasons (involving finances and social standing) for staying in the relationship. She may be understandably loath to admit that she is staying in an abusive relationship out of financial self-interest. As a result of these kinds of dynamics, surveys such as the CVAWS may still misrepresent the class characteristics of abusers.

21 As Kantor and Straus point out, alcohol may not be the link to violence. Rather, alcohol and violence may be both linked to a pivotal third factor. For example, both violence towards women and "heavy" drinking may be related to popular conceptions of manly behaviour (as cited in Johnson 1996, 12).

22 "Learned helplessness" is a psychological term that refers to the psychological state created when organisms "learn that they cannot predict whether what they do will result in a particular outcome" (1993, 135). Lenore Walker applied this term to battered women to describe the sense of confusion and narrowing choices that often accompany an abusive relationship.

23 Other evidence also suggests women are far from passive, helpless victims. The CVAWS found that in one-third of all cases of violence, the women were able to successfully end their husbands' use of violence after one episode by leaving (or threatening to do so), by calling the police, or by some other method (Johnson 1996, 140).

3 CHILD ABUSE: THE DENIAL OF CHILDHOOD

24 As we will further discuss in Chapter 5, psychologists have argued that abusive and neglectful parents can be categorized in terms of certain personality problems. For example, neglectful mothers may be described as "apathetic-futile," "impulse ridden," suffering from "reactive depression," and being "borderline" or "psychotic." Fathers who sexually abuse their children are described in terms of having "poor impulse control," "low frustration tolerance," "social and emotional immaturity," etc. (Tower 1996, 108, 145). While it should be noted that a considerable portion of the child abuse literature is devoted to analyzing the personality types of abusers, the emphasis in this book is on understanding child abuse as a social issue. Evidence indicates that the maltreatment of children is socially and historically constructed; that is, a society's beliefs, values, and rules contribute to the acceptance of abusive behaviours. While personal pathologies may play a part (particularly in extreme cases of abuse), it is the larger societal context that must be understood as the backdrop to child abuse.

25 See Trocmé and Bala (2005) and Bala, Mitnick, Trocmé, and Houston (2007) for analyses of false allegations of child abuse by alienating parents in the 1998 and 2003 CIS cycles.

26 It is not possible to be sure that these negative effects are directly caused by PAS as they could also be related to their parents' divorce or their parents' personal problems, notes Amy Baker (2005).

27 Physical abuse was comprised of six forms: shake, push, grab, or throw; hit with hand; punch, kick, or bite; hit with object; choking, poisoning, or stabbing; and "other physical abuse." Sexual abuse had nine forms: penetration, attempted penetration, oral sex, fondling, sex talk or images, voyeurism, exhibitionism, exploitation, and "other sexual abuse." Neglect was made up of eight forms: failure to supervise: physical harm, failure to supervise: sexual abuse, permitting criminal behaviour, physical neglect, medical neglect (including dental), failure to provide psychiatric or psychological treatment, abandonment, and educational neglect. Emotional maltreatment took six forms: terrorizing or threat of violence, verbal abuse or belittling, isolation or confinement, inadequate nurturing or affection, exploiting or corrupting behaviour, and exposure to non-partner physical violence. Exposure to intimate partner violence was comprised of three forms: direct witness to physical violence, indirect exposure to physical violence, and exposure to emotional violence (CIS 2010, 30).

28 There is also some argument for considering exposure to environmental hazards while pregnant as a form of child abuse. For example, if a woman knowingly exposes her child to second-hand smoke or works long hours on a computer, is she engaging in a form of child abuse? As evidenced in recent legal disputes in Canada, it is not clear how courts can effectively protect fetal rights while not infringing on the rights of the mother.

29 Various religious organizations have sought to examine the ways in which religious

ideologies have traditionally supported domestic violence and abuse (McAteer, *Toronto Star*, 17 June 1995).

30 The belief that children should obey their fathers is embedded in the Ten Commandments and in the story of Abraham and Isaac. In testing Abraham's obedience, God instructs him to kill his only son, and Abraham proves himself by intending to carry out God's will. Throughout the Old Testament, parents (presumably fathers) are exhorted to physically discipline their children. "He that spareth his rod hateth his son: but he that loveth him chasteneth him betimes" (Proverbs 13:24 as cited in Greven 1990, 48). In Deuteronomy, Moses instructs parents that it is appropriate to stone to death "a stubborn and rebellious son" (Greven 1990, 49).

31 See Flynn 2000 regarding battered women and animal companions.

32 Indicative or shifting priorities and increasing governmental cutbacks, *Vis-à-vis* was folded in July 1996 (Denham and Gillespie 1996, 3).

33 The Centres are located at the University of New Brunswick, the University of Western Ontario, the University of British Columbia, the University of Manitoba, and the University of Montreal. They were each allocated $500,000 to be dispensed over five years.

34 Developments occurring in the United States during the eighties and nineties provided further support for these Canadian efforts. In 1984 a major centre for research—the Family Violence and Sexual Assault Institute—was established in Tyler, Texas. Numerous new American journals—*The Journal of Child Abuse and Neglect, The Journal of Child Sexual Abuse, The Journal of Child Maltreatment*—were also launched in response to dramatic increases in both popular and academic interest in the topic, and much Canadian research appears in these sources.

35 In 2008, boys were more commonly maltreated between the ages of eight and eleven, while for girls, substantiated abuse was more common in the adolescent group.

36 Primary caregiver risk factors were alcohol abuse, drug/solvent abuse, cognitive impairment, mental health issues, physical health issues, few social supports, victim of domestic violence, perpetrator of domestic violence, and history of foster care or group home (CIS 2010, 40–41).

37 Hazards consisted of the presence of accessible weapons, the presence of accessible drugs or drug paraphernalia, evidence of drug production or drug trafficking in the home, chemicals or solvents used in drug production, home injury hazards such as poisons, fire implements, or electrical hazards, and other home health hazards such as insufficient heat or unhygienic conditions (CIS 2010, 42).

38 This relationship between poverty and abuse is interrelated with the parents' own socialization and gender.

39 For example, Gelles and Straus report that African-American children are significantly more likely to be abused than their white counterparts (1986, 252).

40 In this regard, it is interesting to note that the McMaster University and Clarke Institute of Psychiatry survey found increased reporting of child abuse amongst younger generations of respondents. For example, in the over-65 group, 7.8 per cent of women report childhood sexual abuse. However, among 25 to 44 year olds, 15.3 per cent revealed such abuse. As the report's authors are quick to point out, it is not clear whether this pattern reflects increased rates of abuse, more willingness to disclose it, or greater ability to remember it (Gadd, *Globe and Mail*, 9 July 1997).

4 ABUSE IN OTHER FAMILY RELATIONSHIPS

41 This cautionary note is not meant to imply that the data gathered for this study are completely invalid, but to call attention to problems with sampling and the possibility of distortion. Wiehe himself points out that the study is exploratory and meant primarily to open the field to discussion and future research (1990, 6).

5 LOOKING FOR EXPLANATIONS: EXPLORING THEORETICAL PERSPECTIVES

42 For a detailed and cogent discussion of patriarchy, see Johnson (1997).

43 The discussion that follows is from a "psychological" perspective in that it focuses on the individual and his or her psyche. However, in this context, both psychoanalytic theories (which address conscious and unconscious behaviour patterns) and psychiatric frameworks (which focus on the treatment of mental illness) are referred to.

44 Michael Smith points out that in both the U.S. and Canada, feminist social scientists have called for a more collaborative relationship with mainstream approaches to research (1994, 123).

45 Based on these results, Lupri et al. have proposed a "dispersion theory" of wife abuse. According to their perspective, wife abuse manifests itself in a variety of ways, including physical and psychological abuse. Patriarchal ideology, which supports violence against women, is dispersed amongst all classes in society. Wife abuse "is a manifestation of men's power to control women, regardless of class position" (1994, 69). This framework is clearly tied to feminist theory.

46 Also referred to as *gender socialization theory*.

47 In a recent review of the research literature, Wallace proposes a list of sixteen abuser traits, including employment problems, isolation, authoritarian personalities, moodiness, wall-punching, excessive attachment to wife, and traditionalism (1996, 174). From the overlap and ambiguities of many of these terms, it is evident that typologies would be a useful line of further research.

48 Dutton suggests from his work that there are three types of abusers: psychopathic, over-controlled, and cyclical/emotionally volatile (1995). Significantly, as with other typologies, a significant minority (20 per cent) are characterized as so psychiatrically impaired that they are impervious to counselling methods typically used with abusive men.

49 The line between sociological and feminist theorizing is often fuzzy (Yllo 1993). In general, feminists distinguish themselves by rejecting any suggestion that intimate violence is gender-neutral and rejecting any psychological or social psychological theorizing that explains woman abuse primarily in terms of pathologies. Rather, feminists argue that woman abuse is rooted in and cannot be understood outside of the patriarchal structure of society.

50 Feminist analysis does not necessarily suggest that all men are more powerful than all women. Rather, the focus is on men and women as social groups. Clearly, there are women who are more powerful (in terms of wealth, corporate position, and so on) than some men. However, there are social patterns in society that suggest that men as a group are privileged over women as a group. For example, women comprise about 9 per cent of the directors of Canadian corporate boards while men comprise 91 per cent (McHutchion, *Toronto Star*, 7 February 1997). The old feminist axiom "where power is, women are not" is not always true, but a power differential between women and men as groups is apparent throughout our society.

51 Wife killings are typically precipitated by "real or imagined insubordination" by the wife. The husband accuses her of sexual infidelity or confronts her unilateral decision to terminate the relationship, or he simply wants to control her. In contrast, wives often kill husbands in defence against their aggression (Wilson and Daly 1994, 4).

52 Victim-blaming refers to the tendency in society to hold victims accountable for their victimization rather than laying the blame firmly at the feet of the perpetrators. For example, rape victims are often implicitly or explicitly blamed for wearing the wrong clothes, for being in the wrong place, or for not taking adequate precautions. Blaming the victim serves to take attention away from those parties who are actually responsible for the violence or abuse.

53 As Wilson and Daly point out, it is not clear if the act of separation triggers the lethal

violence. It may be that the violence becomes so intolerable that the woman leaves—but whether or not she leaves, her life is at risk.

54 Walker argues that her notions of learned helplessness and battered woman syndrome (BWS) are in fact consistent with feminist theories (1993, 144). She argues, for example, that BWS is consistent with the feminist view that normal women are victimized by batterers, that normal women may stay in abusive relationships, and that the violence is not women's fault (145). Other feminists reject Walker's approach on the grounds that it is overly psychological and focuses too much on personality while putting too little emphasis on the relevant structural and cultural factors (Bowker 1993).

55 Ironically, while the decision to stay may be based on a rational calculation of the alternatives, by staying the woman often is providing her husband with a "license to hit" (Hoff 1990, 44).

56 Intersectionality has been criticized as vague and open-ended, but Davis (2008) points out that this may be the secret of its success. Intersectionality incorporates the postmodern insistence on the situatedness of knowledge, including that of the researcher conducting the study. It allows for attention to be focused not only on the fact of intersecting power structures in a woman's life, but on the material consequences of this intersection. For these reasons, the theory of intersectionality allows for much variation and adaptability in definition. As Davis asserts, "In short, intersectionality, by virtue of its vagueness and inherent open-endedness, initiates a process of discovery which not only is potentially interminable, but promises to yield new and more comprehensive and reflexively critical insights. What more could one desire from feminist inquiry?" (2008, 77). Despite her admiration for the theory, Davis raises the point that a successful theory is not necessarily a "good" theory because it does not necessarily provide "encompassing or irrefutable explanations of social life" (2008, 78).

57 Theoretical work on child abuse tackles a wide variety of questions. For example, models have been developed to explain the treatment stages characteristic of child sexual abuse (Orenchuk-Tomiak, Matthey, and Christensen 1989). While the emphasis here is on the central question—Why do parents abuse their children?—it should be noted that theorizing has pursued a variety of avenues.

58 Social learning theory is also often termed socialization theory, social psychological theory, or the cycle of violence approach.

59 It should be noted that some victims of physical abuse may deploy other abusive actions (such as psychological or sexual abuse) as adults. It would be inaccurate to conclude from this lack of a necessary relationship between childhood abuse and adult victimizing that children can escape completely unscathed from an abusive childhood.

60 For example, the social learning impact of being exposed to wife assault may vary

depending on the child's ability to distance her-/himself from the situation, her/his self-esteem, and proclivity to internalize the conflict (Moore et al. 1989, 81).

61 Amongst the numerous celebrities who have come forward to describe themselves as abuse survivors are Sinead O'Connor, Roseanne, Brian Wilson, Gary Crosby (son of Bing Crosby), LaToya Jackson, Marilyn Van Derber Atler (former Miss America), and Christina Crawford (daughter of Joan Crawford). Many of these people grew up in affluent surroundings.

62 For a Canadian application of the ecological model, see Krishnan and Morrison (1995).

63 Needless to say, feminist analysts have addressed a much broader range of issues than suggested by this one question. For example, Karen Swift's work on child neglect, which examines the ways in which child welfare work processes characterize certain mothers (notably, low-income, single-parent mothers) as neglectful (1995).

64 There clearly are many ways in which one can "be a man." Masculinities range from Phil Donohue's sensitive male to Arnold Schwarzenegger's robotic fighting machine. However, not all masculinities are equally valued and legitimated by our society. As many analysts in male studies now point out, there is a "hegemonic masculinity" which represents the prevailing image of what a "real" man should be.

65 To gauge the social pressure on women to have and raise children, consider social stereotypes of women who explicitly choose not to have children or the societal stigmatization of women who give up custody of their children in divorce. As Cole (1988) points out, reproductive policies that make it difficult or impossible for women to terminate unwanted pregnancies also function to compel women to become mothers.

6 LOOKING FOR SOLUTIONS

66 The White Ribbon Campaign has its own website (www.whiteribbon.ca), newsletter, blog, and Facebook group.

67 Since the inception of the modern women's movement, feminist psychologists, social workers, and counsellors have developed both a thoroughgoing critique of traditional psychodynamic therapy and feminist alternatives. Feminist therapy seeks to encourage women to question, for example, the self-denial and self-sacrifice that are built in to the traditional woman caregiver role. The intent of therapy is to empower women and to provide them with the skills to question the role of the larger social order in their personal problems (Pressman 1989).

68 Dutton, however, counters that his approach to group counselling is effective. Based on a ten-year review of treated and untreated abusers, he concludes that for every 1,000 men,

there were 350 fewer arrests and 10,500 fewer attacks than if the men were untreated. Not surprisingly, given this ongoing controversy about the benefits of treatment groups and treatment approaches, therapists and policy analysts are currently debating how to establish standards for batterer intervention (including treatment approaches, training of therapists, goals of programs, and so on) (see Gondolf 1995; Geffner 1995).

69 According to the Health Canada survey, treatment programs last from eight weeks to one year (1994).

70 For more information about Domestic Violence Courts, see www.justice.gc.ca/eng/pi/fv-vf/rep-rap/for2001.html.

71 The Ad Hoc Federal-Provincial-Territorial Working Group Reviewing Spousal Abuse Policies and Legislation is referred to in the text as "Federal-Provincial-Territorial Working Group."

72 Major assault includes aggravated assault and aggravated assault with a weapon/causing bodily harm.

73 The incarceration rate for the most serious offences such as major assault was 32 per cent, almost double that of the rate for common assault at 17 per cent. Incarceration was also common in criminal harassment convictions involving spouses (32 per cent). However, the prison terms were relatively short—one month or less for common assault, uttering threats, and criminal harassment, with the average sentence being about 123 days for two-thirds of convictions of spousal major assault. Terms of longer than six months were imposed in about 14 per cent of major assaults. Probation, on the other hand, was generally longer than six months and shorter than twelve months in length, except in the case of criminal harassment. Over half of spouses convicted of criminal harassment who received probation were sentenced to two years or more. The fact that probation is mandatory when conditional discharges or suspended sentences are imposed may be one reason why probation is so common.

74 Twenty-three per cent of men aged 18 to 24 were incarcerated as opposed to 18 per cent of men aged 35 to 44, and 11 per cent of men 55 and over.

75 This unintended consequence was alleviated by instructing police officers not to automatically countercharge, but rather, to record the details of the charge and present them to a Crown to decide whether further action is warranted (MacLeod 1995a, 22).

76 The names of child welfare agencies vary to some extent from province to province and region to region.

77 Trocmé reports a growing emphasis on involving police in child abuse investigations (1994, 78).

78 For example, a Calgary woman sued a BC man for sexual abuse that had taken place fifty years earlier (*The Standard* [St. Catharines], 31 December 1993).

79 For more information on the recent evolution of child welfare policy, see Ministry of Children and Youth Services, July 2005.

80 Research indicates that on average, children under sixteen who become permanent wards of the state will be sent to eight different foster families and many will be placed in institutional settings (Dunsdon 1995, 453).

81 For a more comprehensive discussion of Canadian strategies for dealing with elder abuse, see MacLean 1995.

82 McDonald et al. (1991) provide more detailed references to the sections of the *Criminal Code* that deal with particular kinds of abuse. In addition, they provide an account of legislation that deals with elder abuse in institutional settings. Such legislation generally consists of government regulation of the institutions themselves and tort or civil contract law.

83 This publication is *Transition Houses and Shelters for Abused Women in Canada 2008*.

SELECTED BIBLIOGRAPHY

Ahmad, Farah, Sheilah Hogg-Johnson, Donna E. Stewart, and Wendy Levinson. 2007. "Violence Involving Intimate Partners." *Canadian Family Physician* 53 (March): 461–68.

Aitken, Gail, and Andy Mitchell. 1995. "The Relationship Between Poverty and Child Health: Long-Range Implications." *Canadian Review of Social Policy*, 35 (Spring): 19–36.

Alaggia, Ramona, Angélique Jenney, Josephine Mazzuca, and Melissa Redmond. 2007. "In Whose Best Interest? A Canadian Case Study of the Impact of Child Welfare Policies in Cases of Domestic Violence." *Brief Treatment and Crisis Intervention* 7: 275–90.

Alaggia, Ramona, and Sarah Maiter. 2006. "Domestic Violence and Child Abuse: Issues for Immigrant and Refugee Families." In Ramona Alaggia and Cathy Vine (eds.), *Cruel But Not Unusual: Violence in Canadian Families*. Waterloo, ON: Wilfrid Laurier University Press. 99–126.

Anderson, Veanne N., Dorothy Simpson-Taylor, and Douglas J. Herrmann. 2004. "Gender, Age, and Rape-Supportive Rules." *Sex Roles* 50(1) (January): 77–90.

Aronson, Jane, Cindy Thomewell, and Karen Williams. 1995. "Wife Assault in Old Age: Coming Out of Obscurity." *Canadian Journal on Aging* 14(2) (supplement): 72–88.

Association for Women's Rights in Development. 2004. "Intersectionality: A Tool for Gender and Economic Justice. Toronto: Association for Women's Rights in Development.

AuCoin, Kathy. 2005. *Family Violence in Canada: A Statistical Profile*. Ottawa: Statistics Canada.

Badgley, Robin F. 1984. *Sexual Offences Against Children in Canada: Volumes 1, 2, and Summary*. Ottawa: Minister of Supply and Services.

Bagley, Christopher, and Kathleen King. 1990. *Child Sexual Abuse: The Search for Healing*. London: Tavistock/Routledge.

Baker, Amy J. L. 2005. "The Long-Term Effects of Parental Alienation on Adult Children: A Qualitative Research Study." *The American Journal of Family Therapy* 33: 289–302.

Baker, Maureen, ed. 1996. *Families: Changing Trends in Canada*. 3rd ed. Toronto: McGraw-Hill Ryerson.

Bala, Nicholas M. C., Mindy Mitnick, Nico Trocmé, and Claire Houston. 2007. "Sexual Abuse Allegations and Parental Separation: Smokescreen or Fire?" *Journal of Family Studies* 13(1): 26–56.

Bargh, John A., and Katelyn Y. A. McKenna. 2004. "The Internet and Social Life." *The Annual Review of Psychology* 55: 573–90.

Bartholomew, Kim, Katherine V. Regan, Monica A. White, and Doug Oram. 2008. "Patterns of Abuse in Male Same-Sex Relationships." *Violence and Victims* 23(5): 617–36.

Bartholomew, Kim, Katherine V. Regan, Doug Oram, and Monica A. White. 2008a. "Correlates of Partner Abuse in Male Same-Sex Relationships." *Violence and Victims* 23(3): 344–60.

Baskin, Cyndy. 2006. "Systemic Oppression, Violence, and Healing in Aboriginal Families and Communities." In Ramona Alaggia and Cathy Vine (eds.), *Cruel But Not Unusual: Violence in Canadian Families.* Waterloo, ON: Wilfrid Laurier University Press. 15–48.

Baxter, Kate, Eliza Sasakamoose, and Darlene Little. 1995. "Ducking Bullets." In Leslie Timmins (ed.), *Listening to the Thunder.* Vancouver: Women's Research Centre. 281–97.

Beaulieu, Marie. 1992. *Intervention for Victimized Elderly People.* (September). Association quebecois Plaidoyer-Victimes.

Bishop, Patricia. 1991. *Child Abuse: Emotional, Psychological and Sexual.* Toronto: Canadian Mental Health Association.

Bograd, Michele. 1988. "Feminist Perspectives on Wife Abuse: An Introduction." In Kersti Yllo and Michele Bograd (eds.), *Feminist Perspectives on Wife Abuse.* Newbury Park: Sage. 11–26.

Bograd, Michele. 1999. "Strengthening Domestic Violence Theories: Intersections of Race, Class, Sexual Orientation, and Gender." *Journal of Marital and Family Therapy* 25(3): 275–89.

Bond, Jr., John B., Roland L. Penner and Penny Yisllen. 1995. "Perceived Effectiveness of Legislation Concerning Abuse of the Elderly: A Survey of Professionals in Canada and the United States." *Canadian Journal on Aging* 14:2 (supplement): 118–35.

Bonisteel, Mandy, and Linda Green. 2005. "Implications of the Shrinking Space for Feminist Anti-Violence Advocacy." Conference paper presented at the 2005 Canadian Social Welfare Policy Conference, Forging Social Futures, Fredericton, New Brunswick.

Bowker, Lee H. 1993. "A Battered Woman's Problems Are Social, Not Psychological." In Richard Gelles and Donileen Loseke (eds.), *Current Controversies on Family Violence.* Newbury Park: Sage. 154–65.

Bowlus, Audra, Katherine McKenna, Tanis Day, and David Wright. 2003. *The Economic Costs and Consequences of Child Abuse in Canada.* Ottawa: Law Commission of Canada.

Briere, John, and Carol E. Jordan. 2004. "Violence Against Women: Outcome Complexity and Implications for Assessment and Treatment." *Journal of Interpersonal Violence* 19(11) (November): 1252–76.

Brinkerhoff, M., and E. Lupri. 1988. "Interspousal Violence." *Canadian Journal of Sociology* (13): 407–34.

Brownridge, Douglas A. 2006. "Partner Violence Against Women With Disabilities: Prevalence, Risk, and Explanations." *Violence Against Women* 12(9) (September): 805–22.

Brownridge, Douglas A., and Shiva Halli. 2000. "'Living in Sin' and Sinful Living: Toward Filling a Gap in the Explanation of Violence Against Women." *Aggression & Violent Behaviour* 5(6): 565–83.

———. 2001. "Marital Status as Differentiating Factor in Canadian Women's Coping with Partner Violence." *Journal of Comparative Family Studies* 32(1) (Winter): 117-25.

Cameron, Gary. 1989. "Community Development Principles and Helping Battered Women: A Summary Chapter." In Barbara Pressman, Gary Cameron, and Michael Rothery (eds.), *Intervening with Assaulted Women: Current Theory Research and Practice.* Hillsdale, New Jersey: Lawrence Erlbaum Associates. 157–65.

Campbell, Marcie, Peter Jaffe, and Tim Kelly. n.d. "What About the Men? Finding Effective

Strategies for Engaging Abusive Men and Preventing the Reoccurrence or Escalation of Violence Against Women." www.crvawc.ca/documents/United%20Way%20Write-Up.pdf. Accessed on November 14, 2010.

Caplan, Paula. 1985. *The Myth of Women's Masochism*. New York: E. P. Dutton.

Card, Claudia. 1995. *Lesbian Choices*. New York: Columbia University Press.

Cardozo, Andrew. 1996. "Domestic violence doesn't know any ethnic boundaries." *Toronto Star* (April 16): A21.

Carson, Ashley B. 2009. "Elder Abuse: A Women's Issue." *Elder Abuse: A Women's Issue— Mother's Day Report 2009*. Washington DC: OWL—The Voice of Midlife and Older Women.

Cartwright, Glenn F. 2002. "The Changing Face of Parental Alienation Syndrome." Paper presented at the Symposium: The Parliamentary Report For The Sake of the Children, Ottawa, April 5–6, 2002.

Choo, Hae Yeon, and Myra Marx Ferree. 2010. "Practicing Intersectionality in Sociological Research: A Critical Analysis of Inclusions, Interactions, and Institutions in the Study of Inequalities." *Sociological Theory* 28(2) (June): 129–49.

Cole, Susan G. 1988. "Child Battery." In Bonnie Fox (ed.), *Family Bonds and Gender Divisions*. Toronto: Canadian Scholars' Press Inc. 517–37.

Collin-Vézina, Delphine, Jacinthe Dion, and Nico Trocmé. 2009. "Sexual Abuse in Canadian Aboriginal Communities: A Broad Review of Conflicting Evidence." *Pimatisiwin: A Journal of Aboriginal and Indigenous Community Health* 7: 27–47.

Conry, Maura. 2009. "The Role of Medication Mismanagement in Abuse and Neglect." *Elder Abuse: A Women's Issue—Mother's Day Report 2009*. Washington DC: OWL—The Voice of Midlife and Older Women.

Conway, John F. 1993. *The Canadian Family in Crisis*. Revised Edition. Toronto: James Lorimer and Company Ltd.

Coomaraswamy, Radhika. 1995. "Some Reflections on Violence Against Women." *Canadian Woman Studies* 15(2–3) (Spring/Summer): 19–23.

Coser, Lewis. 1956. *The Functions of Social Conflict*. New York: Free Press.

Cottrell, Barbara. 2001. *Parent Abuse: The Abuse of Parents by Their Teenage Children*. Ottawa: Health Canada.

Cranswick, Kelly, and Donna Dosman. 2008. "Eldercare: What We Know Today." *Canadian Social Trends* Catalogue No. 11-008-X: 48–56.

Crichton-Hill, Yvonne, Nikki Evans, and Letitia Meadows. 2006. "Adolescent Violence Towards Parents." *Te Awatea Review* (December): 21–22.

Crook, Farrell. 1992. "Wife is acquitted in man's mutilation." *Toronto Star* (October 2): A4.

Cross, Pamela. 2001. "Ontario's Domestic Violence Protection Act: Will It Prevent Violence?" March 27. Ontario Women's Justice Network (www.owjn.org). Accessed on December 16, 2010.

Cunningham, Alison, and Linda Baker. 2004. *What About Me? Seeking to Understand a Child's View of Violence in the Family*. London, ON: Centre for Children & Families in the Justice System.

Currie, Cheryl L. 2006. "Animal Cruelty by Children Exposed to Domestic Violence." *Child Abuse & Neglect* 30: 425–35.

Davis, Kathy. 2008. "Intersectionality as Buzzword: A Sociology of Science Perspective on What Makes a Feminist Theory Successful." *Feminist Theory* 9(1): 67–85.

DeKeseredy, Walter S. 2007. Review of Donald G. Dutton's Rethinking Domestic Violence. *Canadian Journal of Sociology Online.* November. www.cjsonline.ca/ reviews/domesticviol. html. Accessed on February 10, 2010.

DeKeseredy, Walter S., and Ronald Hinch. 1991. *Woman Abuse: Sociological Perspectives.* Toronto: Thompson Educational Publishing.

DeKeseredy, Walter S., and Desmond Ellis. 1994. *Pretest Report on the Frequency, Severity and Patterning of Sibling Violence in Canadian Families.* Ottawa: Family Violence Prevention Division, Health Canada.

DeKeseredy, Walter S., Hyman Burshtyn, and Charles Gordon. 1995. "Taking Wife Abuse Seriously: A Critical Response to the Solicitor General of Canada's Crime Prevention Advice." In E. D. Nelson and Augie Fleras (eds.), *Social Problems in Canada Reader.* Scarborough: Prentice Hall Canada Inc. 67–69.

DeKeseredy, Walter S., and Martin D. Schwartz. 1998. "Measuring the Extent of Woman Abuse in Intimate Heterosexual Relationships: A Critique of the Conflict Tactics Scales." *National Online Resource Center on Violence Against Women* (www.vawnet.org). Accessed on February 10, 2010.

———. 2005. "Backlash and Whiplash: A Critique of Statistics Canada's 1999 General Social Survey on Victimization." http://sisyphe.org/articles.php3?id_article=1689. Accessed on November 24, 2009.

DeKeseredy, Walter S., and Molly Dragiewicz. 2007. "Understanding the Complexities of Feminist Perspectives on Woman Abuse." *Violence Against Women* 13(8) (August): 874–84.

Denham, Donna, and Joan Gillespie. 1996. "Ending violence against women and children requires new outlook." *Perception* 20(2) (Fall): 3.

Department of Justice. 2009. *Family Violence: Department of Justice Canada Overview Paper.* May. Ottawa: Department of Justice.

———. 2009. *Abuse of Older Adults: Department of Justice Canada Overview Paper.* June. Ottawa: Department of Justice.

———. 2003. *Dating Violence Fact Sheet. Ottawa: Department of Justice.* Accessed on March 16, 2010.

DiMaggio, Paul, Eszter Hargittai, W. Russell Neuman, and John P. Robinson. 2001. "Social Implications of the Internet." *Annual Review of Sociology:* 307–36.

Dobash, Russell P., and R. Emerson Dobash. 2004. "Women's Violence to Men in Intimate Relationships: Working on a Puzzle." *British Journal of Criminology* 44(3): 324–49.

Doherty, Deborah, and Dorothy Berglund. 2008. *Psychological Abuse: A Discussion Paper.* Ottawa: Minister of Health.

Drake, Betty, and Shanta Pandey. 1996. "Understanding the Relationship Between Neighbourhood Poverty and Specific Types of Child Maltreatment." *Child Abuse and Neglect* 20 (11): 1003–18.

263

Duffy, Ann, and Norene Pupo. 1992. *Part-time Paradox: Connecting Gender, Work & Family.* Toronto: McClelland & Stewart.

Dunsdon, Kelly. 1995. "Child Sexual Abuse: A Comparative Case Comment." *Canadian Journal of Family Law* 12(2): 441–56.

Durrant, Joan E. 2000. *A Generation Without Smacking: The Impact of Sweden's Ban on Physical Punishment.* London: Save the Children.

Dutton, Donald, G. 1995a. *The Batterer: A Psychological Profile.* New York: Basic Books.

———. 1995b. *The Domestic Assault of Women.* Vancouver: UBC Press.

Dutton, Donald G., Marilyn J. Kwong, and Kim Bartholomew. 1999. "Gender Differences in Patterns of Relationship Violence in Alberta." *Canadian Journal of Behavioural Science* 31(3): 150–60.

Duxbury, Linda, and Christopher Higgins. 1994. "Far lilies in the Economy." In Maureen Baker (ed.), *Canada's Changing Families: Challenges to Public Policy.* Ottawa: The Vanier Institute of the Family. 29–40.

Economy Watch. n.d. "Canada Economy." www.economywatch.com /world_economy/ canada. Accessed September 19, 2010.

Edelson, Jeffrey L., Zvi Eisikovits, and Edna Guttman. 1985. "Men Who Batter Women." *Journal of Family Issues* 6(2) (June): 229–47.

Educaloi. "Family Violence—Spousal Abuse and Family Violence." www.educaloi.qu.ca. Accessed on December 16, 2010.

Elizabeth Fry Society. 2010. Aboriginal Women. www.elizabethfry.ca/eweek2010e/pdf/ Aboriginal%20Women.pdf. Accessed on December 26, 2010.

Ellison, Nicole B., Charles Steinfield, and Cliff Lampe. 2007. "The Benefits of Facebook 'Friends': Social Capital and College Students' Use of Online Social Network Sites." *Journal of Computer-Mediated Communication* 12: 1143–68. Accessed on October 5, 2010.

Environics Research Group. 2008. *Awareness and Perceptions of Canadians Toward Elder Abuse.* Ottawa: Human Resources and Social Development Canada.

Family Violence in Canada: A Statistical Profile. 2006. Ottawa: Statistics Canada.

———. 2007. Ottawa: Statistics Canada.

———. 2008. Ottawa: Statistics Canada.

———. 2009. Ottawa: Statistics Canada.

Feder, Lynette, and Kris Henning. 2005. "A Comparison of Male and Female Dually Arrested Domestic Violence Offenders." *Violence and Victims* 20(2): 153–71.

Federal-Provincial Working Group on Child and Family Services Information. 1994. *Child Welfare in Canada: The Role of Provincial and Territorial Authories in Cases of Child Abuse.* Ottawa: Minister of Supply and Services.

Felson, Richard B., Jeff Ackerman, and Seong-Jim Yeon. 2003. "The Infrequency of Family Violence." *Journal of Marriage and Family* 65(3): 622–703.

Finkelhor, David, and Kersti Yllo. 1995. *License to Rape: Sexual Abuse of Wives*. New York: Free Press.

Finkelhor, David, Heather Turner, and Richard Ormrod. 2006. "Kid's Stuff: The Nature and Impact of Peer and Sibling Violence on Younger and Older Children." *Child Abuse & Neglect* 30: 1401–21.

Firestone, Shulamith. 1970. *The Dialectic of Sex*. New York: William Morrow and Company.

Flynn, Clifton P. 1999. "Exploring the Link Between Corporal Punishment and Children's Cruelty to Animals." *Journal of Marriage and the Family* 61(4): 971–81.

Foucault, Michel. 1979. *Discipline and Punish: The Birth of the Prison*. New York: Vintage Books.

Forrester, Trina. 2009. *Hidden From Sight: A Look at the Prevalence of Violence Against Women in Ottawa*. Ottawa: Ottawa Coalition to End Violence Against Women. www.octevaw-cocvff.ca/en/pdf/reports/Hidden_from_Sight.pdf. Accessed on September 14, 2010.

Fox, Greer Litton, and Velma McBride Murry. 2000. "Gender and Families: Feminist Perspectives and Family Research." *Journal of Marriage and the Family* 62(4) (November): 1160–72.

Gadd, Jane. 1997. "More boys physically abused than girls." *Globe and Mail* (July 9): Al, A6.

Gannon, Maire, and Jodi-Anne Brzozowski. 2004. "Sentencing in Cases of Family Violence." *Family Violence in Canada: A Statistical Profile* 2004: 53–67.

Garbarino, James. 1977. "The Human Ecology of Child Maltreatment: A Conceptual Model for Research." *Journal of Marriage and the Family* 39 (November): 721–35.

Garbarino, James, and Gwen Gilliam. 1980. *Understanding Abusive Families*. New York: Lexington Books.

Gardner, Richard A. 2002. "Parental Alienation Syndrome vs. Parental Alienation: Which Diagnosis Should Evaluators Use in Child-Custody Disputes?" *The American Journal of Family Therapy* 30(2): 93–115.

Geffner, Robert. 1995. "Editor addresses readers' concerns." *Family Violence and Sexual Assault Bulletin* 11(3–4) (Fall/Winter): 29–32.

Gelles, Richard J. 1993. "Through a Sociological Lens: Social Structure and Family Violence." In Richard J. Gelles and Donileen R. Loseke (eds.), *Current Controversies on Family Violence*. Newbury Park: Sage. 31–46.

Gelles, Richard J., and Claire P. Cornell. 1990. *Intimate Violence in Families*. 2nd ed. Newbury Park: Sage.

Gelles, Richard J., and Murray A. Straus. 1988. *Intimate Violence*. New York: Simon and Schuster Inc.

Genuis, Mark, B. Thomlison, and C. Bagley. 1991. "Male Victims of Child Sexual Abuse: A Brief Overview of Pertinent Findings." *Journal of Child and Youth Care* (Fall): 1–6.

Gil, David G. 1980. "Unraveling Child Abuse." In J. Cook and R. Bowles (eds.), *Child Abuse: Commission and Omission*. Toronto: Butterworths. 119–28.

Gillis, J. Roy, and Shaindl Diamond. 2006. "Same-sex Partner Abuse: Challenges to the

Existing Paradigms of Intimate Violence Theory." In Ramona Alaggia and Cathy Vine (eds.), *Cruel But Not Unusual: Violence in Canadian Families*. Waterloo, ON: Wilfrid Laurier University Press. 127–44.

Gnaedinger, Nancy. 1989. *Elder Abuse: A Discussion Paper*. Ottawa: National Clearinghouse on Family Violence.

Goffman, Erving. 1963. *Stigma: Notes on the Management of Spoiled Identity*. New York: Simon & Schuster, Inc.

Gold, Svea J. 1986. *When Children Invite Child Abuse*. Eugene, Oregon: Fern Ridge Press.

Goldner, Virginia, Peggy Perm, Marcia Sheinberg, and Gillian Walker. 1990. "Love and Violence: Gender Paradoxes in Volatile Attachments." *Family Process* 29(4): 343–64.

Goldstein, Stanley E., and Arthur Blank. 1988. "The elderly: abuse or abusers." In Benjamin Schlesinger and Rachel Schlesinger (eds.), *Abuse of the Elderly: Issues and Annotated Bibliography*. Toronto: University of Toronto Press. 86–90.

Gondolf, Edward W. 1995. "Gains and Process in State Batterer Programs and Standards." *Family Violence and Sexual Assault Bulletin* 11(3–4) (Fall/Winter): 27–28.

Gonzalez, Miriam, Joan E. Durrant, Martin Chabot, Nico Trocmé, and Jason Brown. 2008. "What Predicts Injury From Physical Punishment? A Test of the Typologies of Violence Hypothesis." *Child Abuse & Neglect* 32: 752–65.

Goodman, Marilyn S. 1990. "Pattern Changing: An Approach to the Abused Woman's Problem." *Family Violence Bulletin* 6(4) (Winter): 14–15.

Goodwin, Megan P., and Bruce Rosco. 1990. "Sibling Violence and Agonistic Interactions Among Middle Adolescents." *Adolescence* XXV(98) (Summer): 451–67.

Government of Canada. 1992. *Family Violence in Canada: A Call to Action*. Ottawa: Minister of Supply and Services.

Gracia, Enrique, and Juan Herrero. 2008. "Is It Considered Violence? The Acceptability of Physical Punishment of Children in Europe." *Journal of Marriage and the Family* 70 (February): 210–17.

Greven, Philip. 1990. *Spare the Child: The Religious Roots of Punishment and the Psychological Impact of Physical Abuse*. New York: Alfred A. Knopf.

Griffiths, C. T., and J. C. Yerbury. 1995. "Native Indian Victims in Canada: Issues in Policy and Program Delivery." In E. D. Nelson and Augie Fleras (eds.), *Social Problems in Canada Reader*. Scarborough, ON: Prentice Hall Canada Inc. 124–35.

Gurr, Jane, Michelle Pajot, David Nobbs, Louise Mailloux, and Dianne Archambault. 2008. *Breaking the Links Between Poverty and Violence Against Women*. Ottawa: Public Health Agency of Canada.

Gurr, Jane, Louise Mailloux, Diane Kinnon, and Suzanne Doerge. 1996. *Breaking the Links Between Poverty and Violence Against Women*. Ottawa: Ministry of Supply and Services Canada.

Hackett, Karen. 2000. "Criminal Harassment." *Juristat* 20(11): 1–17.

Haight, Wendy L., Woochan S. Shim, Linda M. Linn, and Laura Swinford. 2007. "Mothers' Strategies for Protecting Children from Batterers: The Perspectives of Battered Women Involved in Child Protective Services." *Child Welfare* 86(4) (July/August): 41–62.

Hanes, Tracy. 1994. "Women's shelter counts up its victories." *Toronto Star* (September 9): Cl, C3.

Hannah-Moffat, K. 1995. "To Charge or Not to Charge: Front Line Officers' Perceptions of Mandatory Charge Policies." In Mariana Valverde, Linda MacLeod, and Kirsten Johnson (eds.), *Wife Assault and the Canadian Criminal Justice System: Issues and Policies.* Toronto: Centre of Criminology, University of Toronto. 35–61.

Harbison, Joan, Pam McKinley, and Donna Pettipas. 2006. "Older People as Objects Not Subjects: Theory and Practice in Situations of 'Elder Abuse'." In Ramona Alaggia and Cathy Vine (eds.), *Cruel But Not Unusual: Violence in Canadian Families.* Waterloo, ON: Wilfrid Laurier University Press. 467–502.

Harman, Lesley D. 1995. "Family Poverty and Economic Stuggles." In Nancy Mandell and Ann Duffy (eds.), *Families: Diversity, Conflict and Change.* Toronto: Harcourt Brace & Company, Canada. 235–69.

Harrison, Deborah, and Lucie Laliberte. 1994. *No Life Like It: Military Wives in Canada.* Toronto: James Lorimer and Company Ltd.

Hayes, Jasmine, Nico Trocmé, and Angélique Jenney. 2006. "Children's Exposure to Domestic Violence." In Ramona Alaggia and Cathy Vine (eds.), *Cruel But Not Unusual: Violence in Canadian Families.* Waterloo, ON: Wilfrid Laurier University Press. 201–35.

Health Canada. 1994. *Canada's Treatment Programs for Men Who Abuse their Partners.* Ottawa: Ministry of Supply and Services Canada.

———. 1996. *Breaking the Links Between Poverty and Violence Against Women.* Ottawa: Ministry of Supply and Services Canada.

Hegarty, Kelsey, Robert Bush, and Mary Sheehan. 2005. "The Composite Abuse Scale: Further Development and Assessment of Reliability and Validity of a Multidimensional Partner Abuse Measure in Clinical Settings." *Violence and Victims* 20(5): 529–47.

Hindberg, Barbro. 2001. *Ending Corporal Punishment: Swedish Experience of Efforts to Prevent All Forms of Violence Against Children—and the Results.* January. Sweden: Ministry of Health and Social Affairs, Sweden; Ministry for Foreign Affairs, Sweden.

Hoff, Lee Ann. 1990. *Battered Women as Survivors.* London: Routledge.

Hotaling, G. T., and D. B. Sugarman. 1986. "An analysis of risk markers in husband-wife violence: The current state of knowledge." *Violence and Victims* 1: 101–24.

Hudson, J. Edward. 1988. "Elder Abuse: An Overview." In Benjamin Schlesinger and Rachel Schlesinger (eds.), *Abuse of the Elderly: Issues and Annotated Bibliography.* Toronto: University of Toronto Press. 12–31.

Jaffe, Peter G., David A. Wolfe, and Susan Kaye Wilson. 1990. *Children of Battered Women.* Newbury Park: Sage.

Jamieson, Wanda, and Lee Gomes. 2010. *Family Violence Initiative: Performance Report for April 2004 to March 2008.* Ottawa: National Clearinghouse on Family Violence.

Jasinski, Jana L. 2004. "Pregnancy and Domestic Violence: A Review of the Literature." *Trauma, Violence & Abuse* 5(1) (January): 47–64.

Johnson, Holly. 1995. "Response to Allegations About the Violence Against Women Survey." In Mariana Valverde, Linda MacLeod, and Kirsten Johnson (eds.), *Wife Assault and the*

Canadian Criminal Justice System. Toronto: Centre of Criminology, University of Toronto. 148–56.

———. 1996. *Dangerous Domains: Violence Against Women in Canada*. Toronto: Nelson.

———. 2000. "The Role of Alcohol in Male Partners' Assaults on Wives." *Journal of Drug Issues* 30(4): 725–40.

———. 2003. "The Cessation of Assaults on Wives." *Journal of Comparative Family Studies* 34(1): 75–91.

Johnson, Holly, and Valerie Pottie Bunge. 2001. "Prevalence and Consequences of Spousal Assault in Canada." *Canadian Journal of Criminology* 43(1): 27–45.

Johnson, John M. 1989. "Horror Stories and the Construction of Child Abuse." In Joel Best (ed.), *Images of Issues: Typifying Contemporary Social Problems*. New York: Aldine de Gruyter. 5–19.

Johnson, Michael P. 2006. "Conflict and Control: Gender Symmetry and Asymmetry in Domestic Violence." *Violence Against Women* 12(11) (November): 1003–18.

Johnson, Michael P., and Kathleen J. Ferraro. 2000. "Research on Domestic Violence in the 1990s: Making Distinctions." *Journal of Marriage and the Family* 62(4): 948–63.

Jones, Ann. 1996. "'Domestic Violence' Is Not Clearly Defined." In A. E. Sadler (ed.), *Current Controversies: Family Violence*. San Diego, CA: Greenhaven Press. 17–21.

Kaufman, Michael. 1987. 'The Construction of Masculinity and the Triad of Men's Violence." In Michael Kaufman (ed.), *Beyond Patriarchy: Essays by Men on Pleasure, Power, and Change*. Toronto: Oxford University Press. 1–29.

Kaukinen, Catherine. 2004. "Status Compatibility, Physical Violence, and Emotional Abuse in Intimate Relationships." *Journal of Marriage and the Family* 66(2): 452–71.

Kelly, Joan B., and Michael P. Johnson. 2008. "Differentiation Among Types of Intimate Partner Violence: Research Update and Implications for Interventions." *Family Court Review* 46(3) (July): 476–99.

Kelly, Ryan. August 12, 2009. "Twitter Study—August 2009." www.pearanalytics.com /blog/ wp-content/uploads/2010/05/Twitter-Study-August-2009.pdf. Accessed on April 16, 2011.

Kelly, Ursula A., Rosa M. Gonzalez-Guarda, and Janette Taylor. 2011. "Theories of Intimate Partner Violence." In Janice Humphreys and Jacquelyn C. Campbell (eds.), *Family Violence and Nursing Practice*. 2nd ed. New York: Springer Publishing Company, LLC. 51–90.

Kempe, C. Henry et al. 1980. "The Battered Child Syndrome." In J. V. Cook and R. T. Bowles, *Child Abuse: Commission and Omission*. Toronto: Butterworths. 49–61.

Kennedy, Leslie W., and Donald G. Dutton. 1989. "The Incidence of Wife Assault in Alberta." *Canadian Journal of Behavioural Science* 21(1): 40–54.

Kirkland, K. 2004. *Abuse in Gay Male Relationships: A Discussion Paper*. Ottawa: National Clearinghouse on Family Violence.

Kiselica, Mark S. and Mandy Morrill-Richards. 2007. "Sibling Maltreatment: The Forgotten Abuse." *Journal of Counseling and Development* 85(2): 148–61.

Knudsen, Dean. 1992. *Child Maltreatment: Emerging Perspectives*. Dix Hills, New York: General Hall, Inc.

Knudsen, Susanne V. 2006. "Intersectionality—A Theoretical Inspiration in the Analysis of Minority Cultures and Identities in Textbooks." www.caen.iufm.fr /colloque_iartem/pdf/ knudsen.pdf. Accessed on October 20, 2010.

Koziol-McLain, Jane, Daniel Webster, Judith McFarlane, and Carolyn Rebecca Block. 2006. "Risk Factors for Femicide-Suicide in Abusive Relationships: Results from a Multisite Case Control Study." *Violence and Victims* 21(1): 3–21.

Krishnan, Vijaya, and Kenneth B. Morrison. 1995. "An Ecological Model of Child Maltreatment in a Canadian Province." *Child Abuse and Neglect* 19(1): 101–13.

Kryk, Vicki. 1995. "Three Case Studies of Elder Mistreatment: Identifying Ethical Issues." *Journal of Elder Abuse and Neglect* 7(2–3): 19–30.

Kuypers, Joseph A. 1992. *Man's Will to Hurt*. Toronto: Fernwood.

La Novara, Pina. 1993. *A Portrait of Families in Canada*. Ottawa: Minister of Industry, Science and Technology.

Laporte, Lise, Depeng Jiang, Debra J. Pepler, and Claire Chamberland. 2009. "The Relationship Between Adolescents' Experience of Family Violence and Dating Violence." *Youth & Society* 43(1) (March 2011): 3–27.

LaRocque, Emma D. 1994. *Violence in Aboriginal Communities*. Ottawa: Royal Commission on Aboriginal Peoples.

Larzelere, Robert E. 1994. "Should the Use of Corporal Punishment by Parents be Considered Child Abuse? No." In M A. Mason and E. Gambrill (eds.), *Debating Children's Lives*. Newbury Park: Sage. 204–209.

Lasch, Christopher. 1977. *Haven in a Heartless World*. New York: Basic Books, Inc.

Lavergne, Chantal, Sarah Dufour, Nico Trocmé, and Marie-Claude Larrivée. 2008. "Visible Minority, Aboriginal, and Caucasian Children Investigated by Canadian Protective Services." *Child Welfare* 87(2): 59–76.

Lenton, Rhonda L. 1990. "Techniques of child discipline and abuse by parents." *Canadian Review of Sociology and Anthropology* 27(2) (May): 157–85.

Lerner, Gerda. 1986. *The Creation of Patriarchy*. New York: Oxford University Press.

Leroux, Thomas G., and Michael Petrunik. 1990. "The Construction of Elder Abuse as a Social Problem: A Canadian Perspective." *International Journal of Health Services* 20:4: 651–63.

Letourneau, N. L., C. B. Fedick, and J. D. Willms. 2007. "Mothering and Domestic Violence: A Longitudinal Analysis." *Journal of Family Violence* 22(8): 649–59.

Lew, Mike. 1990. *Victims No Longer*. New York: Harper and Row.

Liddle, A. Mark. 1989. "Feminist Contributions to an Understanding of Violence against Women—Three Steps Forward, Two Steps Back." Canadian Review of Sociology and Anthropology 26(5) (November): 758–75.

Litwin, Howard, and Sameer Zoabi. 2003. "A Multivariate Examination of Explanations for the Occurrence of Elder Abuse." *Research on Aging* 25(3): 224–46.

Loseke, Donileen R. and Demie Kurz. 2005. "Men's Violence Toward Women Is the Serious

Social Problem." In Donileen R. Loseke, Richard J. Gelles, and Mary M. Cavanaugh (eds.), *Current Controversies on Family Violence.* 2nd ed. Thousand Oaks, CA: Sage Publications. 79–95.

Lupri, Eugen, Elaine Grandin, and Merlin B. Brinkerhoff. 1994. "Socioeconomic Status and Male Violence in the Canadian Home: A Re-examination." *Canadian Journal of Sociology* 19(1): 47–73.

Luxton, Meg. 1988. "Thinking About the Future." In K. Anderson (ed.), *Family Matters: Sociology and Contemporary Family Matters.* Scarborough: Nelson Canada. 237–60.

Lynn, Marion, and Eimear O'Neill. 1995. "Families, Power, and Violence." In Nancy Mandell and Ann Duffy (eds.), *Canadian Families: Diversity, Conflict and Change.* Toronto: Harcourt Brace & Company, Canada. 271–305.

MacDonald, John A. 1995. "The Program of the Spallumcheen Indian Band in British Columbia as a Model of Indian Child Welfare." In R. B. Blake and J. Keshen (eds.), *Social Welfare Policy in Canada: Historical Readings.* Toronto: Copp Clark Ltd. 380–91.

Mackie, Marlene. 1991. *Gender Relations in Canada: Further Explorations.* Toronto: Butterworths.

MacLean, Michael J., ed. 1995. *Abuse and Neglect of Older Canadians: Strategies for Change.* Toronto: Thompson Educational Publishing, Inc.

MacLeod, Linda. 1994. *Understanding and Charting Our Progress Toward the Prevention of Woman Abuse.* Ottawa: Minister of Supply and Services.

———. 1995a. "Expanding the Dialogue: Report of a Workshop to Explore the Criminal Justice System Response to Violence Against Women." In M. Valverde, L. MacLeod, and K. Johnson (eds.), *Wife Assault and the Canadian Criminal Justice System: Issues and Policies.* Toronto: Centre of Criminology, University of Toronto. 10–32.

———. 1980. *Wife Battering in Canada: The Vicious Circle.* Ottawa: Canadian Advisory Council on the Status of Women.

———. 1987. *Battered But Not Beaten...: Preventing Wife Battering in Canada.* Ottawa: Canadian Advisory Council on the Status of Women.

MacLeod, Linda, and Cheryl Picard. 1989. "Towards a More Effective Criminal Justice Response to Wife Assault: Exploring the Limits and Potential of Effective Intervention." Working Paper. Ottawa: Department of Justice Canada.

MacMillan, Ross, and Rosemary Gartner. 1999. "When She Brings Home the Bacon: Labor-Force Participation and the Risk of Spousal Violence against Women." *Journal of Marriage and the Family* 61(4): 947–58.

Makin, Kirk. 2008. "Judge Rules Father Brainwashed Son Into Hating Mother." *Globe and Mail,* May 15. www.theglobeandmail.com. Accessed September 16, 2008.

Makinen, Gail. 2002. *The Economic Effects of 9/11: A Retrospective Assessment.* Congressional Research Service: Library of Congress. Accessed on April 15, 2011.

Mandell, Nancy, ed. 1995. *Feminist Issues.* Scarborough: Prentice Hall, Inc.

Manion, Ian G., and Susan Kay Wilson. 1995. *An Examination of the Association Between Histories of Maltreatment and Adolescent Risk Behaviours.* Ottawa: Minister of Supply and Services.

Mann, Ruth M. 2007. "Intimate Violence in Canada: Policy, Politics, and Research on Gender and Perpetration/Victimization." In Les Samuelson and Wayne Antony (eds.), *Power & Resistance: Critical Thinking About Canadian Social Issues.* 4th ed., Black Point, NS: Fernwood Publishing. 50–74.

Mardorossian, Carine M. 2002. "Toward a New Feminist Theory of Rape." *Signs: Journal of Women in Culture and Society* 27(3): 743–75.

Margolin, Leslie. 1992. "Beyond Maternal Blame." *Journal of Family Issues* 13(3) (September): 410–23.

Mathews, Benjamin P., and Donald C. Bross. 2008. "Mandated reporting is still a policy with reason: empirical evidence and philosophical grounds." *Child Abuse and Neglect* 32(5): 511–16.

McAteer, Michael. 1995. "Churches probe roots of domestic violence." *Toronto Star* (June 17): K16.

McCallum, Maureen, and Al Lauzon. 2005. "If There's No Mark, There's No Crime." *Canadian Woman Studies* 24(4): 130–35.

McDonald, Lynn, and Blossom Wigdor. 1995. "Editorial: Taking Stock: Elder Abuse Research in Canada." *Canadian Journal on Aging* 14(2) (supplement): 1–13.

McDonald, P. Lynn, Joseph P. Hornick, Gerald B. Robertson, and Jean E. Wallace. 1991. *Elder Abuse and Neglect in Canada.* Toronto: Butterworths.

McDonald, Lynn, April Collins, and Julie Dergal. 2006. "The Abuse and Neglect of Older Adults in Canada." In Ramona Alaggia and Cathy Vine (eds.), *Cruel But Not Unusual: Violence in Canadian Families.* Waterloo, ON: Wilfrid Laurier University Press. 425–66.

McEvoy, Maureen, and Judith Daniluk. 1995. "Wounds of the Soul: The Experience of Aboriginal Women Survivors of Sexual Abuse." *Canadian Psychology* 36(3): 221–35.

McGillivray, Anne, and Joan E. Durrant. 2006. "Child Corporal Punishment: Violence, Law, and Rights." In Ramona Alaggia and Cathy Vine (eds.), *Cruel But Not Unusual: Violence in Canadian Families.* Waterloo, ON: Wilfrid Laurier University Press. 177–200.

McHutchion, John. 1997. "Canada tops U.S. in unaligned directors." *Toronto Star* (February 7): E3.

McInnes, Elspeth. 2003. "Parental Alienation Syndrome: A Paradigm for Child Abuse in Australian Family Law." Paper presented at the Child Sexual Abuse: Justice Response or Alternative Resolution Conference convened by the Australian Institute of Criminology and held in Adelaide, 1–2 May 2003.

Merkle, Erich R., and Rhonda A. Richardson. 2000. "Digital Dating and Virtual Relating: Conceptualizing Computer Mediated Romantic Relationships." *Family Relations* 49(2): 187–92.

Messerschmidt, James W. 1993. *Masculinities and Crime: Critique and Reconceptualization of Theory.* Lanham, MD: Rowman & Littlefield Publishers, Inc.

Meszaros, Peggy S. 2004. "The Wired Family: Living Digitally in the Postinformation Age." *American Behavioral Scientist* 48(4) (December): 377–90.

MetLife Mature Market Institute. 2009. *Broken Trust: Elders, Family, and Finances.* Westport CT: MetLife Mature Market Institute.

Michalski, Joseph H. 2004. "Making Sociological Sense Out of Trends in Intimate Partner Violence." *Violence Against Women* 10(6) (June): 652–75.

Miller, Alice. 1981. *The Drama of the Gifted Child.* New York: Basic Books.

———. 1983. *For Your Own Good: Hidden Cruelty in Child-Rearing and the Roots of Violence.* New York: Farrar, Straus, Giroux.

Miller, Leslie. 1990. "Violent Families and the Rhetoric of Harmony." *British Journal of Sociology* 41(2) (June): 263–88.

Mills, C. Wright. 1959. *The Sociological Imagination.* New York: Oxford University Press.

Minaker, Joanne C., and Laureen Snider. 2006. "Husband Abuse: Equality With a Vengeance?" *Canadian Journal of Criminology and Criminal Justice* 48(5) (September): 735–52.

Ministry of Children and Youth Services, July 2005. www.cdrcp.com/pdf/CWTransformation-FINAL-rev'd%20July%2011.ek.pdf. Accessed on December 1, 2010.

Mones, Paul. 1991. *When a Child Kills: Abused Children Who Kill Their Parents.* New York: Pocket Books.

Moore, Timothy E., Debra Pepler, Reet Mae, and Michele Kates. 1989. "Effects of Family Violence on Children: New Directions for Research and Intervention." In Barbara Pressman, Gary Cameron, and Michael Rothery (eds.), *Intervening with Assaulted Women: Current Theory, Research and Practice.* Hillsdale, New Jersey: Lawrence Erlbaum Associates. 75–91.

Moore, Todd M., and Gregory L. Stuart. 2005. "A Review of the Literature on Masculinity and Partner Violence." *Psychology of Men and Masculinity* 6(1): 46–61.

Morrow, Marina, Olena Hankivsky, and Colleen Varcoe. 2004. "Women and Violence: The Effects of Dismantling the Welfare State." *Critical Social Policy Ltd.* 24(3): 358–84.

Muller, Robert T. 1995. "The Interaction of Parent and Child Gender in Physical Child Maltreatment." *Canadian Journal of Behavioural Science* 27(4): 450–65.

National Clearinghouse on Family Violence. 1986. *Abuse and Neglect of the Elderly.* Ottawa: Minister of Supply and Services.

———. 1994. *Summaries of Projects Funded in Aboriginal Communities (1986–1991).* Ottawa: Minister of Supply and Services.

———. 2002. *Family Violence and People With Intellectual Disabilities.* Ottawa: Public Works and Government Services Canada.

———. 2004a. *Intimate Partner Abuse Against Men.* Ottawa: Public Works and Government Services Canada.

———. 2006. *Child Sexual Abuse.* Ottawa: Minister of Health.

———. 2008. *Transition Houses and Shelters for Abused Women in Canada.* Ottawa: Minister of Public Works and Government Services Canada.

———. 2008. *Canada's Treatment Programs for Men Who Abuse Their Partners.* Ottawa: Public Works and Government Services Canada.

———. 2009. *Federal Elder Abuse Initiative.* July. Ottawa: Public Health Agency of Canada. Accessed on November 21, 2010.

———. 2009. *Domestic Violence Courts in Canada*. E-Bulletins, March. Accessed on November 21, 2010.

———. 2010a. *Engaging Men & Boys in Family Violence Prevention*. E-Bulletins, January. Accessed November 21, 2010.

———. 2010b. "Social Media in Elder Abuse Prevention." E-Bulletins, September. Ottawa: Public Health Agency of Canada. Accessed on January 1, 2011.

———. 2010c. Family Violence Initiative Performance Report for April 2004 to March 2008. Ottawa: National Clearinghouse on Family Violence.

National Council of Welfare. 1997. *Poverty Profile 1995*. Ottawa: Minister of Supply and Services.

Nemr, Racha. 2009. "Fact Sheet: Police-Reported Family Violence Against Children and Youth." *Family Violence in Canada: A Statistical Profile* Catalogue no. 85-224-X: 32–42.

Northrup, David A. 1997. "The Problem of the Self-Report in Survey Research." *Institute for Social Research Newsletter* 12(1) (Winter): 1–2.

Nwosu, L. Ngozi. 2006. "The Experience of Domestic Violence Among Nigerian-Canadian Women in Toronto." *Canadian Woman Studies* 25(1–2): 99–106.

O'Neill, John. 1994. *The Missing Child in Liberal Theory*. Toronto: University of Toronto Press.

One Voice, the Canadian Seniors Network. 1995. *National Action Plan to Reduce the Abuse of Older Adults in Canada*. Ottawa: One Voice, the Canadian Seniors Network.

Orenchuk-Tomiak, Natalie, Gemma Matthey, and Carole Christensen. 1989. "The Resolution Model: A Response to the Treatment of Child Sexual Abuse." *SIECCAN Journal* 4(4) (September): 3–10.

Paintal, Sureshrani. 2007. "Banning Corporal Punishment of Children: An ACEI Position Paper." *Childhood Education* 83(6): 410–13.

Painter, Susan Lee, and Don Dutton. 1985. "Patterns of Emotional Bonding." *International Journal of Women's Studies* 8(4): 363–75.

Payne, Brian K., and Richard Cikovic. 1995. "An Empirical Examination of the Characteristics, Consequences, and Causes of Elder Abuse in Nursing Homes." *Journal of Elder Abuse and Neglect* 7(4): 51–74.

Peterman, Linda M., and Charlotte G. Dixon. 2003. "Domestic Violence Between Same-Sex Partners: Implications for Counseling." *Journal of Counseling and Development* 81(1): 40–47.

Pillemer, Karl. 1993. "The Abused Offspring Are Dependent: Abuse Is Caused by the Deviance and Dependence of Abusive Caregivers." In Richard J. Gelles and Donileen R. Loseke (eds.), *Current Controversies on Family Violence*. Newbury Park, CA: Sage Publications. 237–49.

Pillemer, Karl, and David Finkelhor. 1988. "The Prevalence of Elder Abuse: A Random Sample Survey." *Gerontologist* 28(1): 51–57.

Pillemer, Karl, and David W. Moore. 1990. "Highlights from a Study of Abuse of Patients in Nursing Homes." *Journal of Elder Abuse and Neglect* 2(1): 5–29.

Pinheiro, Paulo Sérgio. 2006. *World Report on Violence Against Children*. Geneva: United Nations.

273

Pittaway, Elizabeth Dow, Anne Westhues, and Tracy Peressini. 1995. "Risk Factors for Abuse and Neglect Among Older Adults." *Canadian Journal on Aging* 14(2) (supplement): 20–44.

Pleck, Elizabeth. 1987. *Domestic Tyranny*. New York: Oxford University Press.

Pleck, Joseph H. [1974] 1995. "Men's Power With Women, Other Men and Society: A Men's Movement in Analysis." In Michael S. Kimmel and Michael A. Messner (eds.), *Men's Lives*. 3rd ed. Boston: Allyn and Bacon. 5–12.

Podnieks, Elizabeth. 1988. "Elder abuse: it's time we did something about it." In Benjamin Schlesinger and Rachel Schlesinger (eds.), *Abuse of the Elderly: Issues and Annotated Bibliography*. Toronto: University of Toronto Press. 32–44.

———. 1992. "The Lived Experience of Abused Older Women." *Canadian Woman Studies* 12(2): 38–44.

———. 2008. "Elder Abuse: The Canadian Experience." *Journal of Elder Abuse & Neglect* 20(2): 126–50.

Podnieks, Elizabeth, Karl Pillemer, J. Phillip Nicholson, Thomas Shillington, and Alan Frizzel. 1990. *National Survey on Abuse of the Elderly in Canada*. Toronto: Ryerson Polytechnical Institute.

Pope, Al. 2004. "B.C. Court Ignores Aboriginal Women's Plea." *Canadian Dimension* 38(3): 10–11.

Pressman, Barbara. 1989. "Treatment of Wife Abuse: The Case for Feminist Therapy." In Barbara Pressman, Gary Cameron, and Michael Rothery (eds.), *Intervening with Assaulted Women: Current Theory, Research and Practice*. Hillsdale, New Jersey: Lawrence Erlbaum Associates. 21–45.

Pressman, Barbara, and Michael Rothery. 1989. "Introduction: Implications of Assaults Against Women for Professional Helpers." In Barbara Pressman, Gary Cameron, and Michael Rothery (eds.), *Intervening with Assaulted Women: Current Theory, Research and Practice*. Hillsdale, New Jersey: Lawrence Erlbaum Associates. 1–19.

Price, E. Lisa, E. Sandra Byers, Heather A. Sears, John Whelan, and Marcelle Saint-Pierre. 2000. "Dating Violence Amongst New Brunswick Adolescents: A Summary of Two Studies." *Research Paper Series Number 2*, January. University of New Brunswick: Muriel McQueen Fergusson Centre for Family Violence Research.

Pron, Nick. 1997. "Custody is child abuse dilemma, Ecker says." *Toronto Star* (April 24): A2.

Public Health Agency of Canada. 2010. *Canadian Incidence Study of Reported Child Abuse and Neglect—2008: Major Findings*. Ottawa: Public Health Agency of Canada.

Pupo, Norene. 1997. "Always Working, Never Done: The Expansion of the Double Day." In A. Duffy, D. Glenday and N. Pupo (eds.), *Good Jobs, Bad Jobs, No Jobs*. Toronto: Harcourt Brace. 144–65.

Quann, Nathalie. 2006. *Offender Profile and Recidivism among Domestic Violence Offenders in Ontario*. Ottawa: Department of Justice.

Radbill, Samuel X. 1980. "Children in a World of Violence: A History of Child Abuse." In C. Henry Kempe and Ray E. Heifer (eds.), *The Battered Child*. 3rd ed. Chicago: University of Chicago Press. 3–20.

Ramsey-Klawsnik, Holly, and Bonnie Brandl. 2009. "Sexual Abuse in Later Life." *Sexual*

Assault Report (July/August): 1–4.

Rajan, Doris. 2004. *Violence Against Women with Disabilities*. Ottawa: National Clearinghouse on Family Violence, Public Works and Government Services.

Renzetti, Claire M. 1992. *Violent Betrayal: Partner Abuse in Lesbian Relationships*. Newbury Park: Sage.

Ristock, Janice L. 2002. *No More Secrets: Violence in Lesbian Relationships*. New York: Routledge.

Rossman, B. B. Robbie. 1994. "Children in Violent Families: Current Diagnostic and Treatment Considerations." *Family Violence and Sexual Assault Bulletin* 10 (3–4): 29–34.

Royal Canadian Mounted Police. 2007. *Stalking: It's NOT Love*. Ottawa: Government of Canada.

Ruby, Clayton. 1996. "Spousal abuse: Establishment agenda just won't work." *Toronto Star* (November 16): D3.

Rush, Florence. 1980. *The Best Kept Secret: Sexual Abuse of Children*. Englewood Cliffs, New Jersey: Prentice-Hall, Inc.

Saewyc, Elizabeth M., Carol L. Skay, Sandra L. Pettingell, and Elizabeth A. Reis. 2006. "Hazards of Stigma: the Sexual and Physical Abuse of Gay, Lesbian, and Bisexual Adolescents in the United States and Canada." *Child Welfare* 85(2): 195–214.

Sauvé, Julia, and Mike Burns. 2009. "Residents of Canada's Shelters for Abused Women, 2008."

Juristat 29(2) (May) Catalogue no. 85-002-X: 1–21.

Scheff, Thomas. 1990. *Microsociology: Emotion, Discourse, and Social Structure*. Chicago: University of Chicago Press.

Schlesinger, Rachel. 1988. "Grannybashing." In Benjamin Schlesinger and Rachel Schlesinger (eds.), *Abuse of the Elderly: Issues and Annotated Bibliography*. Toronto: University of Toronto Press. 3–11.

Segal, Uma. A. 1995. "Child Abuse by the Middle Class? A Study of Professionals in India." *Child Abuse and Neglect* 19 (2): 217–31.

Sev'er, Aysan. 2009. "More Than Wife Abuse That Has Gone Old: A Conceptual Model for Violence against the Aged in Canada and the US." *Journal of Comparative Family Studies* 40(2): 279–92.

Sinclair, Judge Murray, Donna Phillips, and Nicholas Bala. 1996. "Aboriginal Child Welfare in Canada." In N. Bala, J. Hornick, and R. Vogl (eds.), *Canadian Child Welfare Law*. Toronto: Thomson Educational Publishing, Inc. 171–94.

Smith, M. D. 1987. "The Incidence and Prevalence of Woman Abuse in Toronto." *Violence and Victims* 2(3): 173–87.

————. 1990a. "Patriarchal Ideology and Wife Beating: A Test of a Feminist Hypothesis." *Violence and Victims* 5(4): 257–73.

————. 1990b. "Sociodemographic Risk Factors in Wife Abuse: Results from a Survey of Toronto Women." *Canadian Journal of Sociology* 15(1): 39–58.

————. 1994. "Enhancing the Quality of Survey Data on Violence Against Women: A Feminist Approach." *Gender and Society* 8(1) (March): 109–27.

Sobsey, Richard, and Sonia A. Sobon. 2006. "Violence, Protection, and Empowerment in the Lives of Children and Adults With Disabilities." In Ramona Alaggia and Cathy Vine (eds.), *Cruel But Not Unusual: Violence in Canadian Families*. Waterloo, ON: Wilfrid Laurier University Press. 49–78.

Spangler, Deb, and Bonnie Brandl. 2007. "Abuse in Later Life: Power and Control Dynamics and a Victim-Centered Response." *Journal of the American Psychiatric Nurses Association* 12(6): 322–31.

Statistics Canada. 1993. *The Violence Against Women Survey*. The Daily. November 18. Ottawa: Statistics Canada.

————. 2000. *Family Violence in Canada: A Statistical Profile*. Ottawa: Statistics Canada.

————. 2006. *2006 Census: Family Portrait: Continuity and Change in Canadian Families and Households in 2006: Highlights*. www12.statcan.ca/census-recensement/2006/as-sa/97-553/ p1-end.cfm. Accessed February 11, 2010.

————. 2009a. *Canada Year Book Overview: Information and Communications Technology*. www41.statcan.gc.ca/2009/2256/cybac2256_000-eng.htm. Accessed on October 18, 2010.

————. 2009b. *Fact Sheet: Family Violence against Children and Youth*. Ottawa: Statistics Canada.

Steinmetz, Suzanne K. 1977. *The Cycle of Violence: Assertive, Aggressive, and Abusive Family Interaction*. New York: Praeger Publishers.

————. 1993. "The Abused Elderly Are Dependent: Abuse Is Caused by the Perception of Stress Associated With Providing Care." In Richard J. Gelles and Donileen R. Loseke (eds.), *Current Controversies on Family Violence*. Newbury Park, CA: Sage Publications. 223–36.

Stewart, Michel, Debra Jackson, Lesley M. Wilkes, and Judy Mannix. 2006. "Child-to-Mother Violence: A Pilot Study." *Contemporary Nurse* 21(2): 297–310.

Strange, Carolyn. 1995. "Historical Perspectives on Wife Assault." In Mariana Valverde, Linda MacLeod, and Kirsten Johnson (eds.), *Wife Assault and the Canadian Criminal Justice System*. Toronto: Centre of Criminology. 293–304.

Straus, Murray A. 1979. "Measuring Intrafamily Conflict and Violence: The Conflict Tactics (CT) Scales." *Journal of Marriage and the Family* 41: 75–88.

————. 1993. "Physical Assaults by Wives: A Major Social Problem." In Richard J. Gelles and Donileen R. Loseke (eds.), *Current Controversies on Family Violence*. Newbury Park: Sage. 67–87.

————. 2004. "Prevalence of Violence Against Dating Partners by Male and Female University Students Worldwide." *Violence Against Women* 10(7) (July): 790–811.

————. 2006. "Dominance and Symmetry in Partner Violence by Male and Female University Students in 32 Nations." Paper presented at conference on Trends In Intimate Violence Intervention, sponsored by the University of Haifa and New York University. New York University, May 23, 2006.

Straus, Murray A., and G. Hotaling. 1979. *The Social Causes of Husband-Wife Violence*. Minneapolis: University of Minnesota Press.

Straus, Murray A., Richard J. Gelles, and Suzanne K. Steinmetz. 1980. *Behind Closed Doors: Violence in the American Family.* Garden City, NY: Anchor Books.

Straus, Murray A., and Richard J. Gelles. 1986. "Societal Change and Change in Family Violence from 1975 to 1985 as Revealed by Two National Surveys." *Journal of Marriage and the Family* 48 (August): 465–79.

———. 1992. *Physical Violence in American Families.* New Brunswick, NJ: Transaction Publishers.

Straus, Murray A., and Stephen Sweet. 1992. "Verbal/Symbolic Aggression in Couples: Incidence Rates and Relationships to Personal Characteristics." *Journal of Marriage and the Family* 54 (May): 346–57.

Strega, Susan. 2006. "Failure to Protect: Child Welfare Interventions When Men Beat Mothers." In Ramona Alaggia and Cathy Vine (eds.), *Cruel But Not Unusual: Violence in Canadian Families.* Waterloo, ON: Wilfrid Laurier University Press. 237–66.

Struthers, Marilyn. 1994. "At a Crossroads in the Work to End the Violence: A Rural Perspective." *Canadian Woman Studies* 14(4) (Fall): 15–18.

Stubbs, Julie. 1995. "'Communitarian' Conferencing and Violence Against Women: A Cautionary Note." In M. Valverde, L. MacLeod, and K. Johnson (eds.), *Wife Assault and the Canadian Criminal Justice System: Issues and Policies.* Toronto: Centre of Criminology, University of Toronto. 260–89.

Swift, Karen J. 1995. *Manufacturing "Bad Mothers": A Critical Perspective on Child Neglect.* Toronto: University of Toronto Press.

Synnott, Anthony. 1983. "Little angels, little devils: a sociology of children." *The Canadian Review of Sociology and Anthropology* 20(1) (February): 79–95.

Taylor, Lauren R., and Nicole Gaskin-Laniyan. 2007. "Sexual Assault in Abusive Relationships." *NIJ Journal* 256 (January): 12–14.

Taylor-Butts, Andrea. 2007. "Canada's Shelters for Abused Women, 2005/2006." *Juristat* 27(4): 1–20. Statistics Canada Catalogue no. 85-002-X. Accessed on January 31, 2010.

Teichroeb, Ruth. 1997. *Flowers on My Grave: How an Ojibwa Boy's Death Helped Break the Silence on Child Abuse.* Toronto: HarperCollins.

Thomlison, Barbara, M. Stephens, J. Cunes, R. Grinnell, and J. Krysik. 1991. "Characteristics of Canadian Male and Female Child Sexual Abuse Victims." *Journal of Child and Youth Care* (Fall): 65–76.

Thorne-Finch, Ron. 1992. *Ending the Silence: The Origins and Treatment of Male Violence Against Women.* Toronto: University of Toronto Press.

Tindale, J. A., J. E. Norris, R. Berman, and S. Kulack. 1994. *Intergenerational Conflict and the Prevention of Abuse Against Older Persons.* Ottawa: Family Violence Prevention Division, Health Canada.

Tjaden, Patricia, and Nancy Thoennes. 1998. *Stalking in America: Findings From the National Violence Against Women Survey.* Washington: Department of Justice National Institute of Justice Centers for Disease Control and Prevention.

Tjaden, Patricia, Nancy Thoennes, and Christine J. Allison. 1999. "Comparing Violence Over the Life Span in Samples of Same-Sex and Opposite-Sex Cohabitants." *Violence and Victims* 14(4): 413–25.

Todd, Sarah and Colleen Lundy. 2006. "Framing Woman Abuse: A Structural Perspective." In Ramona Alaggia and Cathy Vine (eds.), *Cruel But Not Unusual: Violence in Canadian Families.* Waterloo, ON: Wilfrid Laurier University Press. 327–69.

Tower, Cynthia Crosson. 1996. *Understanding Child Abuse and Neglect.* 3rd ed. Boston: Allyn and Bacon.

Trocmé, Nico, Debra McPhee, Kwok Kwan Tam, and Tom Hay. 1994. *Ontario Incidence Study of Reported Child Abuse and Neglect.* Toronto: Institute for the Prevention of Child Abuse.

Trocmé, Nico, B. MacLaurin, B. Fallon, J. Daciuk, D. Billingsley, M. Tourigny, M. Mayer, J. Wright, K. Barter, G. Burford, J. Hornick, R. Sullivan, and B. McKenzie. 2001. *Canadian Incidence Study of Reported Child Abuse and Neglect: Final Report.* Ottawa, Ontario: Minister of Public Works and Government Services Canada.

Trocmé, Nico M., Marc Tourigny, Bruce MacLaurin, and Barbara Fallon. 2003. "Major Findings from the Canadian Incidence Study of Reported Child Abuse and Neglect." *Child Abuse & Neglect* 27: 1427–39.

Trocmé, Nico, and Nicholas Bala. 2005. "False Allegations of Abuse and Neglect When Parents Separate." *Child Abuse & Neglect* 29: 1333–45.

Trocmé, Nico, Barbara Fallon, Bruce MacLaurin, Joanne Daciuk, Caroline Felstiner, Tara Black, Lil Tonmyr, Cindy Blackstock, Ken Barter, Daniel Turcotte, and Richard Cloutier. 2005. *Canadian Incidence Study of Reported Child Abuse and Neglect—2003: Major Findings.* Minister of Public Works and Government Services Canada, 2005.

Turcotte, Martin, and Grant Schellenberg. 2007. *A Portrait of Seniors in Canada.* Ottawa: Statistics Canada.

Turner, Jan. 1995. "Saskatchewan Responds to Family Violence: The Victims of Domestic Violence Act, 1995." In M. Valverde, L. MacLeod, and K. Johnson (eds.), *Wife Assault and the Canadian Criminal Justice System: Issues and Policies.* Toronto: Centre of Criminology, University of Toronto. 183–97.

Tyler, Tom R. 2002. "Is the Internet Changing Social Life? It Seems the More Things Change, the More They Stay the Same." *Journal of Social Issues* 58(1): 195–205.

Ulman, Arina, and Murray A. Straus. 2003. "Violence by Children Against Mothers in Relation to Violence Between Parents and Corporal Punishment by Parents." *Journal of Comparative Family Studies* 434: 41–60.

Umberson, Debra, Kristin L. Anderson, Kristi Williams, and Meichu D. Chen. 2003. "Relationship Dynamics, Emotion State, and Domestic Violence: A Stress and Masculinities Perspective." *Journal of Marriage and the Family* 65(1): 233–47.

Ursel, E. Jane. 1995. "The Winnipeg Family Violence Court." In M. Valverde, L. MacLeod, and K. Johnson (eds.), *Wife Assault and the Canadian Criminal Justice System: Issues and Policies.* Toronto: Centre of Criminology, University of Toronto. 169–82.

Vadasz, Mish. 1988. "Family abuse of the elderly." In Benjamin Schlesinger and Rachel Schlesinger (eds.), *Abuse of the Elderly: Issues and Annotated Bibliography.* Toronto: University of Toronto Press. 91–94.

Van Wormer, Katherine. 2009. "Restorative Justice as Social Justice for Victims of Gendered Violence: A Standpoint Feminist Perspective." *Social Work* 54(2): 107–17.

Van Stolk, Mary. 1978. *The Battered Child in Canada*. Revised ed. Toronto: McClelland and Stewart.

Vienneau, David. 1992. "Court ruling helps woman overcome child incest horror." *Toronto Star* (October 30): Al, A36.

Vine, Cathy, Nico Trocmé, and Judy Finlay. 2006. "Children Abuse, Neglected, and Living With Violence: An Overview." In Ramona Alaggia and Cathy Vine (eds.), *Cruel But Not Unusual: Violence in Canadian Families*. Waterloo, ON: Wilfrid Laurier University Press. 147–76.

Vogl, Robin. 1996. "Initial Involvement." In N. Bala, J. Hornick, and R. Vogl (eds.), *Canadian Child Welfare Law*. Toronto: Thomson Educational Publishing Inc. 33–54.

Voumuakis, Sophia E., and Richard V. Ericson. 1984. *New Accounts of Attacks on Women*. Toronto: University of Toronto Centre of Criminology.

Wachholz, Sandra, and Baukje Miedema. 2000. "Risk, Fear, Harm: Immigrant Women's Perceptions of the 'Policing Solution' to Woman Abuse." *Crime, Law & Social Change* 34: 301–17.

Walker, Gillian. 1990. *Family Violence and the Women's Movement*. Toronto: University of Toronto Press.

Walker, Lenore. 1979. *The Battered Woman*. New York: Harper Colophon Books.

———. 1993. "The Battered Woman Syndrome." In Richard Gelles and Donileen Loseke (eds.), *Current Controversies on Family Violence*. Newbury Park: Sage. 133–53.

Wallace, Harvey. 1996. *Family Violence: Legal, Medical and Social Perspectives*. Boston: Allyn and Bacon.

Warshak, Richard A. 2000. "Remarriage as a Trigger of Parental Alienation Syndrome." *The American Journal of Family Therapy* 28: 229–41.

———. 2001. "Current Controversies Regarding Parental Alienation Syndrome." *American Journal of Forensic Psychology* 19(3): 29–59.

Washburne, Carolyn. 1983. "A Feminist Analysis of Child Abuse and Neglect." In David Finkelhor, Richard J. Gelles, Gerald T. Hotaling, and Murray A. Straus (eds.), *The Dark Side of Families: Current Family Violence Research*. Beverly Hills: Sage Publications. 289–92.

Watchel, Andy. 1994. *Child Abuse and Neglect: A Discussion Paper and Overview of Topically Related Projects*. Ottawa: Minister of Supply and Services.

Wekerle, Christine, Eman Leung, Anne-Marie Wall, Harriet MacMillan, Michael Boyle, Nico Trocmé, and Randall Waechter. 2009. "The Contribution of Childhood Emotional Abuse to Teen Dating Violence Among Child Protective Services-Involved Youth." *Child Abuse & Neglect* 33: 45–58.

Welsh, Moira, and Kevin Donovan. 1997a. "How to save the children." *Toronto Star* (June 21): Al, A16, A17.

———. 1997b. "CAS seeks power to combat abuse." *Toronto Star* (April 22): Al, A26.

Wharf, Brian. 1994. "Families in Crisis." In Maureen Baker (ed.), *Canada's Changing Families: Challenges to Public Policy*. Ottawa: The Vanier Institute of the Family. 55–68.

Wiebe, Ellen R., and Patricia Janssen. 2001. "Universal Screening for Domestic Violence in Abortion." *Women's Health Issues* 11(5) (September/October): 436–41.

Wiehe, Vernon R. 1990. *Sibling Abuse: Hidden Physical, Emotional, and Sexual Trauma*. Lexington, MA: Lexington Books.

Wilson, Johanna. 1996. "Physical Abuse of Parents by Adolescent Children." In Dean M. Busby (ed.), *The Impact of Violence on the Family: Treatment Approaches for Therapists and Other Professionals*. Boston: Allyn and Bacon. 101–22.

Wilson, Margo, and Martin Daly. 1994. "Spousal Homicide." *Juristat Service Bulletin* 14(8): 1–15.

Wright, Lisa. 1996. "24-hour hotline to help domestic abuse victims." *Toronto Star* (November 22): A3.

Yalnizyan, Armine. 2010. *The Problem of Poverty Post-Recession*. Ottawa: Canadian Centre for Policy Alternatives.

Yllo, Kersti A. 1993. "Through a Feminist Lens: Gender, Power and Violence." In Richard J. Gelles and Donileen R. Loseke (eds.), *Current Controversies on Family Violence*. Newbury Park: Sage. 47–66.

Zilney, Lisa Anne, and Mary Zilney. 2005. "Reunification of Child and Animal Welfare Agencies: Cross-Reporting of Abuse in Wellington County, Ontario." *Child Welfare* 84(1): 47–66.

INDEX